The Canadian Labour Movement

A Brief History

Second Edition

Craig Heron

James Lorimer & Company, Publishers
Toronto, 1996

James Lorimer & Company Ltd. acknowledges with thanks the support of the Canada Council and the Ontario Arts Council in the development of writing and publishing in Canada.

Cover photo: David Hartman

Canadian Cataloguing in Publication Data

Heron, Craig
    The Canadian Labour Movement

2nd ed.
Includes bibliographical references and index.

ISBN 10: 1-55028-522-X ISBN 13: 978-1-55028-522-2

1. Trade unions — Canada — History. I. Title.

HD6524.H47 1996   331.88'0971 C95-933262-6

James Lorimer & Company Ltd., Publishers
317 Adelaide St. West
Suite #1002
Toronto, ON
M5V 1P9

Printed and bound in Canada

Contents

Preface to the First Edition

There are now many excellent books on Canadian labour history, in which readers can find dramatic stories and illuminating analyses of Canadian working-class life and struggles. This book is not intended to be the definitive synthesis of all that writing. It is simply a brief interpretive history setting out the large patterns and broad themes in the development of workers' movements in this country. It was written primarily for those who know little about the Canadian labour movement, but perhaps its general arguments may also give specialists in the field of labour history and activists in the labour movement something to mull over.

I am grateful to Ruth Frager, James Naylor, and Ian Radforth for helpful comments and to Curtis Fahey for patience and editorial efficiency.

Preface to the Second Edition

When I was pressed to update this book, I took the opportunity not only to correct the unfortunate errors that readers and reviewers had pointed out, but also to give greater attention to gender and the distinct experience of Quebec. More daunting was the need to assess the profound changes that had swept over working-class Canada since I finished the last version seven years ago. The last three chapters therefore contain a great deal of new information and reflections on a process of social transformation that is far from complete. I am grateful for the many helpful comments I received, especially from David Langille, and for the editorial prowess of Diane Young and Eileen Koyama.

Introduction

June 15, 1885. Harry passes his union card across the kitchen table. He arrived in Winnipeg only yesterday, but he has wasted no time in looking up the secretary of the local union. Harry is a printer. He finished his apprenticeship in London, England, five years ago and has been moving from city to city in Canada and the United States to get some experience and to see the world. He headed west to take a job in a Winnipeg newspaper office. There is no question in anyone's mind that Harry is a skilled man. His trained hands set each piece of type, his keen mind organizes the work to be done, and his sharp eye watches for errors. His boss knows that there is simply no way to get the work done except to entrust it to men like Harry; no machines can replace him. In his travels, however, this proud craftsman has met bosses who have tried to cut down his wages, or to bring in poorly trained boys — or worse yet, women! So Harry became a dedicated member of the International Typographical Union. Meeting with his fellow craftworkers each week makes him feel good. He knows that his trade is a little more secure as a result of union protection, but he also has a chance to flex his pride in craft traditions running all the way back to Gutenberg. He also likes the sense of manliness that his skills, his good wages, and the companionship of other male printers give him. White men in the British Empire should expect no less, he believes. Sharing a cup of tea with his new union secretary, he asks about local labour conditions and once again feels the bonds uniting skilled men like them across international borders.

April 12, 1910. Rose jostles and jokes with the other women from the shop as they file into the meeting hall. She is a seamstress. At age eighteen she has worked in women's cloak factories in Montreal off and on for seven years. She learned to sew at home, but found that her skills with a needle mean little to her bosses. Clothing is now mass-produced; each worker stitches up the same part of the garment over and over. Female workers like Rose get the least skilled work, such as sewing in linings. She works long hours at piece-work, but still makes far less than the men in the shop. Last spring she decided she had had enough. An organizer for the International Ladies' Garment Workers Union spoke to a crowd of the "girls" outside the factory at lunch-time a few weeks ago, and Rose immediately paid her dues to join the new Montreal local. She does not understand much about unions. The leaders have been sending the women to separate meetings and continue to keep them in the dark about negotiations. Now these leaders want to know if the women are ready to strike. Taking her seat near the front of the hall, Rose knows she is ready.

May 1, 1923. Sandy shakes his fist along with the others as the procession passes the company office. Lifting his end of the banner higher, he launches into a new chorus of a labour song. He is a coal miner. He followed his father into the Cape Breton mines as a trapper boy in the early 1900s, and now works at the coal face several miles underground from the pit head at Glace Bay. With little more than his muscle, a few simple tools, and his invaluable experience, he digs out the fuel that is crucial for so much industrial production. He knows the fine physical details of the mine and always has his eye trained on the veins of coal and an ear tuned to the "bumps" in the rock. His work is hard and, except for the presence of his helper, socially isolated. Yet he has always been deeply attached to his workmates, and he attends the local meetings of the United Mine Workers of America faithfully. In fact, he has served on the union pit committee for his mine for the past three years. For Sandy the union symbolizes the importance of the coal miners to society and, as breadwinners, to their families. It is also a weapon against the giant corporation that now controls most Nova Scotia mining. He has walked some angry picket lines in recent years and has been listening with increasing conviction to the radicals who lead the local union. This spring the steelworkers who have been organizing in Sydney are marching with the miners in a grand celebration of the workers' holiday, May Day. Singing lustily in the windy streets of Glace Bay, Sandy again allows himself to believe that this more radical kind of labour movement is going to bring a new world for workers, without bosses and with compassion for all.

April 8, 1937. Ernie glances at his watch as he slips the next part into his machine. In five minutes he will follow the plan and lead his department out. Ernie is an autoworker. Born on a farm near Oshawa, Ontario, he quit school after Grade 10 to take a job at the General Motors plant. Fifteen years later, he has worked his way up to the position of semiskilled machine operator. His job looks boring and repetitive, but it demands careful concentration and experience. Like the other workers in his department, he feels a little bit of pride in the cars he helps to produce. He resents his supervisors' harassing him from morning to night, however. He hates the unnecessary gruffness, the favouritism, and the constant pressure to speed up. Most of all, he is bothered by the low wages the company pays. At lunch breaks last winter everybody was talking about the union "sit-down" strikes in the U.S. auto plants. Ernie saw the first glimmer of hope for better wages and working conditions, and eagerly signed a card to join the new GM local of the United Automobile Workers of America. He even agreed to serve as shop steward for his department. Glancing around, Ernie spots a dozen union buttons pinned on grimy work shirts. He has a hunch that life at GM will never be the same again.

May 5, 1949. Henri hears shots as he staggers out of the clouds of tear gas and runs toward the sound. He finds his workmates angrily beating four men. Someone tells him the intruders are undercover cops, who used their guns to threaten the strikers. The truck carrying the scabs is backing up the road in the grey light of dawn. The picket line remains unbroken. Henri is a mineworker. Born and raised in the town of Asbestos, Quebec, he and his family have worked for Canadian Johns Manville for many years. When Henri began work there twenty years ago, the workers had a Catholic organization with a chaplain running the meetings, but few employees joined. Over the past ten years, however, the union has been pushing harder to get decent wages and safer working conditions. The church is no longer holding the workers back: the chaplain has been helping them organize, and even the archbishop in Montreal has announced his support for their strike. But these swaggering bullies from the provincial police and the new scabs are not listening. So Henri and his fellow strikers have decided to fight back the way they know best. They will show the company and the Quebec premier that they are serious about winning this strike. Henri jokes nervously with the other pickets about when the Riot Act will be read.

October 5, 1969. Helen joins in the applause as the vote is announced in the Prince George convention hall. She has just helped to rechristen her organization the British Columbia Government Employees Union. Helen is a secretary. She left school in Vancouver with a Grade 12 commercial diploma in the 1950s and eventually found work in a provincial government office. She quit for a few years after her sons were born, but she came back knowing that unlike her mother or grandmother she would hold a paying job for most of her life. For years she has been feeling the frustration building in her office. Although she likes the work and thinks she does a first-rate job, she feels that she is losing touch with her manager as the office gets bigger and more bound up in red tape. She also resents the low wages that the government pays her. She did not need much convincing to join the government employees' association, even though it was a weak organization without legal collective-bargaining rights. As one of the loudest, liveliest members in her office, Helen was soon elected to the local executive. Now she sits smiling amid the convention delegates, confident that a defiant new spirit among government workers will make a difference to secretaries like her.

February 10, 1988. Wendy finds it much easier to bear the subzero temperatures on the picket line than the news that a provincial court judge has just levied a five-hundred-dollar fine on her union president. This fine is the ultimate insult. Wendy is a nurse. With three years training in a nursing school, she thinks of herself as a competent professional who plays a vital role in the country's health care system. Yet the hospital administration has been steadily increasing her workload while holding down her salary. Now, after taking away the nurses' right to strike five years ago and then offering a paltry wage increase, the Alberta government has virtually forced them out on strike. Wendy would probably never call herself a feminist, but Florence Nightingale would be horrified at the way that she and the other nurses are refusing to be pushed around. As picket captain, Wendy lets the women's anger fill the chilly air with a flurry of insults against the provincial politicians, before re-forming the picket line and leading a chorus of "Solidarity Forever."

These seven Canadians never actually existed. But the events did happen, and thousands of wage-earners like them were involved. This book is about the Canadian workers like these seven people who have struggled over the years to form a labour movement that can promote and defend their interests. For some readers these workers will be unfamiliar figures. Far too many Canadians, including many union members, assume that the labour movement consists of a few men with flashy suits and big salaries, sitting behind desks in sumptuous offices. Certainly many unions now have sizable full-time staffs, but a few highly publicized leaders — villains such as Hal Banks and heroes such as Bob White — overshadow the small army of committed men and women who have taken time after work to keep their unions going, without any expectation of material reward for themselves. These people often played leadership roles in their workplaces and communities, once workers had been convinced to listen. This is a history, then, of a social movement, not simply of a bureaucracy.

It is not a history of all workers in Canada in all the phases of their lives; that would be a much bigger project and a much longer story. This study is limited in two important ways. First, the men and women who took up the union cause sometimes won over most of the workers in their own communities, but never enlisted a majority of the Canadian working class. Only in the early 1980s did the proportion of unionized workers in Canada reach 40 per cent (although, according to the oddly Canadian "Rand Formula," which will be discussed later, nearly 60 per cent were covered by union contracts). Those left out have generally been the most vulnerable and the most difficult to organize: the least skilled, the transient, immigrants, women. Or they have been the most ambivalent about their status as workers — the clerical and professional workers in particular. Many workers, moreover, found ways to resist their bosses that were less formal than unionization: many quietly agreed among themselves to set their own production quotas on the job, while others simply stayed home from work or quit. Canadian labour thus remained a minority movement frequently trying to enlist a larger portion of the country's wage-earners. Second, the terrain that unions in Canada contested was primarily the world of paid work; they have been institutions organized on the basis of occupation or industry. Consequently, unions paid little attention to the unpaid domestic sphere that defined most women's lives — except in men's demands for a family wage or for more time with their families. Nor did they show great interest in neighbourhood or larger community associations among workers. The workplace remained the primary focus of labour activity. Much of this story, then, will be about relatively skilled, white, English-speaking (and some French-speaking) male workers in their places of work.

Yet, however narrowly focused unions were in the beginning, they reached out to create something larger than the sum of their parts — a labour *movement* with wider social and political concerns. Despite its narrow base within the working class, that movement has frequently aspired to speak on behalf of all workers and to promote a broad program of social reform or even revolutionary transformation. It has been particularly concerned with confronting the state over larger issues that can affect many aspects of workers' lives: education, health, housing, environment, and so on. So this is not a history of an entire class, but of the most active, articulate, independent, and cohesive elements within that class.

It is important to understand this labour movement within its social context. We cannot expect to find its history only by looking into offices and convention halls. Certainly we have to examine labour's main goals, ideologies, leadership, and strategies over the years. But we must also consider how these activities and ideas were shaped by specifically Canadian factors, especially the economy, the class structure, and the state. The economy that provided the job opportunities was crucial. It was, of course, a capitalist economy, with control over economic decision making in private hands. To the end of the nineteenth century, individual entrepreneurs, their families, and their limited partnerships (most of them based in local communities) held the levers of economic power; from the early twentieth century, large corporations grew to dominate most sectors of economic life in Canada. Since 1900, and even more dramatically since World War II, many of those corporations have been U.S. controlled. Moreover, since the mid-nineteenth century, this capitalist economy has had, roughly speaking, two parallel spheres of production. One sphere has been oriented to the extraction and export of natural resources for use elsewhere, especially in the imperial centres of first Britain and then the United States. This sector has largely shaped Canada's economic relationship with the world economy. The other sphere has been organized to manufacture goods for the domestic market of resource producers (especially the thousands of farmers) and urban dwellers. Canada has therefore seen a wide range of occupational groups, from loggers and miners to mass-production factory workers, often working in enterprises as sophisticated as any in the Western World. For all the unevenness of development, the Canadian economy was no Third World backwater.

Yet this economy has been relatively small and often fragile. International markets for resource products have fluctuated widely, leaving Canadian producers in desperate straits. Canadian manufacturers then had difficulty selling their products domestically, especially when farmers were in trouble. More recently, Canadian industries have increasingly had to adjust to a new "international division of labour," which is dominated by transnational corporations and which has effectively removed certain kinds of manufacturing from Canadian soil. The ghost towns that dot the northern Canadian landscape, the long history of out-migration before World War II, and the frequent plant shut-downs in recent years testify to the instability of employment for Canadian workers. It is thus not surprising that, since the mid-nineteenth century, so many Canadian unionists in the widely scattered, isolated industrial centres linked up with larger, stronger labour movements based in the United States — a pattern found nowhere else in the industrialized world.

Perhaps even more important, the Canadian economy has shown severe regional imbalances throughout this century. By the 1920s, financial control and most manufacturing had been concentrated in central Canada around the Toronto-Montreal axis, while the Maritimes lost industries, and the West and the North were restricted primarily to resource extraction. Workers experienced quite different opportunities and pressures, as the regions followed their own rhythms of development (and underdevelopment). The regions also developed their own relations with workers in neighbouring U.S. regions: for example, the factory workers of southern Ontario and the U.S. industrial heartland, or the West Coast miners and loggers in both countries. Not surprisingly, then, we cannot speak of a single Canadian labour movement any more than we can hypothesize about a homogeneous Canadian working class. With such a small-scale, insecure, and fragmented economy, moreover, Canada was no imperialist superpower and thus never developed the jingoistic nationalism that has provided so much social cement in the United States.

The second factor to greatly influence the Canadian labour movement, social structure, has also had its own peculiarities. Canada was a settler society, in which the native population was pushed back and European social patterns were transplanted. There was also a colonized population of Europeans — the French Canadians centred in the future province of Quebec — which kept alive its distinct culture, despite English hostility and assimilationist efforts. Throughout the British North American colonies, the landed aristocracy, once a distinct social class, quickly disappeared in the nineteenth century, and an ambitious, powerful capitalist class of merchants, manufacturers, bankers, and sundry financiers took shape, initially regionally based and competitive, but increasingly cohesive after the turn of the century. Yet we do not find any simple dichotomy of workers and owners in this country. Before World War II, there was an enormous group of resource-industry producers who were not wage-earners — the thousands of small-scale, independent farm and fishing families. Many farmers produced large crops for sale; however, many others, and most fishers, barely subsisted on the margins of the commercial economy. Occasionally the more successful farmers added hired help to the family work teams for a season, but most often they remained outside the framework of employment relations. Their large numbers and their determined independence made these primary producers a major force in Canadian politics before World War II — a force which was not always sympathetic to the labour movement's concerns.

Some of the more marginal farmers, fishers, and their children left home periodically to work for wages. They provided a flexible pool of labour for employers and a source of frustration for union organizers, since these men and women seldom thought of themselves as full-time wage-earners. The fact that the family farm or fishing village could reabsorb these workers when they were no longer needed by outside employers helped to delay the arrival of the modern welfare state in Canada compared to that in the rest of the industrialized world. This large class of independent commodity producers has shrunk dramatically since World War II. As farmers disappeared from sight over the course of the twentieth century, their place in the social structure was taken by increasing numbers of clerical and professional workers, who began to appear in the early 1900s and who reached massive numbers after World War II. This change constituted the major shift in what has been loosely known as the "middle class."

The working class itself has undergone some major changes over the past century. The particular mix of workers, skill levels, and ethnicity or race has been determined primarily by the recruitment and employment practices of owners and managers, with some help from the immigration authorities of the Canadian state. There were four waves of major changes in the organization of work: after 1840, after 1890, after 1940, and after 1975. Each disrupted the previous mix by altering the technological base of production, dispensing with old skill requirements, and creating new ones. Native-born Canadian wage-earners have met some of these needs, but employers have also relied heavily on immigrants: for less skilled labour, they have drawn on the Canadian agricultural hinterland and the peasant villages of Asia, southern and eastern Europe, and most recently the Caribbean; for skilled labour, they have drawn on Britain, sometimes western Europe, and most recently Asia. Often these workers have brought their own particular traditions of collective resistance, whether in the form of British craft unionism, Ukrainian peasant organizing, or Jewish socialism. But, with their distinctive languages and cultures, they did not blend easily into a common working class. Many were peasants with only limited experience in wage labour and with plans to return home or re-create their peasant lifestyles on the Canadian Prairies as soon as possible. Many Anglo-Canadian workers nonetheless greeted these newcomers with suspicion and occasional hostility. Ethnic and racial fragmentation thus became a central feature of the Canadian working-class experience. Yet most often, within these fragments, class identity was not obliterated; rather, parallel and distinct working-class experiences emerged.

Workers also grouped themselves in family units in households, where most of the strategizing for daily survival took place. Here the fundamental gendered division of labour within the working class was laid down, as male heads of household left each day to earn wages (often accompanied by older children), while the mothers and daughters stayed behind to carry out the unpaid tasks for family maintenance and to manage the household economy. This patriarchal arrangement was mirrored in the wider society in the narrow range of job options for females in the paid labour market and in the regular exclusion of women from public life (including parliamentary elections and many union meetings). There were numerous departures from this pattern — widows and single mothers coping on their own, or bachelor sojourners sharing a bunkhouse, for example — but, for both women and men, it was the organization and power dynamics of their family households that established many limits and opportunities, as well as the basis of a gendered working-class identity.

Finally, as a colony and then a largely self-governing dominion within the British Empire, Canada developed liberal-democratic state institutions more or less the same as those in Britain. Like British workers (and those in other Commonwealth countries), Canadian workers were therefore integrated into two processes with mixed blessings: the "rule of law" and parliamentary democracy. Under British common law, individual workers had a set of civil rights, but, in practice, as we will see, their rights to freedom of speech, association, and assembly were regularly violated by military troops, police, and hostile magistrates. These rights were only secured once unions and political organizations had enough political clout to have them entrenched in legislation and properly enforced. Even more important, workers had to call on the legislatures to restrain the courts' enthusiasm for the rights of private capital in the potent legal notion of the "contract of employment," a lopsided concept that left individual workers almost legally powerless, compared to their employers.

Electoral rights were similarly ambiguous. Parliamentary democracy in Canada operated formally on the notion of popular sovereignty, and politicians and civil servants could never completely ignore the concerns of a working-class constituency. At each peak of labour militancy and agitation, for example, the federal government launched a major investigation into what was once known as "the labour question," and introduced some new legislation aimed at protecting workers. But organized workers had difficulty obtaining leverage in this parliamentary arena. Well into the twentieth century, the right to vote was restricted on the basis of property, gender, or race. (For example, in Ontario, property qualifications on the municipal franchise lasted until 1921; in Quebec, women could not vote until 1940; and in British Columbia, Asians were barred from voting until 1947.) Workers, therefore, seldom sat in legislatures. Moreover, for the labour movement, the problem of trying to find some political space within the liberal state was compounded by the movement's minority status within a class that was itself a minority within the Canadian social structure until well into the twentieth century. Put simply, farmers' votes tended to matter more. For a labour movement with parliamentary ambitions, then, building coalitions became essential — first, with farmers, later with white-collar professionals.

The constitutional structure of the Canadian state posed additional problems. In the crucial area of property rights that governed relations between capital and labour, the several provincial jurisdictions were supreme. The process of nailing down favourable legislation for workers was thus slow and fragmented. Within those provinces, moreover, the executive branch was extremely powerful, and governing parties tended to establish long, almost impregnable dynasties rooted in patronage networks. Yet, despite all these obstacles, Canadian workers have nonetheless shown a deep and abiding commitment to the rule of law and liberal-democratic electoral politics, and have often been provoked to outrage when those in control of the state disrupted these orderly processes, especially with troops or police, to suppress labour organizing.

With this background in mind, it is perhaps now clearer why Canada has never really had a single national labour movement that grew steadily from humble origins in the nineteenth century to its current healthy size. Relatively few hallowed traditions have been handed down from the nineteenth-century labour pioneers to their modern heirs. (Labour activists may still call themselves "brother" and "sister" in the traditional way, but the world of the local craft union in the mid-nineteenth century is light years away from the highly centralized, bureaucratic milieu of the late twentieth century.) Rather, a long series of often independent, locally or regionally based movements rose and declined, depending on the opportunities for organizing that were created within the economy, class relations, and the state.

No national working class is always united and struggling. Industrial capitalism creates too many pressures that undermine solidarity and atomize men and women surviving on nothing but wages. Misery itself is rarely enough to cause workers to revolt: resistance to subordination within capitalist society stems from a mixture of resentment at the violation of accepted standards of natural justice and hope about alternative possibilities. These conditions appear most often in periods of prosperity, when workers' material conditions are actually improving, but workers' aspirations are frustrated. What we will see in Canada, accordingly, is a pattern, not of slow and steady growth, but of surging and receding. There was really no "golden age" when workers were more united than ever again; rather, each labour resurgence brought a reconstituted working class into motion against quite different odds.

There were four brief but dramatic moments of working-class resistance when the labour movement expanded its membership and its goals: the mid-1880s, the end of each world war, and the decade after 1965. (This pattern closely parallels the struggles of U.S. workers.) Each time, the upsurge of labour revolt occurred well into a period of economic transformation, after new groups of workers had become sufficiently accustomed to their new workplaces and to their fellow workers to be able to coalesce into a unified force capable of articulating and pursuing common goals. Each time, Canadian workers carried over a few lessons and even some leadership from the past, but more important was the experimentation in new circumstances; major defeats would often discredit certain ideologies or forms of organizing and thus shape subsequent responses. Each time, the peak moment of solidarity came in a period of relatively full employment and in the wake of some major social crisis, most often a war. Each time, a new crop of articulate, usually young, local and middle-level leaders sprang up; these leaders were closely linked to working-class communities and were often immersed in radical politics. Each time, there was a remarkable degree of working-class unity, mobilization, and determination to win a new place for workers within industrial society. And each time, Canadian employers resisted the new challenge vigorously with some combination of iron fist and velvet glove, while the state helped to keep the inevitable conflict within safe bounds, both through the repression of more radical and militant tendencies and through the creation of new institutions and laws to guide class tensions into safe channels. Each of these explosions of militancy and radicalism was followed by a new stabilization of class relations.

The great watershed was the 1940s. Before that point, almost every effort by various labour movements to win a permanent place in Canadian industrial and political life was beaten back by hostile employers and a generally unsympathetic state. It was only during and immediately following World War II that unions made the breakthrough that allowed them to operate, within a tightly controlled framework, in most mass-production, resource, and transportation industries. Many workers were left out — notably those in smaller-scale industries, in white-collar occupations, and in less prosperous regions, especially Atlantic Canada. But the base was broadened in the 1960s and 1970s with the organization of public-sector workers (and fishers). The basic institutional forms of the modern labour movement are nonetheless rooted in the great surge of organizing that began in the late 1930s and early 1940s.

Within each of these periods of renewed struggle, there was often plenty of conflict within the labour movement over how to organize and what to demand. Many of the more skilled workers tended to be most interested in protecting the small bit of industrial turf that they held onto, and resisted any suggestion that unions should be watered down by including the less skilled. Entrenched union leaders also tended to be fearful about endangering the organizational structures they had created or inherited (and often their own jobs, of course). Against them have often been arrayed younger, more impatient, more militant, and more radical workers who wanted aggressive action or radical change. In short, there was recurrent conflict between the spark of spontaneous or principled defiance and the desire to hold fragile organizations together. In the process of union consolidation, the challenge was to keep the organization together without smothering the spark. The story of the Canadian labour movement, then, is one of hostility from employers and the state, but also of frequent internal turmoil, of craft unionist against industrial unionist, of rank-and-filer against bureaucrat, of marxist against labourist or social democrat, of women against men.

Whatever their disagreements, however, labour activists in Canada have shared a commitment to taking the sting out of uncontrolled market relations in a capitalist society. They provided a relentless reminder to owners and managers of Canadian industry and to politicians and state officials that the private accumulation of wealth and the consolidation of capitalist power could not proceed without recognizing human needs. All of Canada's various labour movements have insisted that the dignity and material well-being of Canadian workers must be made a social priority. They have yet to achieve that goal, but, in their efforts to get there, they have shaken up Canadian society profoundly.

In chapter 1, we meet the first movement of organized craftworkers beginning to take shape in the mid-nineteenth century in response to the new capitalist organization of work and labour markets. By the end of the century, the militant craftworkers were leading a much broader working-class confrontation with the new industrial capitalist order, but their efforts collapsed by the 1890s. In chapter 2, we find a new wave of organization and agitation rolling through the corporate capitalist world of the early twentieth century, this time involving both revived craft unions and a new, more radical movement for all-inclusive industrial unionism. These two strands converged briefly at the end of World War I and extended into independent working-class politics, but both were crushed in the early 1920s. Chapter 3 explores the slow, uphill battle to shake the solid hegemony of Canadian employers in industrial life in the two decades between the wars and then the breakthrough that took place at the end of World War II to give unions a permanent, if constrained and largely depoliticized, place in key sectors of the economy. In chapter 4, we watch the industrial regime of legalized collective bargaining, established in the 1940s, come apart in the 1960s and 1970s under pressure from angry rank-and-file unionists and militant newcomers to the labour movement from the public sector. Chapter 5 traces the vigorous counterattack from the state and capital to weaken Canadian unions permanently. Chapter 6 presents the internal pressures and new dilemmas facing the labour movement today. Finally, chapter 7 assesses the emerging agenda for labour in the hostile climate of the 1990s.

1

The Craftworkers' Challenge

A bird's-eye view of British North America in the early nineteenth century would have found a tiny population clustered along the eastern coasts and major waterways of a great wilderness. The oldest European settlers were the French peasants in the St. Lawrence valley and the English and Irish fishers on the East Coast. Fur traders had penetrated far inland to gather pelts from the thousands of native peoples, who still controlled most of what is now Canada. New waves of U.S. and British immigrants were slowly penetrating the densely wooded hinterland of what was to become Ontario and the Maritime provinces. Fish, furs, timber, and wheat were the only goods produced in quantity for sale abroad. The colonies' major urban centres, a few busy ports on the Atlantic and the St. Lawrence, handled this commerce in primary products, but most of the population could be found on small, fairly self-sufficient farms. A sprinkling of artisans in the towns and countryside manufactured what little was not imported or produced around the household. These self-employed men (and a few women) made goods from scratch in their small workshops with simple tools, a well-developed expertise, and the help of an apprentice or a family member, and then sold them out the front door of the shop.

Over the course of the nineteenth century, Canada became an industrial nation. By the 1890s, farming, fishing, and logging still kept most Canadians busy, and the Prairies and British Columbia were still thinly settled, but there were now large islands of industrialized life in central and eastern Canada. These communities were connected not simply by waterways but by new "ribbons of steel" — railway lines. For some fifty years, capitalist entrepreneurs had been seizing opportunities to start up or reorganize their firms to turn out new products for new markets. In these efforts, they tended to locate in larger urban centres, although industrial production was still remarkably widely dispersed throughout the settled provinces. They had drawn in many of the thousands of new immigrants who had made their way to these shores, mostly from the British Isles and especially from Ireland. Now each morning, the country's first generation of full-time wage-earners trudged off to the factories and mines that had replaced much production by artisans: Canada's first working class had been born. And the most skilled within that class had become the most vocal and the most active in challenging the place of workers within this new industrial capitalist society.

Preindustrial Protest

In preindustrial British North America, wage earning was most often a transition in life or a seasonal interlude, not a permanent status. There were opportunities for waged work, but few lasted year-round. At particular points in the annual cycle, especially harvest time, farmers might need to hire temporary help. The great fur-trading companies sent workers inland from Montreal and Hudson Bay, but in many cases only on a seasonal basis. Logging operations in New Brunswick or the Canadas required workers to head into the bush each fall, but turned them loose a few months later. East Coast merchants sent crews of fishers out to the offshore fisheries for only a season. In the busy summer months a man could find a short-term job, day-labouring in the towns or digging on the construction sites for the new canals. A woman could find similarly limited work in town or country as a servant. The majority of the population, however, lived and worked with their families on their own farms, or hoped to be doing so quite soon. Many wage-earners came from farms where extra cash was needed, or had recently debarked from immigrant ships and needed cash to establish their own farms. In the Atlantic colonies, fishing was a similarly independent activity, carried on by family groups. Much smaller numbers of independent artisans also worked out of their own households throughout the colonies. Outside the settled areas, most native peoples who gathered furs or provisions for the fur-trading companies maintained key features of their traditional way of life. Indeed, what appears to be wage labour in that early society was often just one form of barter among members of a local community. In this context, few people worked regularly for wages and thought of themselves as a distinct group in society. That pool of labour began to appear around the middle of the nineteenth century, when land became less accessible and setting up shop on your own became more difficult.

The experience of those who spent a long period in wage labour was quite different from that of their modern counterparts. Like the seasonal workers, most of these individuals probably thought of themselves as moving through wage labour to an independent economic status (or, in the case of women, into marriage). But in the interim, they were bound quite tightly to their employers. Girls working as domestic servants and boys, as farm labourers, were generally just extra pairs of hands for the family production team. They lived in the same household as the family, ate at the same table, and worked with them in the household or on the land. Boys learned a craft in the same way, whether it was blacksmithing, silversmithing, or shipbuilding. All these youngsters were considered apprentices and were often formally bound to their employers by contracts of indenture that lasted many years. In return for faithful service to their masters, these children received room, board, clothing, and sometimes schooling.

This kind of relationship might not end with adulthood. In the urban crafts, young workers who had finished their apprenticeships became "journeymen," working for wages before setting up on their own as "masters," who then hired apprentices and journeymen. During those years, a journeyman's relationship with a master went far beyond what we now expect in an employment contract. It was not uncommon for a single worker to live in his master's house, though this practice declined in the early nineteenth century. Even more important, masters and journeymen were united in their dedication to their craft. They did not transplant the tightly structured European craft guilds, but they did keep alive old customs and practices attached to particular occupations and often organized ritualized celebrations in the larger towns and cities. They held lavish banquets with speeches and toasts glorifying their craft and marched together in colourful parades, displaying the banners, symbols, tools, and products of their trades. In more isolated settings, where preindustrial employers had to assemble and hold onto a larger workforce, their bond with many of their workers was based more on their personal leadership in the community and on their willingness to take care of the workers' material needs. They typically provided some combination of housing, stores, churches, and schools for workers and their families. The men who wintered inland for the fur trade companies, the loggers sent into the bush, the sailors on overseas vessels, the skilled workers at such small industrial sites as Les Forges Saint-Maurice, and the first groups of miners lived and worked in this kind of environment. Both craftworkers and resource workers might also be legally indentured for a fixed term of service.

This highly personal bond of service, loyalty, and mutual obligation, based on the scarcity of labour (and of jobs) in the colonies, has been called "paternalism." We should be wary, however, of conjuring up images of kindly father-figures patting the heads of respectful workers. The system was ripe for cruelty and abuse. There is evidence that in the early nineteenth century masters were toughening up the contracts of indenture to get more work out of their workers and to discipline them more strictly. Small wonder so many apprentices were reported to have run away. Under a cluster of legislation known as the Master and Servant Acts, English employers had legal recourse if a worker absconded or was willfully disobedient. Some of the colonies added their own legislation to enforce these contracts of employment: Nova Scotia in 1765, Lower Canada in 1802, and the United Province of Canada in 1847 (separate legislation also governed sailors and, after 1850, railway employees). In addition, the owner's control over all community institutions, especially housing and company stores, could be used to keep the workforce in line in the more isolated resource communities.

It is hard to imagine much collective activity among workers who passed only briefly through the labour force or who were bound so closely to employers by welfare provisions and legal constraints. There is nonetheless scattered evidence that, when workers had more regular contact with each other and were assembled in larger groups, they banded together to confront their employers with their concerns. These struggles were sporadic and isolated. There were also sharp differences between those confrontations in the resource industries and transportation construction work and those involving urban craftsmen.

At various points before the 1870s, scattered groups of fur traders, fishers, miners, and construction labourers stood up to their employers with collective demands for improvements in the terms of their employment. Never was there any formal or permanent organization to carry on these battles. Instead, the workers, generally of the same ethnic background, simply organized spontaneously in defence of the values and customs of their individual community.

In the 1830s and 1840s Irish workers in the woods and on the canals reasserted their long-standing sense of injustice and their styles of organizing learned in the hard-pressed Irish countryside. Often these traditional methods were turned against competitors in the labour market, whether French Canadians or other Irish workers with whom feuds had raged for generations. The contractors who hired these workers also faced this wrath. These workers banded together to threaten their opponents and, if necessary, to crack their skulls in bloody skirmishes to secure jobs or better wages. Similarly, from the 1840s to the 1860s, English and Scottish coal miners and Cornish tin miners brought over to work mines in Nova Scotia, Vancouver Island, and central Ontario carried with them well-established standards of acceptable wages and workloads and bristled at incursions on these practices. Frequently that meant resistance to a cut in their customary wage rates.

These workers formed what historians have called "crowds," that is, loosely structured but well-disciplined groups who marched off together to take immediate, direct action against the alleged wrong. Crowd behaviour was usually purposeful and followed some kind of familiar ritual. At some gatherings, effigies were burned; at others, participants blackened their faces and created the noisy ruckus of the charivari (the old community ritual designed to ridicule ill-matched newlyweds). The threat of violence always hung over these activities, and violence often erupted, especially when the employers responded in kind by calling in the troops. The result of these confrontations was what authorities liked to call a "riot," but the violence was usually controlled and directed at specific targets, such as the manager's house or the company store. The whole community sometimes became involved, as in Albion Mines, Nova Scotia, in 1841, when women and children surrounded the house of the mine manager and broke a few shutters and windows to demand that he restore their coal allowances during the local miners' strike. The apparent informality of these crowd activities did not prevent some workers from waging long, determined battles, sometimes lasting months. The Nova Scotia miners' strike stretched over three winter months and ended in victory for the miners. A similar episode erupted at Nanaimo on Vancouver Island in 1870 and lasted five months. None of these situations involved a formal union, though the workers sometimes chose an ad hoc committee to speak on their behalf. This form of working-class protest lasted in mining towns until the 1870s, and on major railway construction sites, pitched battles were still breaking out among migrant peasant-labourers in the early twentieth century.

In the preindustrial towns, this kind of "collective bargaining by riot" occasionally took place, but a different form of worker organization also developed. Here journeymen craftworkers took the initiative when they sensed that their interests and those of their masters were no longer identical. In the first half of the nineteenth century, some of their employers began to think in more capitalistic terms about labour, reducing the employment relationship to no more than a wage and looking for ways to cut labour costs, such as slashing wages or reducing apprenticeship requirements. The proud traditions of the crafts now seemed to mean less than the possibilities of profitable expansion. To counteract the economic insecurity of this new situation and to try to maintain the integrity of their craft customs and practices, small groups of journeymen began to form local craft unions or "societies." These institutions were familiar to the craftworkers who were arriving from Britain or the United States, where "friendly societies" had been active since the late eighteenth century. Their main purpose was to provide a benefit fund to help members through periods of distress (illness, accident, unemployment, or death), but gradually they also began to represent the journeymen's interests to employers.

Typically a craft union drew its membership from only one occupational group — printers, carpenters, stonemasons, and so on — and admitted only the skilled wage-earners in the trade, the journeymen. Apprentices, women, and unskilled labourers found the union's gates closed to them. In this early period the range of craftworkers' competence was still broad. For example, a printer was expected to be able to do all the work in producing a newspaper from setting the type to running the small presses.

No one can put a date on the formation of the first society in British North America, but the economic boom of the War of 1812 seems to have encouraged the earliest organizing efforts. In 1816 the Nova Scotia legislature passed an act to curb the "great numbers of ... Journeymen and Workmen, in the Town of Halifax, and other parts of the Province, [who] have, by unlawful Meetings and Combinations, endeavoured to regulate the rate of wages, and to effectuate illegal purposes." Despite such official hostility, most of the larger towns and cities had a handful of unions of printers, carpenters, shoemakers, tailors, cabinet-makers, and the like by the 1830s and 1840s, though they tended to become inactive after a few years and had to be rebuilt. In a few cases these societies were prepared to strike to support their demands. One of the most famous examples involved the illustrious Upper Canadian radical William Lyon Mackenzie and the other print-shop owners in Toronto in 1836. The printers wanted a wage increase and apprenticeship guarantees, but Mackenzie led the employers' resistance to these demands and successfully broke the strike. The other bastion of Upper Canadian liberalism, George Brown, made even more aggressive moves against his printers in the 1840s.

The early craft unions, however, were far less confrontational than these incidents might suggest. More often they were found in processions holding high their craft emblems or in banquets with the masters extolling the glorious merits of their particular crafts. Perhaps to forestall legal prosecution for conspiracy under the common law or colonial legislation, several such unions insisted that they were "united to support, not combined to injure." The distinction between masters and journeymen was still too blurred for entrenched hostility to develop. The fact that none of these local unions affiliated with larger organizations and that only in Toronto, Kingston, Montreal, and Quebec City were there short-lived attempts in the 1830s to unite these craftsmen across occupational lines suggests that attachments to craft and local employers were far stronger than any kind of working-class identity.

Coping with Industrial Capitalism

By 1850 British North America's economic life was undergoing a major transformation that would take the shape of an industrial revolution over the next half century. Many master artisans expanded their workshops into good-sized "manufactories," while some merchants decided to set up factories rather than import commodities for sale. Lumber mills proliferated similarly, and by the 1870s canning factories were opening on the West Coast. The great accelerator was the railway, which began to spread out over the countryside in the 1850s, linking up more isolated communities and widening the markets for consumer and producer goods. To supply the coal for the steam engines powering ships, locomotives, and factory equipment, new mines opened in Nova Scotia and on Vancouver Island. And, of course, construction projects sprouted across the country to meet the new demand for factories, homes, and commercial outlets in the rapidly expanding urban areas.

Families that became dependent on wages for much of their survival faced changes on many fronts. Within working-class households, the long-standing gendered division of labour was reorganized. The family became much more reliant on the wages brought home by the male head (and children, if paid work could be found) and on the unpaid labour of the women, who both stretched the wages to make ends meet and supplemented such income by taking in boarders, raising pigs or chickens, and so on. Life was full of uncertainty; maintaining security, comfort, and respectability was sometimes extremely difficult. It was nonetheless the setting in which working-class boys and girls learned gender roles and acquired gender identities in the new industrial order. Males expected to become the dominant figures and breadwinners in their family households.

Each day, when these men headed off to workshops, mines, and mills, they encountered many changes on the job. This First Industrial Revolution introduced steam power and new technology, but far more disruption came from the ways that capitalists reorganized work. Perhaps most important, they brought together many workers under one roof, where labour could be better coordinated and monitored, and where discipline could be maintained more effectively. These goals were the central purposes of the first factories in Canada, as in other countries. Bells and clocks were installed to keep better track of time on the job. Strict rules were posted, and punishments for infractions included fines and beatings. At the same time, wherever possible, the new industrialists tried to reduce their reliance on artisans' skills so that they could produce goods more cheaply. In some cases they used the old technique of flooding the labour market with poorly trained workers, often boys and sometimes women, who could be paid less. In others they set out to break down the craftwork process into specialized tasks that could be parcelled out to less skilled workers to do repeatedly and presumably faster. In still others they searched for machinery — the rotary printing press, the sewing machine, the spinning mule, or the rolling mill, for example — to replace slow, expensive manual work. Work was being intensified dramatically.

Yet, despite all these efforts of aggressive entrepreneurs, success was limited. Newspaper editors and other commentators were mesmerized by the fiery rolling mills and by the new textile factories where hundreds of women and children handled fancy machinery. But around these islands of modernity many smaller, more labour-intensive workshops still ran on the skills of the craftworker. In foundries, cigar factories, print shops, buggy shops, and many other workplaces, workers continued to make products by hand in the old-fashioned ways, with little or no help from machinery. In the coal mines, colliers still dug out the coal with their simple tools and their ingenuity. At the same time, some of the new mechanized work processes created new groups of skilled workers: machinists, iron rollers, sawyers, locomotive engineers, clothing cutters, and so on. Many owners of mines and workshops actually found it practical to subcontract much of the work to these skilled individuals on their payroll. Of course, in the booming cities and towns, thousands of skilled building trades workers were still practising their crafts with fewer factory-like disruptions. In short, the first wave of industrialization in Canada did not wipe out the basis for craft unionism. The movement's most vigorous forms emerged in settings where employers who were attempting to produce for a mass market (agricultural implements, newspapers, cast-iron stoves, clothing, shoes, and so on) began to tighten the managerial screws on large groups of craftworkers who still maintained considerable control over the labour process. So, among the older crafts, the moulders, tailors, printers, coopers, cigarmakers, and shoemakers, along with such leading building trades workers as carpenters, were most likely to unionize.

In fact, craft organizations found new sources of support, as the craft union model spread rapidly to many new groups of skilled workers after 1850. The growing numbers of printers, tailors, carpenters, shipbuilders, and other familiar preindustrial craft unionists were joined by several aggressive new locals of coopers, cigarmakers, and moulders (who created some of the most tough-minded and persistent union organizations in late-nineteenth-century industrial Canada). Even the new skilled workers, notably machinists, iron puddlers and rollers, sawmill workers, and by 1865 locomotive engineers, were taking out union charters. The first coal miners' union appeared at Wellington on Vancouver Island in 1877 as the Miners' Mutual Protective Association, and two years later the coal miners of Springhill, Nova Scotia, created that province's first miners' organization, eventually known as the Provincial Workmen's Association (PWA), which soon had branches on the mainland and on Cape Breton Island. Some apparently unskilled workers such as longshoremen and carters also adopted the craft union model.

The attraction of this kind of organization for skilled workers (and for those who aspired to the same status) was that it gave them the opportunity to present a united front to employers who threatened to disrupt customary patterns of work and wages. The craft union model assumed that, by drawing in all practitioners of a particular craft, it would be possible to control the labour market for their skills — to prevent their bosses from destroying their apprenticeship systems by recruiting untrained workers and immigrants, from increasing their workloads unbearably, from scrapping the customary wage levels, and from undermining the respectable standard of living they aspired to. Respectability, in fact, was a touchstone of craft unionism: unionists were motivated by the desire to enjoy the material advantages of industrial "progress," to be able to provide well for their families, to participate fully in social, educational, and political life, to be treated justly and with dignity.

These elements in craft unionism — the attempts to retain exclusive control over who practised the craft and the yearning for respectability — separated these unionists from two other groups of workers. First, the unskilled were shunned if they tried to intrude on the craft and if, in their poverty and misery, they lived a rougher lifestyle. These attitudes could have a racist overlay if, as was often the case, the unskilled were Irish, French, or Asian. In British Columbia the first miners' unions were built on overtly racist attacks on Chinese workers, who were believed to be threatening the white workers' standard of living. Second, respectability incorporated the new "cult of domesticity" that urged women to stay in the household while the menfolk ventured forth into the world to earn the family's wages. Craftsmen tended to want female family members to remain at home, and deeply resented employers who brought in women as unskilled help in efforts to degrade the crafts. Printers, shoemakers, and tailors had all seen women brought in along with new machinery and the subdivision of labour. Their masculine identity as breadwinners and skilled producers — what they dubbed their "manhood" — was at risk. Craft unionists thus remained deeply suspicious and often openly hostile to women in the labour force.

While craftworkers began to use their organizations much more aggressively, only rarely did they try to halt or turn back industrial innovations. Those workers confronted first and most directly by new machines sometimes seized upon familar forms of resistance; Montreal shoemakers, for example, used the cover of an election riot in 1849 to smash a set of new sewing machines, and three years later Toronto tailors staged a mock funeral procession for the same equipment. After 1850, however, it was more common for craftworkers to try to win a secure place for themselves within industrializing society. Craft unionists therefore began to adapt their organizations to the new industrial age.

The widening network of railway lines gave workers much greater mobility in their search for jobs. British or Irish immigrants arriving to look for work in the colonies could try their luck in several different towns and even head south to the United States. On the way they often passed U.S. workers heading north to test the Canadian market for their craft skills. In order to make the conditions of work as similar as possible across the continent for these "tramping artisans," some local unions began in the 1850s and 1860s to affiliate with the emerging national organizations for their crafts in the United States. Gradually these continent-wide organizations changed their names to "international unions." A few locals of British unions also appeared in the 1850s among some machinists and carpenters, but this connection was not as useful for skilled workers as the North American link. The first affiliates were local unions in central Canada, and the region around Hamilton and Toronto became the core of this new continentalism. Gradually some groups of Maritime craftworkers reached southward as well. French Canadian unionists, however, remained suspicious of organizations that showed no sympathy for their separate culture, and smaller numbers of Quebec unions joined the continental movement in the late nineteenth century. In fact, throughout the country, independent local unions remained the norm. Thus, in the beginning, international unionism in Canada was an effort by craftworkers in the larger industrial centres, principally in central Canada, to control an emerging continental labour market in craft skills. Initially it involved mostly a better exchange of information (on the local labour market, union organization, or strikes), access to larger strike funds, and little loss of local control for Canadian craft unionists. For years to come, Canadian employers would nonetheless denounce the "foreign agitators," whom they held responsible for misleading and stirring up their otherwise content workers.

Craftworkers also struggled to gain a more secure footing for their unions and to compel their bosses to deal with them regularly. The inspiration for this more regularized approach to workers' organization was undoubtedly the so-called new-model unions that began to appear in England in the 1850s. The experience of these unions suggested that higher dues would provide more stability and negotiating clout, and that union activities should be more centrally coordinated. North American craftworkers, many of them British immigrants, were quick to adopt these practices. By the 1870s international unions were also beginning to codify their customary practices in union constitutions and rule books. These documents specified apprenticeship requirements, workload, hours of labour, the pace of work, and a host of other work-related matters. Locally each craft announced a "schedule" stating the precise terms, especially the wages to be paid, that employers had to accept if they wanted to hire union members.

The union had no intentions of negotiating these important issues, but plenty of employers balked at the demands. Some unions even banded together themselves and imposed the new tactic known as the "lock-out." Many more strikes resulted from these stand-offs than had ever taken place before — at least 349 across the country in the 1850s, 1860s, and 1870s, according to a recent estimate. In fact, the strike was evolving into a tactic for extracting concessions from employers that was more orderly than the sporadic eruptions of the preindustrial years. Workers now wanted not only to withhold their labour power to halt production, but also to bring community opinion to bear upon their employer. Discouraging strikebreakers might still involve hints of violence; the sober strike parade and quiet picket line became the respectable means of accomplishing both purposes.

The problem was that the courts frowned on such activity. A few Lower Canadian workers were condemned under the Combination Acts passed in Britain in 1799–1800. Eventually, by the mid-nineteenth century, judges had brought the common law into line with the reigning economic orthodoxy of *laisser-faire*, and union organizing and strikes could be construed as conspiracies in restraint of trade. Provincial legislation in Nova Scotia in 1816 and 1864, in Lower Canada in 1821, and in the United Province of Canada in 1847 reinforced these restrictions on union activity. At several points before 1872, workers were arraigned for their strike activities, although there is no evidence that any were successfully prosecuted for conspiracy. Newspaper editors and members of the clergy also regularly fanned public intolerance of collective organization, which, they claimed, violated the central precepts of an individualistic bourgeois, Christian age.

The craftsmanship union, however, was much more than simply a practical institution that facilitated collective bargaining. It was the skilled workers' way of nourishing the traditions of the craft, still celebrated in union meetings with elaborate rituals and in special parades with brass bands and richly adorned banners fluttering in the breeze; the union also allowed them to flex their pride in their craft, a pride which no longer seemed to be shared by their employers.

They regularly asserted a labour theory of value that stressed the importance of manual labour for society: in the words of a labour poet, "The noblest type of mankind / Are they that work to live. / ... The true wealth of a nation / Is in her workingmen!" In trades such as baking, coopering, moulding, shoemaking, and printing, there were even a few fleeting attempts to organize cooperative workshops as more humane alternatives to capitalist enterprise. Craft unionism was, in fact, a way of preserving alternative values that conflicted with the dominant bourgeois individualism that seemed to define the age. As much as these workers aspired to the respectability of middle-class life, they preferred to attain it collectively and in the process to preserve a spirit of solidarity and mutuality. On the job, craftworkers liked to cooperate as much as possible in carrying out their skilled tasks. After work, they shared a drink and a cigar or played baseball together, brought their families to balls and picnics, and generally kept alive a sense of community among themselves. Perhaps most symbolically, they always provided their deceased members with an appropriately respectable funeral.

In their battles for recognition, nineteenth-century craft unionists began to develop a sense of common interests with workers in other occupations. It was a slow and contradictory process, since the essence of craft unionism was to put up walls around each trade and to keep out all competition. But the pride in their crafts and the skills that made it possible easily extended to other skilled workers, as it had in the preindustrial days when artisans were self-employed. The first formal links between unions in different trades occurred at the city level. During 1867 thousands of Montreal workers rallied to an ambitious local project known as the Grand Association of Canadian Workingmen, under the charismatic leadership of Médéric Lanctôt. This lawyer-journalist promoted a broad platform of strike solidarity, cooperative production, nationalism, and liberal reform, but quickly destroyed the organization with his political ambitions. Hamilton, Toronto, and St. Catharines craftworkers organized less flamboyant trades assemblies in 1863, 1871, and 1875, respectively, and a trades council appeared in Ottawa in 1872. None of these organizations lasted more than a few years, but during their brief lifespans they acted as the focal point of community identity for their members. They organized balls, concerts, picnics, lectures, and perhaps a small lending library, coordinated strike activity, mediated industrial disputes, corresponded with workers' organizations in other Canadian cities and abroad, lobbied for legislative reforms, and generally promoted discussion about the worker's place in Victorian society.

The most impressive expression of cross-occupational solidarity emerged in 1872. By that point, the pace of industrialization was accelerating noticeably, and workers were beginning to wonder about their place in the new capitalist order. In Britain and the United States, unionists were already agitating for shorter hours of work as the reward to wage-earners for the new gains in productivity. By the early 1870s in several Canadian towns and cities, workers were pressing their employers for a reduction in the normal ten-to-twelve-hour working day. Early in 1872 a meeting in Hamilton launched the Nine-Hour Movement, which quickly spread across southern Ontario and into Montreal and beyond, to Sherbrooke and Quebec City. Railway-shop craftworkers were at the forefront of the organizing. In each town, workers formed Nine-Hour Leagues, essentially the country's first working-class political organizations, which held public meetings to promote the benefits of shorter hours and to encourage employers to comply. Leaders stressed how workers could become better citizens and have more time with the family, away from the job. "We want to better our physical constitutions, and increase our mental power ...," a prominent labour leader declared. "We want not more *money*, but more *brains*; not richer *serfs*, but better *men* ..." Another insisted that "the increase of intelligence among the masses of the people has opened up a new appetite that must be fed ..."

In the face of employer intransigence, the leagues developed a coordinated strategy of a series of general strikes beginning in Hamilton in May 1872. Their plans were disrupted when the Toronto printers jumped the gun and held a strike in March. The newspaper publishers, led by the irrepressible George Brown, responded by dragging the strike leaders into court on conspiracy charges. Brown's wily political opponent, Prime Minister John A. Macdonald, promptly made a conciliatory gesture to the growing numbers of organized craftworkers by introducing the Trade Unions Act, which was modelled on one passed in Britain the year before. Henceforth trade unions were to be exempt from the liability to common-law conspiracy charges. The momentum of the Nine-Hour Movement was nonetheless broken, and, when fifteen hundred Hamilton workers marched off the job on May 15, they faced their bosses' hostility alone. The strike petered out, and further agitation died, as Ontario employers closed ranks against the reform. Embittered leaders took little comfort later in the year when Canada's first working-class parliamentarian, Tory Henry B. Witton, was elected in Hamilton, since he had played no part in recent labour activity or the nine-hour agitation and would never show much independence from the Tory caucus.

This explosion of broad-based working-class solidarity may have been short lived, but it had two important longer-term consequences. First, it encouraged labour leaders to develop a more permanent presence in Canadian public life. A newspaper that focused on expressing workers' perspectives and concerns, the *Ontario Workman*, began its three-year run in 1872 (albeit with generous support from Macdonald and the Tories). Even more important, in the spring of that year, Nine-Hour League leaders met in Hamilton to establish the first organization to promote workers' interests across local and occupational boundaries. They dubbed it the Canadian Labor Protective and Mutual Improvement Association, but, when craft union leaders met a year later in Toronto, they chose the simpler title of the Canadian Labor Union (no doubt with an eye on the older American Labor Union). Despite the pretensions to national stature, delegates to the annual meetings held until 1878 came only from Ontario. This new body was not intended for negotiations with employers, and set only a limited role for itself in organizing workers. It was above all a political organization that hoped to develop a unified program of workers' concerns and to carry these concerns into the political arena — "to agitate such questions as may be for the benefit of the working classes, in order that we may obtain the enactment of such measures by the Dominion and local legislatures as will be beneficial to us, and the repeal of all oppressive laws which now exist."

While the rhetoric suggested broad working-class interests, and there were calls for free public education, full voting rights for all workers, factory inspection, and a bureau of labour statistics, most of the specific goals centred on the concerns of organized craftworkers. At the annual meetings, delegates passed resolutions for protection against competition from prison labour, child labour, unapprenticed workers, and immigrants who were willing to work for low wages, and for safeguards for such craft union activity as picketing. There was some talk about the need to elect nonpartisan workers to legislative halls to carry out such a program (though never a suggestion of an independent labour party), but, aside from the fact that existing property qualifications denied many workers the vote, most of these labour leaders remained close to the dominant political parties, either the Conservatives or the Liberals (Macdonald got maximum mileage out of his intervention in 1872). Ontario's sole working-class legislator was Ottawa printer Daniel J. O'Donoghue, who was elected to the legislature in 1874 as an independent candidate, but who quickly attached himself to the Liberals. Most of this labour movement's political work, therefore, consisted of intense lobbying, backed where necessary with mass meetings. These efforts paid off in the form of new mechanics' lien legislation (for recovering wages owed to workers) and an act to decriminalize the breach-of-contract provisions of the Master and Servant Act in Ontario, along with an 1876 federal act to protect peaceful picketing from criminal prosecution. Sustaining such an organization nonetheless proved difficult. The Canadian Labor Union quietly expired in the depths of the depression of the late 1870s, but it had given a generation of craft union leaders valuable political experience and compelled the Canadian state to respond.

The second major consequence of the Nine-Hour Movement involved the state's role in labour relations. Macdonald's dramatic gesture that brought the Trade Unions Act onto the statute books in 1872 was hailed as a great breakthrough for the emerging labour movement, since it removed the criminal taint on union activity. The prime minister was treated to labour dinners in his honour in Toronto and Ottawa. Certainly the legislation gave an important nod of approval to union activity, but it was no Magna Carta for Canadian workers. The act required unions to register to be eligible for this protection, a step that virtually no unions ever took. More importantly, the act was tied to another piece of legislation that criminalized numerous vaguely defined activities related to union organizing efforts: "molesting, obstructing, watching and besetting." Indeed, within the next year a few workers were indicted for conspiracy under this second act. It took intense union lobbying in Ottawa to obtain legislative clearance for nonobstructive picketing in 1876. The Canadian state had thus created only a tiny legal space within which unions could operate. Moreover, if employers found the new criminal law less useful in their battles with workers, they still had easy recourse to civil action under common law, and before World War II, unionists were still dragged before judges for civil conspiracy, conspiracy to induce breach of contract, and numerous other offences — all while the Trade Unions Act was in force. In the end, Macdonald's labour legislation was far less important for the security it gave unions than for the recognition of the political power of organized craftworkers it embodied and for the pattern it set for a state initiative as a pacifying force on a militant labour leadership.

Craft unionism, then, was the response of many (though by no means all) skilled workers to the changing nature of work in the second half of the nineteenth century — the demeaning new disciplines and controls, the downward pressure on wages and living standards, the outrage over the threat to dignity and self-worth. The limitations of craft unionism were evident by 1880. These unions had emerged mostly in the larger, industrially dynamic towns and cities in southern Ontario, Quebec, and the Maritimes. Efforts to broaden the connections between local unions beyond southern Ontario never succeeded, and most of the organizations remained fragmented and isolated. In many smaller places, of course, older patterns of paternalism still inhibited any sharp divide between skilled workers and their employers. In places where unionism took hold, the organizations were fragile creatures that often withered and had to be revitalized within a few years. Many fell apart when employers fired and blacklisted unionists and forced the remaining workers to sign so-called iron-clad contracts (promising to stay away from unions), and when the economy forced major shut-downs. The great depression in 1873 shattered the fragile movement that had taken shape early in the decade, and by the 1880s organizers had to begin from scratch in most parts of the country.

The craft union movement also had a narrow social base within the emerging working class. The notion of class unity with the unskilled, especially with female wage-earners, was still weak among men whose primary commitment was to defend craft privilege against industrial capitalist degradation. These craftsmen were struggling for a secure place in the new industrial order where they would be respected for their skills and abilities and allowed maximum independence and self-expression in most aspects of their lives. Their forms of organization reflected this concern with respectability. In contrast to the earlier "collective bargaining by riot," they pursued a sober, peaceful, orderly strategy of organizing and presenting their concerns. In the words of the chairman of the first Canadian Labor Union meeting, these unionists were "honest, earnest, and prudent workers." Such words stood in marked contrast to the blunter actions taken by angry crowds of canal labourers in Montreal who fought with strikebreakers in 1877, or by construction labourers in Quebec City the next year who marched on the provincial legislature to protest wage cuts, who looted a flour warehouse, and who fought troops sent to restore order.

It would be convenient to dub these craft unionists an "aristocracy of labour," and in many ways their eagerness to defend their status in the production process earned them this label. But they were something more as well. Their reverence for manual labour, their commitment to mutual support and solidarity as the means for improving their social condition, and their deep devotion to liberal democracy encouraged many craftworkers to identify and promote the more general interests of "workingmen," transcending their narrow focus on craft-related concerns. This new perspective should not be confused with a full-fledged class consciousness, since it kept the skilled man in the foreground and harboured plenty of ambiguity about other workers. But in the context of industrial conflict, this new approach was able to pull craft unionists closer to a sense of class. It took the new conditions of the 1880s to highlight that possibility more dramatically.

The Great Upheaval

By the 1880s there was no longer any question that an Industrial Revolution was under way in Canada. With the stimulus of the high-tariff National Policy, factory production and coal mining expanded remarkably in the Maritimes, in central Canada, and in British Columbia, and many more workers were drawn into the new structures of industrial capitalist production. Some industrialists now stood atop huge enterprises in their communities; in transportation and finance, even larger corporations with substantial economic power had appeared. This new economy nonetheless gave many Canadians a roller-coaster ride of rapid expansion, followed by overproduction and frequent cut-backs in output and wages. Workers were forcefully reminded of the chronic insecurity of their jobs and their incomes. The shock of this rapidly changing world stirred up renewed working-class concern about living standards and cherished values, and improved employment prospects in the early and mid-1880s gave many workers the opportunity to act on their outrage.

Many workers in the new industries organized spontaneously, without a union to lead them. Among these groups, women factory workers were the most remarkable, especially in textile, boot-and-shoe, and tobacco production. Female cotton workers burst into uncharacteristic militancy in Montreal in 1880; Milltown, New Brunswick, in 1886; Kingston in 1886 and 1887; Cornwall in 1888 and 1889; and Hamilton in 1890. Craft unions revived with new vigour in the 1880s in centres where they had previously taken hold and began appearing in many other cities. Strikes erupted over the same issues that had haunted craftworkers since mid-century. There were also clear signs that craft unionists in many of these localities turned to joint action with other skilled workers as they perceived a growing gulf between themselves and their capitalist employers and a threat to their long-term interests. More unions linked up with internationals in the United States. Local trades councils proliferated in every region of the country; there were thirty-five by the turn of the century. In 1883 many of these unionists met in Toronto to inaugurate a national labour organization, and three years later they established a permanent organization, the Trades and Labor Congress of Canada (TLC), which met annually for the next seventy years.

Regional differences persisted, however. In the Maritimes the most remarkable development was the rise and consolidation of the independent Provincial Workmen's Association. This miners' organization included a few local branches of glass, foundry, and boot-and-shoe workers, but generally it functioned as a fairly loose confederation of skilled colliers' lodges. Watching over its affairs was an articulate miner-turned-journalist, Robert Drummond, who acted as general secretary and chief ideologue. An earnest, preachy teetotaller obsessed with working-class respectability, Drummond was always ready to trumpet the rights of independent workers in the face of unreasonably autocratic mine managers and an undemocratic state. With or without his blessing, local PWA lodges waged surprisingly successful battles to retain their direct control over coal-hewing operations. In 1886 they made their first foray into independent labour politics by nominating workers for election to the legislature; their candidates were defeated. Drummond nonetheless used this new militancy to parlay his connections with the provincial Liberal party into the most impressive concessions to workers from any government in Canada in the period. These measures consisted of a vastly improved system of mine inspection, arbitration services for industrial disputes, an extension of the electoral franchise ("the badge of citizenship") to residents of company housing, and, most important, legislation in 1891 requiring certification of skilled miners. As in the past, however, the miners' struggles remained largely isolated from those of the urban craftworkers in the region and in the rest of the country.

Outside the Maritimes, one new organization swept up the energies of Canadian workers more than any other: the Noble and Holy Order of the Knights of Labor. Founded in Philadelphia in 1869 as a secret society, the Knights were operating openly by the time a group of Hamilton painters met in an unfinished building in 1881 to launch the organization's first "local assembly" in Canada. The order's popularity soared after the Knights used a huge strike to win recognition from the U.S. railway baron, Jay Gould, in 1885. In the wake of such a spectacular victory, the Knights of Labor became the great hope of workers in the United States and in many other countries. People surged enthusiastically into the order; it is estimated that in 1886 the Knights' membership passed one million around the world. At that point, there were more than two hundred local assemblies in Canada — more than three-quarters of them in Ontario, a sprinkling in the West, and most of the rest in Quebec. Between the 1880s and the early 1900s, four hundred assemblies probably existed in the country, often grouped in "district assemblies." Some of these groups simply incorporated older craft unions (though some cautious craftworkers preferred dual membership), but many drew in workers who had never enrolled in a labour organization. Few urban industries were untouched by this new organizing drive, from Montreal garment shops, to Winnipeg railway yards, to Vancouver Island mining towns.

Organizationally, the Knights were flexible. Workers joined either "trade" assemblies specific to a craft or "mixed" assemblies of varied occupations, which might exist in one small community or in a single large factory (such as a cotton or lumber mill, or a farm-machinery plant). Most organizations were trade assemblies, and almost everywhere craftworkers filled the leadership role. Yet what made this organization so different was that all workers, regardless of skill, were welcomed into the noble cause. As a result, female workers in cotton mills, clothing shops, and shoe factories, led by bold young women such as Hamilton's Katie McVicar, entered the ranks of organized labour for the first time in Canadian history. So too did blacks. In both cases these workers were often hived off into their own assemblies, but they were full members of the order nonetheless. In addition, a new sensitivity to francophones brought about separate district assemblies for English and French workers in Montreal in 1889. As in the past, the informal focal point of this international movement in Canada was the Hamilton-Toronto region, where the order's Canadian leaders maintained regular communication with the Philadelphia headquarters. But the movement developed little national cohesion. Its strength lay, quite unevenly, in local communities and subregions around major cities, where in some cases a huge percentage of the local workforce was swept up and in others much smaller numbers were involved.

The Knights of Labor managed to attract such a widespread, diverse membership because of its unique combination of ideology and practice. As the name of the order suggests, the Knights were centrally concerned with protecting and enhancing the nobility of labour. Those who worked with hand or brain and "earned their bread by the sweat of their brow" were worthy of respect; those who lived off the labour of others or who blocked productive labour were not. Looking around in the 1880s, the Knights were dismayed to find this formula reversed. The loosely defined enemy included monopolists and land speculators, and many Knights were avid readers of Henry George and were active proponents of his single-tax theory. But their critique covered a wider range. The Knights challenged the dominant acquisitive tendencies of the industrial capitalist economy. Their Declaration of Principles opened with a ringing denunciation of the "alarming development and aggression of aggregated wealth, which, unless checked, will inevitably lead to pauperization of the toiling masses." Industrial capitalism seemed to have released the moral constraints on society — reducing workers to poverty, forcing women and children into the workforce, bringing in allegedly "uncivilized" Chinese labour, and corrupting politics.

The Knights saw an alternative to the growing economic competitiveness and inequality of wealth that undermined community morality and living standards. They believed that productive labour should be properly rewarded and respected, and that democracy and cooperation should be the organizing principles of industrial society. A century later, their rhetoric may sound socialistic, but they never called for the abolition of private capital or for widespread public ownership of the means of production. They did discuss (and experiment with) producers' cooperatives as an alternative to capitalist ownership, but more often they simply emphasized the need to impose moral restraints on the free play of the market and to preserve a greater sense of community and social responsibility in industrial society. Despite the class-conscious tone of their public statements, the Knights focused on social cohesion and cooperation among "the masses," that is, all those who worked by hand or brain (only bankers, lawyers, gamblers, and saloon-keepers were officially barred from membership in the order). At the core of their analysis was the "honest workingman," who was every inch the self-improving, morally upright Victorian (certainly a teetotaller), who cooperated with his fellow workers to maintain decent living standards and fair working conditions, who bowed his head to no one, and whose pride, independence, and respectability were under attack. Social "progress" toward justice and economic security would come from the collective struggle of such enlightened, morally sound individuals — men and women alike. The outcome, many Knights believed, would be more an ethical than an economic revolution, resulting in a society based on more democratic, humane relationships. Half a century later, the mayor of Hamilton fondly recalled his youth in the order: "I thought its programme would revolutionize the world ... It was a crusade for purity in life generally." In general, the Knights of Labor incorporated many of the learnings of the craft unionists of the 1870s for working-class independence and dignity, but now presented a sharper criticism of industrial capitalist society and a bolder vision of a different future. The calm confidence of the Nine-Hour Movement gave way to a sense of crisis.

To the modern eye, the Knights' local assembly meetings seem strangely archaic. New recruits encountered a complex ritual of passwords and symbols adapted from one of the most popular male recreational settings of the period, the fraternal lodges. The ceremony was intended not only to bind the members together with familiar rituals, but also to celebrate the dignity of toil and the value of the producer. Members meeting on the street were expected to exchange special handshakes and key phrases to acknowledge their solidarity outside the meeting hall: "I am a worker," one would declare; "I too earn my bread by the sweat of my brow," the other would reply with an appropriate gesture. The local assembly meeting had different goals: to respond to particular problems the members had with their employer, as a craft union would do; to help educate the members regarding major social, economic, and political issues with lectures and discussion; and to collect local industrial statistics (on wage rates, employment patterns, and so on). In general, the assemblies strived "to assist members to better their condition — morally, socially, and financially." To link up the individual assemblies, the order sponsored innumerable picnics, balls, musicals, parades, and public celebrations, which drew hundreds, even thousands, of participants in many towns and cities. For active members, these events helped to make the order an all-encompassing network of associations.

The Knights' program of action placed high priority on "spreading the light"; that is, educating workers in the principles of what the order liked to call "labor reform." Assemblies held special meetings featuring guest lecturers, often from the United States. They opened reading rooms and supported several weekly labour newspapers from Montreal to Victoria; a cadre of self-taught working-class intellectuals and talented journalists — notably a brilliant, popular Toronto intellectual, Phillips Thompson — contributed to these publications. Once educated, workers would use the ballot box to send working-class candidates to the legislatures and to put industrial society on the right track. In several cities from Montreal to Nanaimo the Knights helped to create the country's first local independent labour parties, though more often workers ran independently with support from the Knights, from craft unionists, and, occasionally, from middle-class reformers such as those in the temperance movement. Bold speeches about the rights of workers and the evils of monopoly punctuated many campaigns for municipal, provincial, and federal office between 1883 and 1894. For the most part, old-party allegiances and voter cynicism undermined these electoral efforts, and, above the municipal level, only four working-class candidates ran successfully (two in Quebec and two in Ontario), each loosely attached to a mainstream party.

In the meantime, the order supported several experiments in producer and consumer cooperatives to indicate what was possible; however, on the whole, their commercial success was as limited as that of many small capitalist enterprises in the period. The concerns of the Knights' leaders about respectability and community solidarity made them uncomfortable with strikes as a working-class tactic, and they preferred to put industrial disputes before an arbitrator whenever possible. But employers were seldom willing to accept such procedures and generally opted to fire and blacklist members of the order or to bring in strikebreakers to undermine the organization. As a result, the Knights found themselves embroiled in several large strikes against anti-union industrialists.

The Knights' appeal was compelling; membership rose dramatically around 1883 and then soared between 1885 and 1887. (Officially the Canadian membership exceeded 14,000 in 1886, but many thousands more workers undoubtedly passed through the order during these years.) Somehow the Knights' moral outrage and vision of a more communitarian alternative caught the mood of thousands of anxious workers, who were prepared to take a stand against the dominant social and economic developments of the late nineteenth century. The sense of a great moral crusade hung in the air. A few of the major strikes led by the Knights against monopoly companies brought hundreds of citizens into the streets in support. Some newspapers opened their columns to the Knights. Some employers tried to meet the thrust of this new labour challenge with the first company-sponsored welfare and recreation programs. Politicians also sensed the mood and rushed to respond. In Ontario and Quebec, factory acts entered the statute books for the first time. The Ontario legislature also appointed a labour statistician (none other than the ubiquitous Daniel J. O'Donoghue) and passed a minimal workers' compensation act. In 1886 Macdonald's federal government initiated the most dramatic response: the large, perambulating Royal Commission on the Relations of Labour and Capital, which heard extensive testimony throughout eastern and central Canada on all the issues that the Knights were concerned about. Clearly the order was having a profound effect on the industrializing society of the 1880s.

Yet just as abruptly, after 1886, membership slipped away and local assemblies began to crumble. In a few localities, especially in Quebec, local assemblies flourished well into the 1890s, but the mass membership was gone. What had happened? After 1886 another downturn in the economy, which reached a deep trough by the early 1890s, certainly robbed the Knights of the bargaining edge and optimism that fuller employment had allowed. As in each upsurge of labour militancy, this economic context would be decisive. Hostile employers thus had a freer hand to crush strikes, most of which were lost in the late 1880s. In Quebec the higher clergy of the Catholic Church complicated these struggles by labelling the Knights as godless revolutionaries (until the Pope decided to leave the order in peace in mid-1887).

Furthermore, external pressures brought serious tensions within the order to the surface. The most ideologically committed leaders of the Knights envisioned the road to labour reform through enlightened use of the ballot box and the development of producer and consumer cooperatives; these leaders were skeptical, even occasionally contemptuous, of industrial militancy. By 1887 this emphasis had caused conflicts with many rank-and-file Knights of Labor in two important ways. First, the plunge into independent labour politics that was intended to unite workers on election day actually embroiled them in highly partisan wrangles, since many "independent" candidacies involved deals with the Liberals or the Conservatives. Moreover, opportunists with private political ambitions occasionally tried to use the Knights as a springboard. As supporters of each party in the upper echelons of the Knights in Toronto jockeyed for position, some members drifted away in disgust.

Second, and probably more important, the larger political vision of the Knights' leaders made them insensitive to the shorter-term dynamics of workplace struggles. Since strikes were authorized only when "all other means [had] failed," local assemblies often walked out on strike in the face of their leaders' earnest entreaties to wait. The Knights held back workers at Toronto's biggest factory, Massey Manufacturing (agricultural implement works), for at least eighteen months in the mid-1880s, and, by 1887, the order had not only discouraged workers in several Toronto plants from striking, but also ordered them to dismantle their picket lines and return to work prematurely. Later, the degree of caution became almost paralyzing: in 1891 Knights leaders informed seething Ottawa and Hull lumbermill workers that six-months' notice was needed before calling a strike (undaunted, the workers organized on their own, won a partial victory over the lumber barons, and early the next year put together a Knights' assembly of two thousand members). A lengthy, bitter strike against the Toronto Street Railway company in 1886 proved to be a turning point in the clash between the leaders' ideology and the Knights' performance on the picket lines: when leaders directed much money and energy away from the strike into a cooperative bus project, they suffered a serious loss of credibility among local trade unionists.

Weak leadership in strikes was one element in a pattern of increasingly stormy relations with the craft unions that existed alongside the assemblies. For many years the relationship between the two bodies was cordial; they sat together in local and national trades councils and even cooperated on picket lines. But friction was inevitable when the two organizations recruited the same occupational groups. Tensions exploded when the Knights signed up scab cigarmakers in Hamilton, London, and other towns and allowed them to use the order's label in competition with the international cigarmakers' union. The local leaders of international unions were outraged. After 1886 many craft unionists retreated from the order, convinced that for all its high ideals it was not reliable in the all-important, rough-and-tumble world at the point of production.

The Knights leaders in Canada had been articulate craftworkers with a new project to propose to workers. For four or five years in the mid-1880s, these leaders managed to convince thousands to join the order's assemblies, but they later lost their confidence. Disillusioned by the Knights' weak and divided leadership in the face of depression and strikebreaking, most members of the order lost heart and drifted away. The moment of hope and vision had passed by the end of the decade. The memory of this "great upheaval" lingered for a few years, as individuals continued their labour activism in the craft union movement and, in a few cases, in more radical politics. In the 1890s, utopian radicalism flowered briefly among small numbers of urban craftworkers and disillusioned middle-class allies, who carried the moral fervour of the 1880s towards an ethically based socialism (in some cases under the influence of the American Edward Bellamy). But for the new generation of working-class activists, who emerged by World War I, the order was a distant reference point. Organizing had to begin anew within a thoroughly altered workforce in a different economic context. The tension between a narrow focus on workplace resistance and a wider political vision nonetheless returned many times to the Canadian labour movement.

For the most part, working-class organizing in nineteenth-century Canada was an enterprise conducted in factories, mines, and building sites by skilled workers, who were concerned about their deteriorating position in the production process and in the wider society. Isolated wage-earners in agriculture and logging and in stagnant towns and villages remained largely untouched. The growth of craft unions over these decades was neither easy nor smooth; growth spurts appeared in the 1830s, 1850s, 1870s, and most dramatically in the 1880s, each followed by defeat and retreat. Nevertheless, in each wave of militancy, the distance between these craftworkers and their bosses widened, and their outrage grew commensurately. By the 1880s many of these skilled workers were convinced that they had to take a stand against the whole industrial system, which still seemed new enough to accommodate change. For the first time, they reached out to less skilled workers and began to act much more like they were leading a movement of the entire working class, even if their rhetoric was often less precise about class tensions. The failure of that initiative left many of these workers much more sober and cautious about the possibilities of industrial transformation. Much of the new union organizing that began at the close of the 1890s reflected a realization that some form of industrial capitalism was here to stay, and the new goal was to find a secure niche within this structure. Looking around, unionists found a few precedents for a stable collective-bargaining relationship — among printers, locomotive engineers, and, above all, miners. Other workers, however, soon reached more radical conclusions.

2

The Workers' Revolt

Most Canadian workers in the 1920s would scarcely have recognized the wage-earning world of their grandparents. Entering the gate to the factory or pit-head, these workers were now more likely to pass beneath the boldly lettered name of a corporate giant — such as home-grown Massey-Harris or Stelco, or U.S. branch plants Ford or Westinghouse — rather than the name of an individual capitalist. Since the 1890s, capitalists in several major industries had learned to submerge their competitive instincts in large new corporations, in order to command the heights of their respective national, or even continental, markets. They had created what would become known as monopoly capitalism.

In some cases they had brought brand new industries to Canada — steel, auto, pulp and paper, chemicals, electrical parts, and nickel mining, for example. Some of the most sophisticated industrial production in the Western World had thus grown up on Canadian soil. These capitalists had also been responsible, with help from the Canadian state, for the integration and centralization of a national economy, which contrasted with the regional clusters of the late-nineteenth-century economy. Most factories, along with the head offices of finance, transportation, and utilities empires, were now found in southern Ontario and in the Montreal region. Large urban metropolises had become the home of more and more economic activity, and had attracted most of the migrants from the countryside and many of those from abroad. The Maritimes, the North, and the West had been reduced to resource hinterlands, often for U.S. industry. In fact, the rapid growth of the resource sector was one of the most important developments in this new economy; these sectors included wheat farming on the Prairies, logging in British Columbia, and hard-rock mining in northern and western Canada. In consolidating their new regime, these corporate capitalists had met vigorous opposition from farmers, small-business owners, French Canadian nationalists, regional boosters, and, inevitably, workers.

But, by the 1920s, they had triumphed over their opponents and won compliance with their grand projects for capital accumulation.

Inside their new enterprises, these industrialists presided over a Second Industrial Revolution. Few industries escaped the more aggressive attempts to break down skills and to mechanize both skilled and unskilled work in the push for higher productivity. Professional managers were hired to take over the thinking and planning functions formerly performed by workers on the shop floor. With the rigid tools of cost accounting, these managers monitored and coordinated production more rigorously, standardizing tasks, reducing workers' independence and flexibility, and trying to cut labour costs. Many found inspiration in Frederick Winslow Taylor's "principles of scientific management," though few firms implemented Taylor's whole scheme with the infamous stopwatches. Essentially, managers created relentless pressure to work faster and produce more. Henry Ford set up his famous experiments, which culminated in the auto assembly line, in Detroit and Windsor. The new managerial practices appeared in many other factories and mines, but their effect was uneven across the industrial landscape; eastern Canadian logging, for example, proceeded untouched, most coal mines remained highly labour intensive, and many small factories still ran on older principles. Yet, by the 1920s, thousands of Canadian workers who punched the new time clocks every day had become familiar with this more bureaucratically managed workplace.

These technological and managerial changes gave the overall structure of the Canadian workforce a new shape. Skilled workers and labourers had not disappeared, but by the 1920s they coexisted with huge numbers of so-called semiskilled machine operators, who were neither as well rounded in their knowledge of production as the craftworkers nor as dispensable as the unskilled labourers. Alongside these blue-collar workers were thousands of new clerical workers, increasingly women, who handled the growing managerial paperwork and whose jobs were organized on general principles that were the same as those of factory work. Simultaneously, many corporate industrialists altered the ethnic complexion of the working class by recruiting migrant peasant-labourers from China, Italy, Poland, Ukraine, and other parts of the rural periphery of the industrialized world for the massive construction projects of the period and for the least-skilled tasks in factories and mines. In some cases, these newcomers arrived as strikebreakers and incurred the wrath of Anglo-Canadian workers. Almost everywhere, they lived in separate immigrant enclaves. In other parts of the industrial towns could be found even larger numbers of skilled newcomers, such as miners and machinists, and female weavers and knitters, from England and Scotland. These occupational and ethnic changes, in essence, created a new working class. And it took some time for workers to become accustomed to this new industrial life and to their new workmates.

This occupational insecurity was compounded by the unpredictability of a boom-and-bust economy. A few years of full employment with ample overtime would abruptly turn into a deep depression (1907–9, 1913–15, and 1920–25). The costs of such basic necessities as food and rent nonetheless rose steadily before the war and then meteorically in the latter years of World War I. Working-class housewives were hard pressed to make ends meet. Living standards in overcrowded boom-town environments showed little improvement.

Workers in this new industrial age developed many different ways of coping. Many had no intention of staying in the jobs that opened up in railway construction camps, mass-production factories, or corporate mining operations, and huge numbers floated between jobs and between cities and regions. Many Canadian farmers and their youngsters took short-term wage-earning jobs, in search of quick cash. Most of the new immigrants from Asia and southern and eastern Europe were sojourners who intended to stay in Canada temporarily. Not until the 1930s did this transiency in the Canadian labour market wind down, as the huge number of short-term jobs in construction and agriculture dried up and the immigration gates were shut.

Joining a union in the monopoly capitalist era was not always a free and easy choice. The decision to ignore the appeal of a union organizer was sometimes based on unwillingness to abandon an individualistic approach to survival or on disenchantment with union officials; but more often, in the workplace (and sometimes in the wider community), corporate employers created an atmosphere in which it would be folly to show any union sympathies. With "stool-pigeons" in every department and unemployed workers hanging around the factory gate, employees could easily lose their jobs and be blacklisted. Freedom of speech and association meant little in such an autocratic work world.

Despite the drifting between jobs and the severe repression, some workers banded together for a brief moment to confront their bosses over short-term demands, especially wages and customary work routines. In the decade before World War I, there were increasingly frequent explosions of militancy on work sites and inside factories, as small groups of workers — a gang of Italian labourers, a group of textile workers, or a department of skilled machinists — undertook their own informal shop-floor bargaining, without the involvement of any unions. Yet this period is marked by the massive growth in the size and ambitions of the Canadian labour movement. By the end of World War I, a large proportion of the Canadian working class was organized and animated by a renewed vision of a better world for workers. The spark of freedom and independence that was lit between 1916 and 1920 was snuffed out in the early 1920s.

The Crisis of the Craftworker

The craftworkers who had survived the First Industrial Revolution soon found this second phase of industrial transformation traumatic. They confronted the same old pressures of labour markets flooded with poorly trained, underpaid workers, now often recruited by aggressive new employers' associations or professional strikebreaking organizations from the United States, such as the Pinkerton or Thiel detective agencies. But, even more important, cost-conscious managers and tyrannical supervisors were invading the independence of workers in the production process more systematically than ever before, with new machinery to undercut their skills and greater scrutiny of their established work practices. Many craftworkers, still proud, refused to take these changes lying down. Their main strategy was to compel employers, corporate and small-scale, to recognize the autonomous nature of their work, even if earning that recognition meant defending an increasingly tiny space in the workplace.

Since the first burst of prosperity at the turn of the century was largely based on the smaller-scale structures of the late-nineteenth-century economy, Canadian craftworkers were able to rally on familiar industrial turf to regain the wages and working conditions that had been eroded in the 1890s. This time they organized more systematically than ever before. In dozens of Canadian towns and cities, skilled workers listened eagerly to the itinerant full-time organizers of the revived U.S. labour movement (the so-called walking delegates that employers denounced so vitriolically) and decided to cast their lot with the brand of international unionism centred in the American Federation of Labor (AFL). Founded in 1886 and headed for nearly forty years by a shrewd ex-cigarmaker, Samuel Gompers, the AFL consisted of a grouping of craft unions that by 1900 had already adapted to the failure of the all-inclusive Knights of Labor and to rising corporate power by developing a more bureaucratic style of unionism within each craft. This new "business unionism" featured higher dues, more full-time officials and organizers, greater centralization of power over strike funds and benefit plans, and stricter lines of demarcation around the crafts. These boundaries provoked frequent jurisdictional battles between unions and excluded the unskilled. The AFL allowed only one union to exist in each trade, and the idea of uniting all workers in one workplace, regardless of skill, was anathema. Women in the paid workforce were rarely allowed into the crafts and thus played only minor roles in such organizations.

Following the early example of the United Mine Workers of America (UMWA), the AFL unions were committed to consolidating stable collective-bargaining arrangements with employers in formal, mutually binding, written contracts, backed by union strength and not by law, and sometimes backed by a union label (on consumer goods). Union leaders wanted to impose specific rules of behaviour on employers. These arrangements inevitably ruled out sympathetic strikes. Yet the craft union leadership expected that such voluntary agreements throughout industry (or "industrial legality," as it has been called), and not political agitation for the intervention of the state, would spread "fair" work practices and decent living standards across North America. To keep tabs on such local agreements, some craft unions hired full-time "business agents." These agents gradually became part of a new labour bureaucracy, which included the officers and organizers of international unions, and which began to develop a concern with protecting the union organization, its assets, its procedures, and its contractual obligations, as well as their own status and salaries. By denying access to central strike funds or ordering strikers back to work, these full-time officials sometimes put brakes on workers' anger and resentment.

Despite this tendency toward bureaucratic caution, opinions still ranged widely and militancy stirred within this craft union movement. Unionists continued to pursue the elusive goal of respectability, but at the local and even the international level, they were often tough, uncompromising fighters for craft interests and sometimes for wider goals. Curiously, it was the organization of street railway workers across the continent that suggested how the narrow bounds of respectability and craft exclusivism could be burst. In city after city (Toronto in 1902, Hamilton and Winnipeg in 1906, St. John in 1913, and so on), street railway locals were forced to strike against the large, privately owned utilities empires that controlled the street-cars, and each time huge, angry crowds of workers took to the city streets to attack company property and strikebreakers. Of course, the craft unions never mobilized or condoned such action, but many different workers participated in the crowd actions.

In the United States, craftworkers were still aiming to control the continental labour market for each skill, and they reached out to their Canadian counterparts more persistently in the late 1890s and early 1900s to prevent the development of a cheap, non-union labour pool north of the forty-ninth parallel. For their part, Canadian craftworkers saw the chance to increase their bargaining power and expertise enormously, even at the expense of relinquishing power over calling strikes and handling funds to a headquarters south of the border. Between 1899 and 1903, Canadian workers in many industries signed up by the thousands in the biggest organizing campaign since the 1880s. In 1902, moreover, the leaders of the American Federation of Labor conspired with a committed band of young Canadian craft unionists to have the Trades and Labor Congress of Canada expel any independent unions that existed alongside the internationals. The TLC was an independent national organization with a mixture of purely Canadian and international affiliates, but it quickly fell into line with the AFL policy. The last remnants of the Knights of Labor, several French Canadian locals, and a few independents were thus shut out of Canada's "House of Labor" (they regrouped in a weak organization that after 1908 was known as the Canadian Federation of Labour). That victory was crowned with the election of the Cana-dian AFL organizer, John Flett, to the congress presidency. The split isolated roughly one-third of Quebec's unions and the leading labour organization in the Maritimes, the Provincial Workmen's Associa-tion (PWA). By the end of World War I, however, the vast majority of Canadian union members, even those in Quebec, belonged to U.S.-based organizations (though international craft unionism re-mained much weaker in the Maritimes and the West than in Ontario). Over the next half century, Canadian unionists, and particularly the Trades and Labor Congress, had difficulty carving out room to ma-noeuvre in response to specifically Canadian conditions, since the U.S. labour leaders viewed Canada as merely another state. But the Canadians hung on, bound by the ideal of internationalism, the strike funds and benefit plans, and the career interests of their full-time officials — the Canadian vice-presidents, business agents, and organizers, who were concentrated in southern Ontario.

At the same time, the old commitment to wider networks of solidarity lived on. Among Canadian craft unions, only the brotherhoods in the railway running trades remained rigidly aloof from all other unions well into the twentieth century. The Trades and Labor Congress still met each year, gradually drawing in representatives from all regions of the country. Aside from a small part-time executive, the congress remained little more than a national gathering at which unionists enunciated their collective demands, which had hardly changed since the days of the Canadian Labor Union. Once a year, delegations arrived in Ottawa and the provincial capitals, with cap in hand, to present the most recent congress resolutions. Provincial organizations existed in Ontario after 1902, in British Columbia after 1910, and in Alberta after 1912. In a few of the larger cities, craftworkers in the same industry, such as the building or the metal trades, formed councils to develop common negotiating strategies, but these bodies had great difficulty persuading the individual crafts to surrender some independence and seldom survived long.

More important were the only other coordinating bodies, the local trades and labour councils, in which craft union representatives met every couple of weeks to discuss common concerns and to respond quickly to pressing issues. These bodies mobilized strike support, lobbied municipal and provincial governments, sponsored weekly labour newspapers, and even launched short-lived local labour parties. A few built "labour temples" to house the city's labour activities. In fact, most of the active life of the Canadian craft union movement in the early twentieth century revolved around individual communities, in contrast to the larger national and continental focus of corporate capitalists. By World War I, the most important concession that these local bodies had begun to extract from a few provincial governments, through joint lobbying and agitation, was comprehensive workers' compensation legislation.

On a week-by-week basis, then, this union movement resembled a string of relatively independent urban islands, each inhabited by single locals of international unions and each taking on a distinctive flavour from the industrial mix of its community, from relations with local employers, from links with middle-class allies, and from the politics and personalities of key local labour leaders. Thus, feisty delegates from the Vancouver or Winnipeg trades and labour councils often clashed with the more cautious craftworkers of Hamilton or Ottawa (though eventually the westerners would make common cause with Cape Breton coal miners).

Few Canadian employers were prepared to have anything to do with this upstart labour movement. The new management theories left no room for negotiation with organized workers. Employers' associations in individual cities or industries, often with connections to U.S. "open-shop" organizations, were started up to drive out unions and their organizers with strikebreakers, blacklists, and industrial spies. Hostile industrialists also turned to the courts more regularly for injunctions (a new legal tool) to block union action and to sue unions for damages from strikes, boycotts, and hostile labour press coverage. A highly symbolic case against the sheet metal workers of the Metallic Roofing Company in Toronto worked its way up the judicial ladder with substantial support from companies and unions, echoing the famous Taff-Vale case in Britain. Eventually it faded from sight in a private settlement, but not before many unionists had been sufficiently intimidated.

Outside the railway industry, the first wave of organizing at the turn of the century and a second in the five years before the war thus met consistent and concerted resistance and suffered major defeats. Unprecedented numbers of strikes erupted throughout central and eastern Canada in industrialized communities where craftworkers were still heavily involved in production. But, by World War I, craft unions had been driven back from the heart of the new industries and lay in a crippled state.

Workers of the World Unite

Who would organize the thousands of Canadian workers whose level of skill denied them membership in craft unions? The Knights of Labor had opened its ranks to all workers, but it had not promoted a consistent form of labour organization; trade and mixed assemblies had coexisted. By the turn of the century a new model of unionization was emerging that would dissolve these distinctions and unite all workers in the same organization — industrial unionism. Many labour historians have described this new approach as a uniquely western Canadian phenomenon, but it is more accurate to view it as the result of the particular combination of industry and population in both the West and the East, and to a limited extent in the centre. The impetus for this new style of unionism came from industries where workers were concentrated in large numbers and faced more aggressive corporate employers, where key groups of workers still had some independence from their bosses, and where distinctions between crafts were traditionally limited or were dissolving in the Second Industrial Revolution. In many of these communities, there was a high percentage of immigrants. Often, the workers who became the union leaders had recently arrived from the United States, Britain, or eastern Europe, bringing heavy political baggage from struggles in their homelands.

In fact, socialists were the foremost advocates of industrial unionism and leaders of the new unions. Their rejection of industrial capitalist society led these activists to seek the unity of all workers in a common struggle, rather than the division of workers into narrowly exclusive organizations; socialists regularly denounced the policies of the "American Separation of Labor." Many of these radicals theorized, somewhat mechanistically, that industrial unionism was the logical working-class response to the corporate form of capitalist organization. In fact, by World War I, this new unionism had become integrated into many socialists' thinking as the economic component in the socialist revolution. International borders had little meaning for these workers, and, in virtually all cases before World War I, enthusiasts of the new unionism linked up with like-minded organizations in the United States. By World War I, industrial unionism had emerged as a full-fledged alternative to craft unionism, though its success was just as limited.

Before the war, industrial unionism in Canada was most vigorous in the resource industries, and miners were the true pioneers. By the turn of the century, hard-rock miners, who dug out metals for large mining and smelting corporations, were setting the pace. Their history had begun in the 1890s in the mining camps of the Western United States, where some of the most violent, open warfare in North American labour history had raged between corporate mine owners and members of the Western Federation of Miners (WFM), founded in 1893. The experienced miners whom Canadian owners recruited moved freely through the mining regions on both sides of the border, educating others on the principles and tactics of resistance to capitalist aggression. By 1900 these miners had established several Canadian locals, which also included smelter workers. Mine managers refused to recognize the locals. The decisive battle shaped up at Rossland, British Columbia, in 1901, where the largest WFM local in the region was destroyed with spies, special police, professional strikebreakers, and injunctions.

Miners immersed in this no-holds-barred confrontation were no longer willing to listen to moderate voices in their union halls. In 1902 the WFM convention endorsed socialism as the organization's ultimate goal. Even more important, the union took the leading role that year in founding a new national labour centre, the American Labor Union, to compete with the American Federation of Labor. This new body was dedicated to organizing workers ignored by the AFL into industrial unions and to spreading socialist ideas through the ranks of North American workers. Its organizers in western Canada were active socialists who recruited workers in many different occupations, including coal miners on Vancouver Island and in southwestern Alberta. They soon won considerable support in Victoria, Vancouver, and other coastal towns. Predictably, relations with the Trades and Labor Congress became frosty.

This new enthusiasm for industrial unionism peaked in 1903, when the United Brotherhood of Railway Employees, a new affiliate of the American Labor Union reaching out to the unskilled, found itself locked in battle with the region's biggest employer, the Canadian Pacific Railway. The corporation's systematic attack on the organization included the familiar array of spies, imported strikebreakers, and special police. One strike leader, Frank Rogers, was killed in Vancouver by gun-toting hirelings. Despite sympathy strikes and boycotts by other western Canadian workers, the company broke the unionists' resistance after several months. The North American craft union movement contributed to the defeat, as part of its concerted attack on the American Labor Union and its affiliates. The unions in the railway running trades and shop crafts managed to keep their members from joining the strike by reminding them of the benefits each of their unions had won that would be threatened by industrial unionism. A royal commission, with the young Mackenzie King in the secretary's chair, was sent out to investigate the recent militancy in the West. The commission added its denunciation of the new unions. By 1904 the backbone of industrial unionism, the Western Federation of Miners, was disintegrating rapidly. Western Canada's first experiment in radical industrial unionism was in retreat.

In June 1905, however, four Canadians (two from Montreal, two from British Columbia) attended the Continental Congress of the Working Class in Chicago to help found a new organizing centre that would expand the work of the American Labor Union — the Industrial Workers of the World (IWW), eventually known affectionately as the "Wobblies." The socialist influence on the IWW was clear; the constitution denounced monopoly capitalism and called for the uniting of all workers into a single force for the revolutionary struggle. The Wobblies saw improvements in workers' lives coming principally through toughness on the picket lines, not through the binding contracts that the craft unionists favoured. For the first time, these workers raised the possibility of using a general strike to bring capitalism to its knees. Industrial action to achieve workers' goals generally took priority over politics, though there was no sharp distinction in practice, and many Wobbly leaders were active in socialist organizations. The IWW envisioned the new society as being run by workers and built around the industrial organizations workers had created in their struggles against capitalists. These ideas bore some resemblance to the European labour ideology known as syndicalism, but the North American Wobblies were less theoretically inclined and more concerned with the practical questions of building revolutionary industrial unionism.

A revitalized WFM was the driving force behind the IWW in western Canada and northern Ontario, until a major dispute within the Wobblies forced the union to withdraw in 1907 (it would eventually find its way into the American Federation of Labor). Thereafter, the IWW drew its solid base of support from unskilled or semiskilled workers in western Canada. The AFL had spurned this constituency: these transient, poorly paid workers, many of them recent immigrants speaking little English, moved through many jobs in construction, logging, harvesting, longshoring, and general labouring — the self-styled "blanket stiffs." In some cases, especially in the loggers' situation, these workers were being drawn into an organized labour movement for the first time, and the Wobblies made them feel right at home. The IWW ideology gave them pride in themselves as workers and in their importance to the industrial system, and the Wobblies' flexible style of organizing fit their lifestyle. Dues were low, membership cards were interchangeable, literature appeared in several languages, and a lusty, irreverent culture of male sociability and marxist education flourished in the work camps and in Wobbly meeting halls in the towns. The modern labour movement is indebted to several inspired Wobbly writers for much of the music that still animates union events, particularly labour's anthem, "Solidarity Forever." Many of these songs were developed at popular street-corner meetings, which were often suppressed by local authorities and which provoked major "free-speech" fights in Vancouver in 1909 and 1912.

Also in 1912 the West Coast Wobblies staged their most spectacular Canadian strike. Seven thousand workers in the Canadian Northern Railway construction camps, speaking sixteen different languages, joined the battle for better camp conditions, but they ultimately lost. The corporation recruited their usual army of scabs, and the alarmed provincial government moved in to close IWW strike camps and jail Wobbly leaders on such trumped-up charges as vagrancy, unlawful assembly, intimidation, and conspiracy. Further repression followed in other strikes. In 1913–14, when the economy slumped into depression, the IWW turned to organizing the unemployed to demand work for wages. But its transient membership scattered in this depression, as construction and resource-industry jobs dried up. The Wobblies never again carried the clout they had had in the half decade before the war. Even in their heyday, their direct influence had been limited to the least-skilled, footloose workers, and they had existed more as a parallel presence than as a direct challenge to the mainstream labour movement. They had nonetheless made an important contribution to an evolving world of labour ideas and tactics in the North and the West, and many labour activists who cut their teeth in the IWW reemerged in similar struggles, especially among loggers at the end of World War I.

Other resource workers had been organizing during the same period. A few groups of fishers, most of whom were not yet full-time wage-earners but who were stuck in a dependent relationship with merchants and canning companies, began to pull together to raise the price paid for fish. In British Columbia, white, native, and Japanese fishers had organized their own unions by the turn of the century and waged large, bitter strikes against the canners' association for higher fish prices. Only the Japanese were able to keep their union together after 1907. Meanwhile, on the Atlantic coast, an energetic organizer named William F. Coaker began the Fishermen's Protective Union in 1908 to bring together fishers, loggers, and sealers; the highly successful union was a force to be reckoned with in Newfoundland society and politics until the 1920s.

Not all of this ferment unfolded outside the labour mainstream. Coal miners, in particular, remained within the craft-union movement while espousing an aggressively industrial form of organization in an industry where it made sense. Their proud independence and solidarity in the workplace made the miners particularly resistant to

the new managerial style of monopoly capitalism and were strengthened by the immigration of militant young workers such as Cape
Breton's James B. McLachlan. In the early 1900s, coal miners who
wanted effective unionism began to place their faith in the U.S. union
in the field, the United Mine Workers of America. At the turn of the
century local activists in Nova Scotia made the Provincial Workmen's Association truly industrial by integrating all workers in and
around the mines. They even helped other workers in the region to
organize PWA lodges, notably the Sydney steelworkers; none of
these lodges survived. In 1906 some members became frustrated with
the cautious PWA leadership and encouraged the UMWA to move
in. They hoped to bring to Nova Scotia miners the negotiating advantages that the craft unionists enjoyed in their international unions.
A referendum vote in 1908 gave the UMWA a slight edge, and the
PWA lodges began transferring to the new organization. But the
entrenched PWA leaders ignored this verdict and held on to their
closed-shop arrangements with the major coal corporations. In 1909
the UMWA was then forced into a devastating twenty-two-month
strike for recognition in the Nova Scotia coalfields; the unionists
were defeated, but they earned great respect among many miners for
their courage and toughness in facing their bosses, in contrast to the
PWA's apparent weakness and collaborationist policies.

In the British Columbia and Alberta coalfields, the UMWA picked
up the remnants of the WFM after 1903. There, too, lengthy, bitter
strikes ensued. On Vancouver Island the union was driven back in
1903, and then rallied to launch a tumultuous two-year strike for
recognition in 1912; that strike garnered widespread union support
through a Miners' Liberation League and resulted in the threat of a
provincewide general strike, before the UMWA conceded defeat. For
the duration of the strikes in both Nova Scotia and British Columbia,
the Canadian government sent in troops, who provoked otherwise
placid scenes into violence by breaking up picket lines and demonstrations, and by arresting leaders. On both coasts, the outbreak of
World War I found the coal miners' unions in tatters. In contrast,
UMWA organizing in the new Alberta coalfields, especially in
Crow's Nest Pass, was more successful, in large part because of the
fragmented ownership of the mines. After a major strike in 1906,
these Alberta miners engaged in regular bargaining with a mine-
owners' association (this pattern was broken briefly by an eight-
month strike of seven thousand miners in 1911). As in the
Pennsylvania coalfields, this success was based on solidarity across

ethnic lines in a work world where many European tongues were spoken, in contrast to the Vancouver Island divisions that pitted whites against the Chinese and Japanese.

Industrial unionism also won converts among workers in new mass-production industries in Canada. The record in Canada is much more limited than that in the United States for the same period, during which, for example, the Wobblies led massive textile strikes and made inroads at Ford's auto plants. The transformation of Canadian manufacturing lagged far enough behind the U.S. situation that a cohesive workforce capable of cooperating in an industrial union had scarcely begun to emerge by the start of the war. Organizing within these industries tended to remain within the bounds of craft unionism or to arise more or less spontaneously, without any union, inside one department or division of a plant. The major exceptions to this pattern occurred in the textile and garment industries. Union organization swept through the Quebec cotton mills after 1906, briefly as part of a U.S. international union and then as the independent Federation of Textile Workers of Canada, which led six thousand workers out on strike in 1907. Similarly, between 1910 and 1913, Canadian affiliates of the international garment unions signed up thousands of workers in the clothing factories of Montreal, Toronto, and Hamilton, and facilitated major confrontations with employers; these events include a six-week strike in Montreal and a highly publicized battle with the T. Eaton Company in Toronto in 1912. Both industries had a considerable degree of cohesion along ethnic lines; French Canadians dominated in Quebec textiles, and Jewish workers, many of them socialists, were predominant in the clothing plants. The organizing ventures in these two industries brought many more wage-earning women into the labour movement for the first time since the days of the Knights of Labor. But unions in both industries lost their momentum or disappeared by the outbreak of World War I.

Despite the set-backs, industrial unionism had emerged as a practical alternative to craft unionism by the beginning of the war. The British Columbia and Alberta Federations of Labor (formed in 1910 and 1912, respectively) were committed to industrial organization, although they continued to include urban craft unionists in a relatively comfortable alliance. The weekly *B.C. Federationist* was the journalistic mouthpiece for that perspective for more than a decade. When the Trades and Labor Congress met in Calgary in 1911, the strong western representation pushed through a resolution endorsing the new approach to organizing, and got British Columbia socialist James Watters elected president. Although the resolution was weakened the next year, industrial unionists had entered the house of labour, where they continued to press for greater working-class solidarity for the next decade.

One crucial outcome of the vigorous industrial unionism of the pre–World War I era was a significant new form of state intervention. As we have seen, workers regularly encountered the ugly face of the state; they battled troops and legal manoeuvres against their organizing efforts, as well as a string of royal commissions, whose reports rapped them on the knuckles for accepting radical leadership and for lacking sober, respectable restraint. The creation of the federal Department of Labour with a conciliation service in 1900 had done little to soften the state's harsh image. But the young, intellectually inclined deputy minister of labour, Mackenzie King, had some new ideas.

King had studied labour problems at Harvard and in Chicago and confronted them as the labour department's chief conciliator and as royal commission secretary. He saw the need for structural change that would smooth out troubled industrial relations. His solution appeared in 1907 as the Industrial Disputes Investigation Act. This legislation required all workers and employers in transportation, resource, and utilities industries to submit their disputes to an ad hoc, three-person board of conciliation before initiating a strike or lockout; once the board had heard the evidence and issued its report, the parties were still constrained from acting during another "cooling-out" period. The act provided no guiding principles for these boards, leaving them to work out their own solutions without clear precedents. At first, most unionists believed that this measure would promote collective bargaining, but they soon learned that it provided no protection from a company's countermoves — stockpiling, importing strikebreakers, firing and blacklisting organizers — to break the momentum of a strike. In 1911 even the Trades and Labor Congress was convinced that this legislation needed to be repealed. The success of the act in curbing strikes was undoubtedly limited, but it was destined to become a cornerstone of the Canadian state's industrial relations policies.

Independent Labour Politics

Since the 1870s, unionized workers in Canada had recognized the need for action by the state to deal with working-class problems. By the early twentieth century the intensifying battles with employers and the regular defeats had reinforced this belief (in contrast to the position held by the AFL's antipolitical leadership). Many active craft unionists had congregated on the left wing of the Liberal party since the 1880s, sometimes moving into a semi-independent Liberal-Labour, or "Lib-Lab," position, but tugged back by sympathetic gestures from Liberal politicians at the federal and provincial levels. Smaller numbers had submerged themselves in the Conservative party. By the early 1900s, however, many working-class activists were profoundly disillusioned with the insensitivity of the old-line parties to labour's political agenda. A conviction took root that workers had to elect their own representatives to legislatures to have their needs fulfilled.

Independent labour politics faced serious obstacles, however. The Liberal and Conservative parties had cultivated abiding loyalties among many working-class voters. Even more important, many Canadian workers were developing a deep political cynicism, which encouraged more and more voters to stay home on election day. This attitude was not surprising: many workers faced continuing property and residential restrictions on their rights to vote and stand for office, and so much campaigning in the early twentieth century was brazenly corrupt. Labour activists had to not only woo many workers away from their political moorings but also mobilize the political abstainers.

There were also deep disagreements about the appropriate ideology for this new working-class politics. Before the war, the dominant form in Canada east of the Rockies was a working-class liberalism known as labourism. It appeared in what were usually called Independent Labour Parties, which were set up occasionally in towns and cities starting in the 1890s. These parties provided a forum for the political expression of skilled workers in manufacturing, construction, and mining, and reflected their sense of place as proud, independent, self-directed individuals in the production process in particular and in society in general. The leadership of these labour parties usually overlapped with that of the local trades and labour council or the district miners' organization.

Ideologically, leaders of these organizations had not travelled far from their liberal roots. They saw the main problem for workers as the restriction of liberty and equality in Canadian political life. Their solutions involved democratizing the state to the fullest (for example, extending the franchise to all men and women, removing property qualifications, abolishing the Senate, and introducing proportional representation) and thereby allowing workers to share political power and capital with other social groups. In essence, these labour parties carried the new bureaucratic model of collective bargaining into the political sphere, where the liberal heritage of equal rights for individuals incorporated equal rights for classes. Much of the fury of their most class-conscious rhetoric centred on how workers were ignored, neglected, and abused. Only independent labour representatives could fight for the specific concerns of wage-earners, they believed, although paradoxically they held an equally strong commitment that the "common good" of the community should not be sacrificed to narrow class interests.

Change came gradually, just as in the craft unionists' long struggle to win concessions, rather than in one revolutionary sweep. Capitalist economic relations did not need to be changed fundamentally, except to root out "parasitic" monopolists and intermediaries in the production process and to recognize the value of productive labour (an echo of the Knights of Labor). The role of the state in the economy should be limited to taking over monopolies and administering a few social welfare programs for those not able to look after themselves (the aged, the sick, the injured, the unemployed, the single mothers). Above all, labourists wanted fair treatment for all workers; one of their standard electoral promises was "a square deal," by which they meant preservation of customary living and working standards, especially regarding the notions of social equality and honest toil as the basis of social worth.

Canadian socialists, most of whom belonged to the Socialist Party of Canada after 1904, were appalled by all this fuzzy thinking. They, too, tended to be skilled workers who believed in the value of the producer and in producers' rights to liberty and democratic expression. But most of them used marxist tools of analysis to locate the root of workers' problems in the capitalist ownership of the means of production, distribution, and exchange, and conceived of no solution short of dispossessing capitalists in a complete transformation of industrial society. In fact, this highly deterministic analysis convinced them that the concentration of industry and the polarization of classes were leading inevitably to a socialist future. A sizable minority of socialists criticized capitalism on more ethical grounds; this analysis led to just as complete a rejection of that social and economic system. During the first decade of the twentieth century, Canadian socialists were particularly dogmatic and inflexible "impossibilists," who officially refused to consider any reform consisting of less than a full-scale revolution and who heaped scorn on craft unionism and labourist politics in equal measures. (In practice, of course, many socialists were active unionists, and the few who found their way into western legislatures were quite prepared to pursue such short-range reforms as an eight-hour working day.) In 1911 a breakaway group that included most of the central Canadian membership and the sizable European immigrant locals formed the Social Democratic Party of Canada, and adopted a more flexible approach to the question of immediate reforms, without abandoning their class-struggle perspective.

Ironically, both labourism and socialism relied on electoral politics as the road to social change, although the socialists saw the need to combine electoralism with a campaign to educate workers in an anticapitalist perspective. Hence socialists became renowned for sponsoring lectures, distributing marxist literature, and holding street-corner meetings that local police forces regularly broke up (often while ignoring a Salvation Army meeting on the other corner). Before the war neither political grouping made great headway in winning large-scale working-class support. Three labour candidates were elected to the House of Commons: Ralph Smith from Vancouver Island in 1900, Arthur Puttee from Winnipeg the same year, and Alphonse Verville from Montreal in 1906; but each slid quickly into the Liberal caucus. The only committed labourist in a provincial legislature before the war was an aging metalworker named Allan Studholme in Ontario (another labourist spent only a few months in the Alberta house in 1909, and a third was elected the same year from Quebec City to the Quebec house, only to fall quickly from favour among labourists and into the arms of the Liberals). After 1901 the socialists held three or four seats in the British Columbia legislature, where, often holding the balance of power, they won significant concessions for labour, including an eight-hour day for miners. The sole socialist member of the legislative assembly in Alberta from 1909 to 1913, Charlie O'Brien, was similarly outspoken and effective. All of these socialist candidates came from the party's core constituency, the coal-mining communities. Elsewhere in Canada, their influence was much more limited electorally, and often the socialist parties existed as little more than sects on the fringes of working-class life. But, in some towns and cities, handfuls of outspoken, articulate, and energetic socialists regularly gingered up the local labour scene and exerted an influence far beyond their formal membership. Just before the war, socialists began to make tentative alliances with labourists, notably in Vancouver, Winnipeg, Toronto, and Montreal, where a few socialist municipal victories were chalked up. Yet it cannot be denied that compared to many European countries or even parts of the United States, the Canadian socialist movement was a small-scale affair before 1914.

All of this working-class political activity flourished in periods of burgeoning union strength and receded when unions were weak or on the defensive. It developed in the context of intensifying industrial conflict, as workers' resentments began to accumulate and to flow into recognition of common interests across occupational lines. This turn to politics was seldom a swing away from the industrial battleground; rather, it was an attempt to broaden and intensify the same conflict into a more unified class initiative. By 1914 there were a few feeble beachheads of labourist and socialist success, but on the whole, like the rest of the organized labour movement in the country, these parties had little to show for the huge effort expended.

War and Democracy

World War I disrupted Canadian life far more than sabre-rattling enthusiasts had ever anticipated in 1914. The economic insecurity of the depression that lasted from 1913 to 1915 evaporated as military recruitment soaked up many of the unemployed and the war economy gathered steam. After the middle of 1915, Canadian workers enjoyed full employment at the highest wages that they had ever known. Working-class living standards were improving slightly, and workers began to feel some relief from the whip of potential poverty that their employers had always wielded over them. Owners and managers soon complained that workers were not willing to work as hard or as regularly as they used to; absenteeism and labour turnover began to increase noticeably.

Workers nonetheless had plenty of grievances, many of which seemed to be shared widely and did not focus on one employer or one industry. In fact, as the wartime economy and society evolved, resentments began to coalesce into the conviction that the whole system was stacked against workers. Mass production of munitions brought renewed managerial attempts to enhance "efficiency" and "dilute" craft skills, by introducing female labour in many metal shops, for example. In several industries craftworkers thus faced an intensified resistance to their long-cherished goals of controlling their mode of work and the labour market for their skills; workers also felt the pressures of tighter supervision and speed-up. Retail prices were also moving up faster than wages, especially after 1916. As workers struggled to catch up, widespread suspicion of profiteering began to settle in. So too did growing consternation about government mismanagement of the war, fuelled by all-too-frequent scandals. The federal government seemed to be becoming more authoritarian and interventionist in workers' everyday lives: for example, it imposed the industrial disputes act on all munitions industries in 1916, it censored press reports of labour strife, and it confiscated the worker's glass of beer with prohibition legislation the next year. Many labour leaders, especially on the left, greeted the federal government's schemes for national registration of workers and for compulsory military conscription with howls of outrage, since they sensed a centralized attack on workers' power and independence in the workplace. In Quebec the resistance to conscription was vigorous and often violent. Meanwhile, pro-war propaganda had been saturating Canadians with appeals to self-sacrifice and public service in the struggle to defend democracy against "Kaiserism." Labour leaders soon demanded *industrial* democracy on the home front and challenged those they began to call their own local "Kaisers." By the end of the war, workers' visions of the possibilities for life in industrial society had widened considerably.

To meet these challenges, craft union leaders in central Canada tried to avoid picket-line militancy and took the cautious route of lobbying for better protection. The Trades and Labor Congress executive tried repeatedly to use the wartime atmosphere to get "fair-wage" clauses inserted into munitions contracts, but they found politicians and industrialists unwilling to change the prewar patterns of labour's subordination to capital. The Imperial Munitions Board, which administered war production, was especially intransigent. Lobbying to block registration and conscription was similarly unsuccessful. In fact, Robert Borden's Conservative and Unionist governments were consistently reluctant to involve craft union leaders in wartime decision making, in contrast to U.S. and British state policy during the war. The appointment of a conservative railway unionist, Gideon Robertson, to the Unionist cabinet and a few modest gestures towards consultation during 1918 were undermined by the orders in council that autumn banning several radical organizations and their newspapers and then forbidding strikes. Canadian craft union officials continued to urge constraint, and their senior partners in the United States went so far as to threaten suspension of militant locals. But, for the most part, caution did not pay off for Canadian craftworkers. The failure of the bureaucratic élite of the craft union movement to win any concessions left the rank and file to fight for themselves in individual industries and communities.

Few categories of workers were untouched by the organizational surge that began in 1916 and reached a peak in 1918–19, when the federal labour department's undoubtedly low estimate of the number of union members in Canada was 378,000 (more than two and one-third times its size in 1916). Craft unionism bounced back to life with unprecedented vigour, as did industrial unions in coal mining in Nova Scotia and Alberta. Across the country, unskilled workers joined unions of longshoremen, teamsters, freight handlers, retail clerks, waiters and waitresses, laundry workers, and telephone operators. They also became members of catch-all "federal labour unions," which were designed by the AFL for workers without a specific craft, but which functioned more often as industrial unions. In fact, whether through this organizational model or through the widening of craft union membership to the less skilled, industrial unionism began to reach many new sectors, including such mass-production work as steel, pulp and paper, rubber, railway-car building, meat packing, oil refining, textiles, and clothing in 1918–19; hard rock mining in northern Ontario in the same period; and logging in British Columbia and northern Ontario early in 1919.

Government employees also shocked local politicians by taking out union charters; in most major cities, municipal labourers, firefighters, and police officers had developed strong unions by 1918 and frequently won collective-bargaining rights (in Montreal and Toronto the police actually went on strike in 1918). The country's letter carriers revitalized their old union and launched local strikes in 1918 that verged on a full-scale national strike until they won concessions from the government. Even teachers and white-collar clerks in banks, business offices, and the federal civil service embraced unionism with a new fervour.

Barriers that had divided workers for years came down. Despite the caution of the handful of national labour leaders and many international-union representatives, craft exclusiveness began to erode, and the crafts cooperated as never before. Joint councils developed unified bargaining (and if necessary, strikes) among all railway unions in Canada, among the marine trades, and among metalworkers and building-trades workers in several cities. By early 1919 some of these craft unions announced common demands that eliminated distinctions among them and insisted on centralized bargaining; they were well along the road to a new kind of industrial unionism. In fact, serious discussion was under way in many quarters about the gradual amalgamation of similar crafts into one organization. In more isolated communities such as Trail, British Columbia; Gananoque, Ontario; Pictou County, Nova Scotia; and St. John's, Newfoundland, all workers coalesced into one organization to confront all their bosses with the same demands. By the end of the war, cooperation was moving to the regional level, as new provincial federations were created in Nova Scotia and New Brunswick. Canadian workers were exhibiting a vigorous class consciousness that translated into open, flexible, and imaginative organization.

The change in the Canadian labour movement was more than quantitative. Women were recruited in many industries in unprecedented numbers, and a few took active roles on local union executives, though most male unionists continued to assume that women belonged in the home, supported by their menfolk's wages. Unions also built bridges to the long-ignored ethnic groups, and, in resource and mass-production industries, these workers were drawn into industrial unions, though they often remained marginal and transient members. In many cases, moreover, new faces appeared at the forefront of local militancy; these bolder, uncompromising men and women were not well integrated into craft union officialdom and were often more committed than the established leadership to more radical politics. Throughout the industrialized world, the emerging revolt of workers, especially the 1917 Russian Revolution, inspired many radicals to new heights of socialist fervour, particularly within the eastern European enclaves in Canadian industrial cities, mining towns, and logging camps, and gave them new hope for building working-class solidarity.

These changes in the labour movement rode on the crest of waves of massive strikes that spread throughout the country, beginning in 1917 and continuing through 1920. An effervescent militancy, guided and shaped, but by no means created, by local labour leaders with a radical bent, flowed out of the ranks of Canadian wage-earners. With pressing orders and labour shortages, many employers had no choice but to deal directly with their organized workers in some form of begrudging negotiation, but many others refused to let the unusual pressures of the war disrupt their traditionally authoritarian, anti-union management policies. They fought back with their time-honoured strikebreaking tactics, often bolstered by new employers' associations. Frequently these battles erupted in defiance of the legal requirements of the Industrial Disputes Investigation Act and of international union officials' instructions. Even more disturbing to employers during 1918 was the growing threat of generalized sympathy strikes (to support the demands of one group of unionists) that emerged in communities from Cape Breton to Vancouver; in many instances, the firms backed down to avoid triggering a wider labour conflagration.

As in the prewar years, the frustrations of these industrial battles and the growing recognition of common working-class interests brought workers into the political arena. In 1917 in dozens of industrial centres across the country, unionized workers responded to the Trade and Labor Congress's call for a new working-class party by setting up local independent labour parties, which soon federated into provincial organizations. A hastily assembled campaign for the 1917 federal election brought humiliating defeat for all labour candidates, but within a few months this political movement was making substantial inroads in municipal contests. Labour candidates emphasized workers' exclusion from wartime decision making and the erosion of democracy that they believed was under way, as well as demands for conscription of wealth to match conscription of men. Ideologically, much of the socialist left allied with labourism and helped to give it a sharper edge and a clearer vision. Socialists were inspired by what they were hearing from Russia, but also by the new class consciousness of Canadian workers, and they saw the need for working-class unity. They therefore joined various labour parties or worked in cooperation with them, while patiently continuing their work in socialist education. Most of the new provincial labour parties were committed to ethical and structural transformation from production for profit to production for human needs.

Crushing the Revolt

By the time the armistice was signed in November 1918, the expectations of Canadian workers had risen enormously from prewar days. Those who had organized on the industrial and political fronts were voicing long-standing concerns about shoring up living standards with decent wages and ensuring more justice and democracy in their lives; in the words of the Ontario Independent Labor Party, unionists sought "the industrial freedom for those who toil and the political liberation of those who for so long have been denied justice." The almost universal demand for an eight-hour day symbolized the more humane industrial regime workers wanted, and the persistent demand for union recognition indicated how they expected to get and hold onto that regime. More and more, unionists seemed to be discussing a new kind of society in which workers' needs and concerns would be properly addressed. That vision could take many forms, from a reformed capitalist society to a full-fledged socialist alternative.

In whatever form, that vision flew in the face of capitalist plans for a return to prewar normalcy. Canadian industrialists came out of the war determined to find new economic stability in an uncertain world. They wanted no obstacles to increasing productivity and cutting costs, and they assigned a high priority to eliminating the obstreperous unions (especially those with radical leadership) that had emerged within their enterprises. Not only were these unions demanding higher pay, shorter hours, and more say in workplace administration, but they were also developing much greater influence in the political realm. These capitalists correctly saw the situation as a struggle over the distribution of power in industrial society and refused to relinquish or even share power with the working class. Never before in Canada had class lines been drawn so sharply in industrial communities across the country. Over the next two years, thousands of Canadian workers were swept up into dramatic confrontations in which their demonstrations of class solidarity met a solid wall of capitalist resistance.

Unionists were far from united on how to meet this challenge. At the Trades and Labor Congress meetings in 1917 and 1918, the cautious craft union majority soundly defeated the new radical militants' program for aggressive industrial unionism and working-class solidarity. The western dissidents headed home to organize a regional labour conference in March 1919 and then a referendum on creating a new militant organization, the One Big Union (OBU). The union was duly launched in June with a solid socialist leadership, and it quickly enlisted most of the western Canadian and northern Ontario labour movement. While dedicated to industrial unionism, the OBU took in unions of all shapes and sizes, including craft unions. One of its central demands was the six-hour day to relieve unemployment. There was scattered support for the new organization in central and eastern Canada, but the eastern counterparts of the western radicals had generally decided that staying in the mainstream labour movement was a better strategy than going it alone. In Nova Scotia, miners, steelworkers, and many other workers were achieving significant success within the confines of the international labour movement and did not relish retreating into isolation. In the larger central Canadian cities, the radicals had to deal with more complex manufacturing communities that did not always polarize as easily as the western resource or transportation centres and that were less friendly to new labour organizations. Central Canadian radicals also had to face a much more firmly entrenched craft union bureaucracy that feared the dangers of industrial unionism to its craft organizations and that would fight tooth and nail to defend AFL-style unionism. Yet the drift toward craft amalgamation, which was tolerated by these officials, gave radicals such as the industrial union leaders in Montreal and Toronto hope that change from within was still possible. The workers revolt in Canada, then, was perhaps more dramatic in the West, but there was no rigid political division between east and west.

While the patterns of conflict with employers were nationwide, there was no significant coordination among working-class organizations on a scale larger than a regional one. In most cases, the rhythms of battle were highly localized. The spring of 1919 provided the most sound and fury, as craftworkers across the country began their annual ritual of spring bargaining, with demands for higher wages, the eight-hour day, and recognition of their joint union bargaining structures. But in some cities, such as Halifax and Montreal, the final showdowns did not arrive until 1920. In eastern and western coal mining the battles did not begin until 1920 and lasted until 1925. Winnipeg workers, organized and unorganized, staged the most famous event in this period, when they walked out in a six-week general strike in May and June 1919 to show their sympathy with the building and metal trades unions, which had been denied the right to collective bargaining. The attempted repression of that strike sparked lengthy sympathy strikes in towns and cities across western

Canada. In a smaller but no less interesting confrontation at the same moment, the workers of Amherst, Nova Scotia, waged a more successful three week general strike through the centralized bargaining agency of their local Federation of Labor. An attempt to mobilize a general strike in support of similar struggles in Toronto floundered on the caution of craft union bureaucrats and their defence of existing contracts and benefit funds. Elsewhere local strikes of craft and industrial unionists raged on as never before; during May, June, and July 1919 more than 115,000 Canadian workers stood their ground in 210 strikes, and the numbers remained high over the next year. Most of these battles produced only bitter defeats for the workers involved. The One Big Union was hammered particularly hard over the next two years, as employers refused to have anything to do with its affiliates and craft unionists collaborated in undermining its strikes. In Nova Scotia and Alberta the United Mine Workers soldiered on until the two district organizations suffered major defeats in cataclysmic strikes in 1925. Firings, blacklistings, and industrial spying ensured that local union leaders were driven away and new troublemakers, nipped in the bud.

During these postwar years, many employers slipped a velvet glove over their iron fist and blanketed their employees with such new welfare provisions as pension and insurance plans, safety programs, recreation facilities, lunch rooms, and company magazines. In a few cases, they launched "industrial councils" of management and employee representatives, as a toothless alternative to unionism, to debate workers' problems without challenging managerial prerogatives. These measures were intended to promote more loyalty and commitment to the firm and to undermine solidarity among workers. Their effects, though uneven and uncertain, were widely praised by the press and the government nonetheless. In Quebec the Catholic Church had a different but parallel agenda. To nurture francophone culture and to head off secular and socialistic influences, church leaders had been promoting their own brand of Catholic unionism for more than a decade. This unionism discouraged strikes and radical goals, promoted good relations with employers, and placed a Catholic chaplain in a crucial role as advisor to the workers. The Catholic unions grew dramatically at the end of the war, and in 1921 the clergy oversaw the creation of the Canadian and Catholic Confederation of Labour, which embraced about one-quarter of Quebec unionists. Nowhere else in the country was there such a large ethnically and religiously based labour organization.

However, far more important in undermining workers' class-conscious militancy than corporate welfarism or Catholic unionism was the severe depression that began late in 1920. Many union locals dissolved in hopeless strikes against drastic wage cuts. As mass lay-offs spread through all industries, workers became more vulnerable to victimization for their union principles. Union membership rapidly declined, along with the confidence that had surged up during the previous three or four years. Fearfulness, fatalism, and cynicism crept back into working-class consciousness, as thousands of workers turned inward to their families and their neighbourhoods to find the resources to survive in capitalist society.

By this point, the Canadian state was also heavily involved in curbing the workers' revolt. Repression was still the first response. In Winnipeg in 1919 all three levels of government collaborated with the city's business people through the self-styled Citizens' Committee of 1,000 to break the general strike. Federal troops and specially recruited police were sent in to patrol the streets and eventually to break up peaceful demonstrations with bloody violence. (The same tactics would be used wherever labour solidarity had reached this intensity, notably in the 1923 Sydney steelworkers' strike.) The federal government delivered its *coup de grâce* in Winnipeg by arresting and threatening to deport strike leaders under a new provision of the Criminal Code. The extensive secret surveillance of radical and labour movement activities that had begun during the war was put on a permanent footing with the creation of a security service within the new Royal Canadian Mounted Police (RCMP). Simultaneously, however, the Canadian state wanted to bolster the conservative elements in the labour movement by showing interest in minor reforms. After the Royal Commission on Industrial Relations had spent several months holding hearings across the country in mid-1919, the Borden government convened a large, national conference of carefully chosen representatives of labour, capital, and "the public" to debate the commission's report. The only concrete result of the exercise was the mistaken belief among craft union leaders that someone was taking them seriously. Their demand for a legislated eight-hour day was shifted first to the new International Labour Organization, then back to the provinces, which quickly buried it.

During the same period, workers had been stepping up their efforts to win greater control over the state. Labour parties continued to win substantial representation on municipal councils and school boards, but the real triumphs came in provincial elections. In October 1919 the Independent Labor Party of Ontario won almost every industrial seat in the province outside Toronto and sent eleven men to the legislature to join the triumphant farmers' movement in a Farmer-Labour government. Similar sweeps brought labour caucuses into the Nova Scotia, Manitoba, Alberta, and British Columbia legislatures. But the 1921 federal election was far less rewarding for the many labour candidates (only three won seats); it marked the end of labour's political movement. Several of those elected at all levels of government had been at the forefront of the workers' revolt; these individuals included Winnipeg strike leaders and OBU activists. But their influence on the legislatures was too limited to stop the assault on the workers' movements. Farmer-politicians turned out to be uncertain allies who often fundamentally disagreed with labour leaders over such issues as the eight-hour day or prohibition. In national politics in particular, labour's agenda was squeezed out by the epic battle between the free-trade farmers and the high-tariff manufacturers (who appealed to working-class voters with apocalyptic visions of industrial collapse under free trade and who met with modest success). In any case, with unions collapsing and working-class optimism crumbling, the political organizations of labour could not survive.

Moreover, working-class activists were increasingly splitting along familiar lines; the craft unionists retreated from political involvement, and revolutionary socialists lost their patience with the ever cautious labourists (whose dismal record of action in the Ontario house strengthened this radical critique). By 1921 most of the left had gravitated to the new international communist movement and that year founded the Communist Party of Canada. But a defeated, dispirited workers' movement was incapable of sharing the vision of these radicals for renewed struggle and socialist transformation.

The workers' revolt in Canada was thus essentially dead by 1921, though its last gasps echoed through mining towns for a few more years. The movement had not been merely an aberration based on wartime grievances; rather, it had been the culmination of twenty years of workers' resistance to the industrial capitalism that was emerging in the early twentieth century. Not since the 1880s had workers shown such class-conscious solidarity, and never again would its demonstration be as potent. That unity was fractured and the revolt, crushed, by three connected forces: capitalist employers, who had no intention of abandoning either exclusive control of their enterprises or their dominant political influence; the Canadian state, which intensified its prewar pattern of siding overtly and heavy handedly with capital in maintaining the subordination of workers; and international craft unionism, which, when push came to shove, was ultimately unwilling to relax its organizational exclusiveness and its ideological restraint, and which actively collaborated in the undermining of radical, industrial-unionist elements in the labour movement. Revolutionary industrial unionism was destroyed in the early 1920s, but craft unionism was only severely crippled, surviving on what small base was left in construction and on the fringes of other industries and clinging to the labour councils and the Trades and Labor Congress. Craft unionists would think twice before allowing themselves to be tugged so far from their organizational moorings again; henceforth, they would tread much more cautiously.

This emphasis on polarization in the labour movement, however, overlooks two qualifications with great significance for the future. First, the vast majority of organized workers in both craft and industrial unions in the early twentieth century belonged to industries requiring considerable independence and male manual labour, both skilled and unskilled, such as mining, construction, and skilled factory work. Thus, much of the fervour of both wings of the labour movement flowed from workers' sense of being "producers" and male breadwinners. Yet, in the quarter century before 1925, in the mass-production factories that withstood the greatest effects of managerial and technological innovations, thousands of semi-skilled workers, many of them women and new immigrants, were touched by unionism only during the brief interlude from 1918 to 1920. Why did these workers comprise such an insignificant part of the Canadian labour movement for most of this period? Part of the explanation is structural: these industries were so new that factory workforces had had little time to coalesce into a cohesive body. These workers were also highly vulnerable to being fired and replaced for insubordination and were terrorized into supporting their bosses' campaign against free trade for fear of losing their livelihood. Perhaps, too, producer consciousness was less powerful among workers in such highly fragmented labour processes. Ultimately, so many of them still preferred to express their disgust by quitting and moving on.

At the same time, of course, women and immigrants were the wage-earners that skilled men eyed with greatest suspicion, as potential threats to their masculine status in the household and the workplace. These marginalized groups had participated in the workers' revolt to an unprecedented extent, but the male leadership seldom shed its uneasiness about them. Although thousands of women became active unionists and some became local leaders, few moved in the higher circles of the workers' movements, and in labour political activity most women were still relegated to the auxiliaries, in their own labour leagues and independent labour parties. In a spirit of working-class "maternal feminism," these female organizations promoted important issues, especially health and education, for unwaged as well as waged women workers, but the main agenda of the workers' revolt across the political spectrum said little or nothing about the domestic sphere. In a similar way, the Anglo-Canadian (and French Canadian) men made no special effort to address the particular economic and cultural problems of immigrant workers from southern and eastern Europe or Asia. Many mass-production factory workers, then, were never fully integrated into the mainstream of the revolt.

The second qualification of a polarized view is that there was a tamer brand of industrial unionism, practised by the United Mine Workers, which avoided socialist visions and embraced the "industrial legality" sought by craft unionists. It had trial runs in Alberta beginning well before the war and in Nova Scotia for a brief period in the early 1920s (although in both cases the local leaders were committed socialists, to the dismay of the UMW headquarters). A similarly bureaucratic form of industrial unionism appeared at the end of the war under the auspices of the Amalgamated Clothing Workers of America, which established complex collective-bargaining structures in the central Canadian clothing industry. This form of unionism, rather than revolutionary industrial unionism, was the legacy that was passed on to the hitherto quiescent mass-production workers when they began to stir in the 1930s.

3

The Giant Tamed

The years between World Wars I and II were hard times for Canadian workers. There was no longer any question that corporations were solidly in the saddle of Canadian economic life. In several industries, corporations confidently pressed on with the workplace transformation that had begun a quarter century earlier, installing new machinery and hiring more managerial experts. But the Canadian economy remained fragile and unstable. For Canadian workers, the dominant theme of the interwar period was chronic underemployment, which was interrupted by only four or five years of more regular work at the end of the 1920s. The 1920s were anything but "roaring." In contrast to the situation in the United States, employment levels in most Canadian industries did not bounce back from the postwar depression until at least 1925. Canadian workers had become familiar with the ups and downs of the business cycle, but the deep depression that set in for most of the 1930s shook many workers' confidence that capitalism could recover. Not surprisingly, the footloose workforce of the earlier boom years was gradually replaced by a more settled working-class population that clung desperately to available jobs.

World War II brought back the jobs and higher wages that workers had been yearning for. It also brought long-term changes that helped to set in motion the longest period of continued prosperity in the history of capitalism. The Canadian state intervened to provide lucrative munitions contracts, to modernize uncompetitive industries, to control economic fluctuations with the new fiscal and monetary tools designed by the British economist John Maynard Keynes, and to begin to reorient the whole economy towards closer integration with the United States. Canadian workers emerged from the war with a familiar determination to hold onto wartime gains. This time, unlike the period from 1919 to 1920, many of them were successful in winning a permanent place for their unions in the industrial life of the country. But the cost of acceptance was severe constraints on what workers were allowed to contest and how they were allowed to contest it.

Fighting the Open Shop

Canadian corporate capitalists in the interwar period presided over an industrial regime that was based on the assumption that all power flowed from the top and that the workforce at the bottom should accept this idea unquestioningly. Holding onto a job meant working hard without complaint, never mentioning unions or radical politics (since stool-pigeons abounded), and currying the favour of supervisors, sometimes with cash, liquor, or other favours. These managers were usually in a position to guarantee regular work, promotions, wage increases, and even jobs for family members. Compliance with this corporate tyranny was necessary for survival, since the only alternative source of income was a miserly system of private charities. And plenty of unemployed workers hovered around the plant gates, ready to take the jobs of any employees were let go (unlike the United States, Canada reopened the immigration gates in the mid-1920s after a brief period of restriction and then closed them again in 1930). Some workers undoubtedly found this environment to be relatively secure, especially if their corporate employers provided such long-term benefits as pensions or insurance plans. But it is hard to believe that most workers were bound to such a fundamentally harsh system through quiet contentment and loyalty to their corporate employers, still less through dewy-eyed satisfaction with the capitalist system as a whole. Far more effective deterrents to any revival of a Canadian workers' movement between the wars were the fear of losing a job and falling into deep poverty, and the fatalistic view that no alterative had a chance of succeeding.

During those long, bleak years, some workers nonetheless made concerted attempts to challenge that industrial regime. Some experienced organizers and agitators from the earlier revolt refused to give up; other rebels simply learned from scratch to pit their uncompromising spirit against the authoritarianism of their employers in the day-to-day trench warfare in the workplace. In organizing, these workers drew on at least five reservoirs of working-class activity. First, the Second Industrial Revolution had not destroyed all skill in the workplace. Small teams of skilled individuals, rolling-mill workers in steel plants or tire builders in rubber factories, for example, were still crucial to production at many of the most sophisticated factories. Other craftworkers, such as electricians and tool-and-die makers, who performed set-up and maintenance work, were also indispensable. These clusters of production and maintenance workers were allowed considerable independence in their work, and thus kept alive some of the pride and prickliness of the earlier craftworkers. Although these individuals were too isolated and vulnerable within their workplaces to sustain craft unionism at this time, they had the potential, if provoked, to become the cutting edge of a wider organization in their plants.

Second, a few such men and their semiskilled workmates began to challenge their employers within institutions designed to contain their militancy. Some used the new industrial councils in the larger corporations to demand improved terms of employment. By World War II, for example, steelworkers at Hamilton and Sydney had used these bodies to create connections with industrial unionism by organizing the employee representatives on the councils and making increasingly militant demands. Dockers in Vancouver and sailors on the Great Lakes similarly took over company unions, created to control hiring, for their own ends. In a similar fashion, the allegedly docile Catholic union movement in Quebec became a much more militant force in the province's labour relations. It attracted many more members during the 1930s in various industries, especially outside Montreal, where the international unions had long been weak and were now unable to attract discontented workers. Without the rigid jurisdictional boundaries of craft unions, the Catholic *syndicats* organized all workers in an enterprise more easily. Although the chaplains were still powerful, lay leaders such as Alfred Charpentier struggled to make their unions work effectively (a breakaway group shook off clerical control completely). Perhaps most symbolically, in 1937 a Catholic union led several thousand workers into a tumultuous, ultimately unsuccessful strike against Dominion Textile, the industry's biggest employer.

Third, the many communities of new European immigrant workers were becoming more permanent and stable, and offered organizations and informal networks that not only helped these workers cope with unemployment, but also promoted ethnic solidarity in struggles involving members of the community. For instance, the Finns, played a crucial role in the renewed efforts to unionize the logging industry, the Jews, in similar efforts in the needle trades, and the Ukrainians, in hard rock mining. Within even the less radicalized immigrant groups, the second generation was growing restless and resentful of discrimination and of the limited opportunities available to them in Canadian industry. These young people were becoming ripe recruits for new union organizations.

Fourth, the pressures of unemployment threw many workers into new forms of organizing. In the early 1930s, solidarity among working-class families intensified through frequent battles with officials who doled out social assistance and landlords who threatened evictions. These workers soon created local unemployed associations to lobby and demonstrate for less demeaning treatment. Many of these groups joined provincial and national organizations to press for such measures as unemployment insurance. Single unemployed men, who often had no access to local assistance, and had to move on in search of work, were assigned to relief camps run by the Department of National Defence and made to work at menial tasks for twenty cents a day. In 1935 men in relief camps rebelled against these conditions and streamed out of the West Coast camps to converge on Vancouver. They then marched to Ottawa to demand proper work and decent wages. Prime Minister Richard B. Bennett rebuffed their leaders, and the RCMP broke up the On-to-Ottawa Trek with bloody violence in Regina. A planned march from Winnipeg collapsed soon afterward, and a small, tired contingent from Toronto reached Ottawa two weeks later, only to be dismissed by Bennett. Out of these struggles came small cores of angry men and women who carried their resentment and organizational experience with the unemployed movement into any jobs they found.

Finally, perhaps the most important new resource for working-class organization was radical politics, especially communism. The Communist Party of Canada emerged in 1921 with a significantly different approach to political organizing; communists modelled their perspective on the Russian experience. Before 1920 many Canadian radicals believed that unions assumed a central role in socialist transformation. This notion was displaced by the new conviction that the party itself was to be the vanguard of revolution. All other organizing, including union-building, was guided by the party's political analysis and strategy, which took its general direction from the Communist International in Moscow. In day-to-day organizing, the difference might seem moot, since the Communists were just as committed to all-inclusive industrial organizations as their predecessors; but between 1920 and 1950 it became clear that communist-led industrial unionism had to fit the political priorities of the party. A few European immigrant groups had particularly strong communist organizations that combined politics, culture, and social welfare; these groups included the Finns, Jews, Ukrainians, and Hungarians. And scores of Canadian workers active in the unemployed organizations joined marxist study groups and eventually the Communist Party, confirming their disillusionment with capitalism; in fact, communists led many of the unemployed groups. The existence of a major socialist state inspired many Canadian radicals to struggle for the creation of a new society. A tightly knit, disciplined party also gave many communist militants the support necessary to act as spark plugs for on-the-job challenges to bosses and the organizational skills to run meetings, publish leaflets, and lead marches. These resources were crucial in the bitter battles for industrial unionism in the decade before World War II.

During the 1920s the effects of the Communist Party on the Canadian labour movement remained weak. In the first half of the decade, the party rejected the One Big Union's strategy of going it alone and urged their followers to stay within the North American labour movement and transform it through amalgamation of crafts and other unifying measures. This perspective was promoted by a special group known as the Trade Union Education League, which carried on its propaganda at union meetings and which ran candidates against the old guard of the Trades and Labor Congress, especially congress president Tom Moore. In the second half of the decade, however, the communists found themselves hounded out of the labour movement at the same time that the Communist International was moving towards a new line on independent organizing. In 1927 communists in Canada collaborated with the rump of nationalist unions, led by the Canadian Brotherhood of Railway Employees, to launch the All-Canadian Congress of Labour (ACCL) a new central organization that was opposed to the TLC and committed to industrial unionism. As the clouds of economic depression began to lift in the late 1920s, communist militants attempted to organize several new unions in major industrial enterprises: notably the western coal mines after 1925, General Motors (GM) in Oshawa in 1928, and National Steel Car in Hamilton in 1929. Outside of mining, none of these initiatives had lasting results; in addition, these groups strained relations with their nationalist allies. Early in 1930, communists in Canada announced the creation of their own union central, the Workers Unity League, dedicated to militant industrial unionism and socialist revolution.

The league never came close to supplanting the craft union movement as the focal point of labour activity in Canada, but it was nonetheless a storm centre of new unionizing efforts in the darkest years of the early 1930s. The committed communists who organized quietly and persistently in many industrial centres helped to create viable new unions among garment workers, longshoremen, loggers, fishers, furniture workers, and many others. The independent Mine Workers' Union of Canada also incorporated locals in western Canada and Cape Breton (where a merger with UMWA locals also brought the new Amalgamated Mine Workers of Nova Scotia into the fold). In several mass-production industries, these efforts did not extend beyond the creation of small, clandestine cells that hardly dented the industry's labour relations but that were invaluable in the next round of organizing. The majority of strikes in Canada between 1930 and 1934 were led by affiliates of the Workers Unity League. Strike tactics were bold and uncompromising and, in the absence of substantial strike funds, emphasized mass pickets to shut down a company's operations. The results were most often harsh red-baiting from local politicians and the press and vigorous repression by strikebreakers and provincial police or troops; but in a few cases the unions won grudging concessions and promises of ongoing negotiations.

The longer-term possibilities of this new brand of communist-led unionism were never tested because of two new developments outside the country in the mid-1930s. First, the Communist International announced an abrupt change of line. Now communists around the world were instructed to abandon their strident revolutionary rhetoric and independent groupings, and to promote "popular fronts" (that is, alliances of progressive individuals and organizations) against the spread of fascism. Communist politics now concentrated on this single goal. The militants in the Workers Unity League therefore disbanded their organization in 1935 and transferred their activities back into the mainstream North American labour movement.

The other development was a major change in the labour movement itself. Since the early 1930s, U.S. workers had also been actively organizing in response to both communist leadership and the labour legislation that formed part of President Franklin D. Roosevelt's New Deal. The old international craft unions had responded by urging caution and trying to divide up workers in each factory into the various craft organizations. At the 1935 convention of the American Federation of Labor, the leader of the United Mine Workers, John L. Lewis, led the attack on this outdated perspective (symbolized by a right chop to the jaw of the leader of the carpenters' union) and announced the creation of the Committee for Industrial Organization (CIO) within the AFL to organize the unorganized into new industrial unions. A dynamic new unionizing initiative was thus born; Lewis used the resources of his own union to fund organizers across the country. This campaign was not solely a bureaucratic manoeuvre, however; Lewis and the local organizers touched a nerve in the U.S. working class. The letters "CIO" soon held compelling power for thousands of rank-and-file workers, whose determination and imagination created a massive social movement. The open-shop bastions — steel, auto, rubber, electrical parts, and other mass-production industries — were soon under siege, and the new tactic of "sitting in," or occupying a factory, began to spread.

Canadian workers followed this activity avidly through newspapers, radio, and newsreels in their local movie-houses. A few enthusiasts for industrial unionism, chiefly communist militants who had been pushing for change since the late 1920s, travelled south to ask the CIO to extend into Canada, with the familiar hope of overcoming their isolation and powerlessness. When they were told that the CIO lacked the human and financial resources to help (beyond paying the salary of one organizer), the Canadians simply adopted the CIO label and renewed their own efforts to organize industrial unions. As in the United States, seasoned communists were at the centre of this new campaign. In fact, the Canadian CIO head office sat upstairs from the Communist Party headquarters in Toronto. As the economy picked up slightly in 1937, hundreds of Canadian workers joined the new CIO unions. The first major breakthrough came that spring, when autoworkers in Oshawa stood up to General Motors and Ontario premier Mitchell Hepburn in a widely publicized strike; they won both improvements in wages and working conditions and recognition of their union. In Sydney the formerly independent steelworkers' union, which had joined the CIO's Steelworkers' Organizing Committee, won similar concessions from Dosco without a strike, while in Montreal the women's clothing industry was convulsed by a successful strike. Yet by the start of World War II, CIO victories in Canada could be counted on one hand. Many union locals appeared in mining and factory towns, but generally each contained only a handful of members. Many workers had drifted away. Why had Canadian industrial unionists been so much less successful than their U.S. counterparts in implanting their organizations among the thousands of unorganized workers in the country's major industries?

As in the past, craft union resistance to industrial unionism played its part. In the United States, the American Federation of Labor could no longer tolerate industrial unions in its midst by 1937 and expelled the CIO (which promptly changed its name to the *Congress of* Industrial Organizations). In Canada, the craft-dominated Trades and Labor Congress delayed taking the same action against the industrial unions, but, in the face of AFL threats to cut the Canadians loose, the TLC also expelled them in 1939. Local labour councils followed suit. Industrial unionists were thus cut off from the moral and financial support of craft union locals across the country. Since the U.S. CIO could not help out, Canadian organizers operated in greater isolation with slimmer resources compared to their U.S. counterparts. In 1940 the small CIO organizations in Canada amalgamated with the thirteen-year-old All-Canadian Congress of Labour to form the Canadian Congress of Labour (CCL), a new centre for industrial unionism. Meanwhile, in Quebec, Catholic unionism continued to provide another wrinkle in the labour movement. Some Catholic unions were caught up in the North American militancy of the late 1930s (notably for four weeks at Dominion Textiles plants in Montreal and several other towns) and extended to new sectors, but clerical control remained rigid, and relations with other union centres were distant. On the eve of World War II, then, the Canadian labour movement was grouped around three mutually suspicious poles of unionism — craft, industrial, and Catholic — each with its own municipal, provincial, and national organizations.

Employers, too, dug in their heels against renewed unionizing efforts. Firing and blacklisting of union activists and industrial espionage continued, and strikebreakers were recruited freely. As the pro-CIO sentiment spread after 1935, more firms returned to corporate welfarism to deflect workers' interest from unions. One of the most successful examples occurred at the Dofasco plant in Hamilton in 1937. Once the union activists had been fired, that corporation set in motion a carefully designed program, the centre-piece of which was a profit-sharing plan offering the economic security that unions promised. Other companies opted for new industrial councils, and company magazines and recreational programs began to proliferate.

Yet a crucial difference between Canada and the United States in this period was the role of the state. Canadian governments were still most likely to respond with an iron heel to any efforts by workers to organize, especially if acknowledged communists were in their midst. Municipal authorities often refused to tolerate communist activities (for example, Toronto's police commission banned radical street-corner speeches and meetings in foreign languages). The Bennett government outlawed the Communist Party in 1931, deported radical immigrants, and used force to suppress strikers and the unemployed. In 1933 the militia was sent into a strike situation for the last time; in Stratford, Ontario, they descended, with ludicrously heavy artillery, to intimidate the strikers (they failed). But provincial governments stepped into the breach with repressive provincial police forces, which regularly roughed up strikers in the 1920s and 1930s. In 1937 Ontario premier Mitchell Hepburn pulled out all the stops to defeat CIO unionism, which he saw as threatening the province's low-wage economy, especially northern mining. The same year, Quebec premier Maurice Duplessis passed the "Padlock Law," which enabled the government to shut down any labour activities suspected of communist influence, and shortly after banned the "closed shop."

Official repression stood in marked contrast to the new atmosphere that pervaded in Washington after Roosevelt's election to the U.S. presidency. The ambitious New Deal, a grab-bag of measures to revive the economy, included new legislation in both 1933 and 1935 to protect union organizers from the antilabour practices of the past and to guarantee the right to collective bargaining for certified unions. The second measure was known as the Wagner Act, after its congressional sponsor. Canadian provincial governments reacted slowly to such experiments, despite lobbying efforts by national and provincial labour bodies. Ontario and Quebec passed Industrial Standards Acts in 1934 to encourage small-scale companies in such sectors as construction, clothing, furniture, and logging to negotiate labour policies with existing unions, but only limited bargaining developed. Between 1937 and 1939, several provinces introduced legislation with a spirit similar to that of the Wagner Act (in Nova Scotia, based on the long-standing practices of "industrial legality" promoted by the coal miners), but none had a mechanism to compel employers to deal with unions. Meanwhile, Mackenzie King's federal government continued to avoid compulsory recognition of unions. Even a 1939 amendment to the Criminal Code to forbid firing a worker for union membership was nullified in the courts. In fact, judges continued to be a bastion of support for employers throughout this prewar decade. Although the highest court had declared the Industrial Disputes Investigation Act beyond the constitutional jurisdiction of the federal government in 1925, most provinces had agreed to allow federal authorities to use it, and the act remained the most important piece of labour legislation on the books. State support for union organizing in Canada in the 1930s was thus not comparable to that in the United States, where union organizers transformed luke-warm presidential encouragement into the announcement that "the President wants you to join the union."

In the interwar years, working-class efforts to tackle the state directly through the ballot box were few and far between. In the early 1920s the communists joined the remnants of earlier socialist and labourist activity in a federated political organization known as the Canadian Labor Party. In 1926 the noncommunists withdrew and regrouped separately. Henceforth the Canadian left was irrevocably divided between communism and social democracy. The Communist Party proceeded to contest elections in its own name, but seldom won support beyond a few municipal seats (in Blairmore, Alberta, the communist slate won control of the town council and promptly renamed the main street after the party's national leader, Tim Buck). During the 1930s the party attracted wider support among artists and writers, while its leadership of peace and youth organizations in the "popular front" phase attracted many concerned citizens. By the end of that decade, its membership and sympathizers had expanded from the predominantly eastern European working-class base of the 1920s to include more Anglo-Canadians, radicalized professionals and white-collar workers. Membership peaked at about sixteen thousand in 1939, although many thousands more had likely passed through the party by this point.

Meanwhile, in 1933, representatives of numerous small social democratic organizations from several provinces met in Regina with farmer delegates and eastern intellectuals to found a new national social democratic party, the Co-operative Commonwealth Federation (CCF), dedicated to "eradicating capitalism" by gradual reforms and constitutional methods. The organization's ideology reflected the influence of the Toronto and Montreal intellectuals who had formed the League for Social Reconstruction the year before. Great emphasis was placed on the inefficiency of capitalism and on the need for social planning by trained experts; this orientation had never held such a prominent place in independent labour politics. The party's electoral success during the 1930s was limited to five federal mem-bers of Parliament (MPs) in 1935 (most of them former Labour or Farmer members), a sprinkling across the western legislatures, and only one in Ontario. Before the war, the party had few working-class members or leaders (the presence of the nationalist labour leader Aaron Mosher at the founding convention was the kiss of death for craft unionists). The commitment to the "parliamentary road to socialism" kept the party apart from the industrial-union movement, which the communists continued to control until the war. The only major union to affiliate with the CCF was the Nova Scotia district of the United Mine Workers in 1938. Like the earlier Canadian socialists, however, the CCF was convinced of the need for political education of voters (to raise socialist consciousness). During the 1930s, in fact, the most common organizational form was the CCF Club, which served as a propaganda and discussion centre for members. In these circles, small numbers of Anglo-Canadian unemployed workers and trade unionists developed a vision of a different kind of society based on production for need, not profit; this vision carried them through many difficult struggles with bosses and politicians.

Among both the communists and the social democrats were many more women activists. As in past labour and socialist movements, women were weakly represented in the top leadership; exceptions included British Columbia's Helena Gutteridge, Grace MacInnis, and Dorothy Steeves, Manitoba's Beatrice Brigden, Ontario's Agnes Macphail (Canada's first female MP) and Florence Custance, and the highly mobile communists Becky Buhay and Annie Buller. Women nonetheless managed to use their growing numbers in the parties and their own organizations to promote brands of communism and socialism that recognized their needs. Though committed primarily to a common political struggle with their male comrades, groups such as the Women's Labour Leagues, the Women's International League for Peace and Freedom, and many local committees and councils pushed for women's equality as citizens and wage-earners, as well as specific maternal issues (they even tried to politicize Mother's Day in the mid-1930s). Communist women also helped unionize female wage-earners, specifically garment workers, secretaries, domestics, and textile workers, though their leaders were usually much more interested in organizing the male-dominated heavy industries.

Meanwhile, in Quebec quite a different reformist political current took shape and drew in working-class activists. It flowed from the "Program for Social Restoration," drafted by Catholic clergy and lay persons and inspired by the 1931 papal encyclical *Quadragesimo Anno*. A group of young liberals turned these ideas into a political platform in 1934 when they founded L'Action libérale nationale (ALN). The party attacked big business and aimed at a more humane form of capitalism through European-style "corporatism" — that is, reorganization of industrial society into "corporations" including both unions and capitalist organizations, under the supervision of the state. This concept was precisely the ideological thrust of the Catholic unions in this period, and some Catholic labour leaders helped to draft the program and worked in the provincial election campaign. In 1935 the ALN formed a coalition government, l'Union nationale, with the Conservatives, but their program was ultimately shelved by an unsympathetic Maurice Duplessis.

Overall, the weakness of workers' movements in Canada was reflected in the rare and largely unsuccessful forays into independent labour politics. Working-class citizens who bothered to vote helped to turf out numerous governments across the country between 1930 and 1939, but they seldom looked to either of the left-wing parties for an alternative. New political parties with a populist aura, the Social Credit in Alberta and l'Union nationale in Quebec, appeared, but elsewhere left-leaning Liberals managed to harness the discontent and sweep to power in provincial elections.

On the eve of the war, then, the industrial regime of the "open shop" had been confronted by union organizing and strike activity in two small waves that had crested in 1934 and 1937, and withstood the challenge. Local working-class activists in the resource and mass-production industries had amassed a wealth of experience, but, outside the coal mining communities and a few isolated factory towns, they had not managed to build the sporadic explosions of frustration and resentment into a broad-based movement of resistance.

The Breakthrough

Disruptions to Canadian labour relations during World War II resembled those during World War I. Military recruitment and munitions production provided steady employment. The working class expanded and took on new hues, as labour shortages brought in large numbers of new workers from farms and women from their households. This time, however, the federal government introduced wage and price controls to keep the resentment against profiteering from fanning the flames of popular discontent. The Industrial Disputes Investigation Act was once again extended to all "essential" war-related industries to discourage strikes, and eventually strike votes were made compulsory. In addition, the National Selective Service restricted workers' freedom of movement in the labour market.

The state's direction of the wartime economy was actually more extensive than in the earlier war, heightening the sense of national emergency and personal sacrifice. Wartime propaganda about the struggle against fascism was thus even more potent, and, as in the past, it was soon directed towards a struggle for democracy in Canadian society. In contrast both to the central administrative role assigned to Canada's leading corporate barons and to labour's prominent place in Britain's wartime government, the role of the Canadian labour movement was minimal; once again unionists were shut out of wartime decision making, except for representation on a powerless National Labour Supply Council and the national and regional war labour boards set up to handle wage controls. Government officials continued to honour the determination of employers in war industries to have no truck nor trade with union representatives. Canada's national labour leaders lobbied earnestly for greater participation in the wartime state, but with little effect. Consequently, they felt no obligation to make the public "no-strike pledge" that U.S. and British leaders announced early in the war.

All three union centres — craft, industrial, and Catholic — easily recruited members after 1940. By 1943 union membership in Canada soared, and one out of every three unionists was on strike; the number of strikes and strikers exceeded the peak in 1919. Once again, local leaders emerged from the rank and file, often with organizing experience and steeped in some brand of radical politics, to win the confidence of frightened and anti-union workmates and to head up the all-consuming struggles in working-class communities. Many women were active in these campaigns as shop stewards and local union executive members, though seldom rising to higher positions in union officialdom. This mass upsurge exemplified the deep commitment of thousands of Canadian workers to prevent the return of the economic insecurity of the 1930s. They consistently demanded wage increases beyond the controlled levels, as well as recognition of their unions. The international unions, to which almost all workers in English Canada belonged, were better equipped to assist the local struggles. Having won recognition in the United States and therefore financially able to support a staff of organizers in Canada, the new industrial unions in the mass-production and resource industries provided a more extensive central administration than industrial unionists in Canada (other than coal miners) had ever before had at their disposal. The energetic young men and women in these full-time jobs also coordinated negotiation strategies across whole industries and promoted more centralized bargaining than employers in most industries had ever been willing to accept. As in the earlier experience of craft unionists, however, workers found this bureaucracy a mixed blessing, since their national leaders were just as inclined to don the mantle of labour politicians and to attempt to damp down militancy.

Despite these resources, Canadian unionists made little headway in dragging their bosses to the bargaining table. The ponderous machinery of the industrial disputes act slowed them down enormously, and they failed to overcome employers' deep-seated resistance to union recognition. Despite the example of the 1935 Wagner Act in the United States, the Canadian government refused to move beyond a declaration made in 1940 that merely urged employers to negotiate with their employees. Government officials and the appointed controllers of war-related industries preferred to encourage dialogue with a "committee of workmen," rather than a full-fledged union. A major strike of gold miners at Kirkland Lake in northern Ontario in the winter of 1941–42 crystallized the labour movement's anger and frustration. When the mine owners refused to accept a conciliation board recommendation to recognize a local of the International Union of Mine, Mill, and Smelter Workers, the workers marched out to picket in the coldest winter within living memory. Support committees sprang up across the country, but the government remained silent, allowing the strike to be broken by scabs and provincial police and the union's leaders to be blacklisted (they reappeared as labour activists in several other industrial centres). The momentum of worker resistance nonetheless continued to build, including during 1943 in a tie-up of the steel plants at Sydney and Sault Ste. Marie. The Trades and Labor Congress and the Canadian Congress of Labor joined forces in a more concerted campaign for federal legislation requiring compulsory union recognition. Even the Catholic unions in Quebec were shedding their caution, as a new generation of activists began to interact with secular intellectuals.

The federal and provincial Liberals finally began to readjust their course when they saw disturbing political consequences of this working-class discontent. There was new thunder on the left. After several years in the political wilderness, the CCF was catching the imagination of thousands of workers with its call for social planning and social security. In 1942 an unknown CCF member defeated the national Conservative leader in a by-election. In Ontario and British Columbia, the social democrats came close to winning provincial elections in 1943; a national opinion poll showed them inching ahead of the Liberals and the Conservatives. In 1944 they captured the Saskatchewan government. Organized labour contributed to these campaigns, and in 1943 the Canadian Congress of Labor declared the CCF to be labour's political arm. Several CCF members elected to provincial legislatures were local union leaders. Even the communists had made a breakthrough, winning two seats in the Ontario house and one in a federal by-election in Montreal.

In response, the Conservatives promptly shifted their platform in the direction of greater social reform, and added "Progressive" to their name. The Mackenzie King government and its provincial counterparts eventually fell into line as well. Not only did the King government announce a new commitment to social security measures (health insurance, pensions, family allowances, housing, and so on) in an effort to steal the initiative from the CCF, but early in 1944, on the heels of similar moves by the Ontario and British Columbia governments, it also passed an order in council, P.C. 1003, that incorporated the principle of compulsory collective bargaining. If "employee representatives" (the word *union* was avoided) proved to a new labour relations board that they had the support of the majority of workers in a particular workplace, they became legally certified, and employers could not refuse to sit down at the bargaining table. The board was empowered to oversee this process and to rule on any "unfair labour practices." Strikes for union recognition were no longer necessary (or legal). The new legislation also incorporated the old practice of compulsory conciliation (with conciliation boards and the "cooling-out" period before strikes and lock-outs) from the industrial disputes act, giving the measure a uniquely Canadian flavour. The bargaining process was thus guaranteed, but there were no new substantive rights and no outcome was assured; indeed, unions could still be broken in strikes over first contracts. Business interests had lobbied with some success to tame the legislation in various ways, including recognition for company unions ("employee associations"), which many corporations had been promoting with new vigour since 1940. Still, in the last two years of the war, unions across the country used the provisions of P.C. 1003 to nail down their first contracts with employers. The state had thus intervened decisively, in the face of considerable resistance from many capitalists, to keep industrial conflict from overflowing into more serious industrial and political challenges to the existing social order.

The labour movement had to deal with problems in its own back-yard as well, however. By the early 1940s, the divisions between craft and industrial unionists were not the most hotly contested lines of cleavage. Some craft unions (the machinists, electricians, and carpenters, in particular) opened their ranks to less skilled workers in factory production, and by the end of the war the members of affiliates to the Trades and Labor Congress outnumbered those attached to the Canadian Congress of Labor — 360,000 to 315,000 in 1946 (the picture is complicated by the existence of such industrial unions as the textiles workers and the sailors inside the TLC). At the national level, the two congresses learned to cooperate during the war, in spite of the continuing tension between them. Far more divisive were relations between the communists and the social democrats, who vied for control of the new industrial unions and the CCL. Neither side could claim the moral high ground in bitter battles that lasted for more than a decade.

By the end of the 1930s, CCF members had allied themselves with the CIO's U.S. leaders, who wanted to curb communist influence and whose strategy emphasized covert manipulation and scant respect for internal democracy. In the Canadian CIO affiliates (notably the Steelworkers' Organizing Committee, renamed the United Steelworkers of America in 1942, which later provided the crack troops of anticommunism in the Canadian labour movement), seasoned communist organizers were fired, and social democrats, sometimes with little or no labour movement experience, were appointed to key posts. In the 1940 merger that created the Canadian Congress of Labor, the social democrats manoeuvred to assure themselves a majority and forced the communists into the permanent role of outraged opposition. Within the new congress, CCF leaders regularly urged locals to affiliate with the CCF and pushed through resolutions of support for the party in 1943 and subsequent years.

Unlike many social democratic labour leaders, the communists could claim with some legitimacy that they had entered the labour movement at the bottom and dedicated themselves to the painfully slow process of building their unions from the ground up. They could also claim to be the heirs to the long struggles to create democratic, all-inclusive unionism for Canadian workers. The industrial unions in which the communist influence remained strongest encouraged rank-and-file participation through democratic structures and effective communication. But the communists were as concerned about their larger political priorities as the social democrats (or, for that matter, supporters of the Liberal Party, who were active in the Trades and Labor Congress).

In the early 1930s, before the dawn of their popular-front phase, Canadian communists permamently alienated many social democrats by attacking them openly and viciously as "social fascists." In 1939 the Communist Party performed one of the about-faces that its connection with the International demanded all too often: after Stalin signed his pact with Hitler, the party abruptly changed its antifascist campaign to an antiwar crusade. The King government promptly outlawed the party and interned several of its leaders. Then, just as suddenly, Canadian communists responded to Hitler's invasion of the Soviet Union in 1941 with another political pirouette and reemerged as the Labour Progressive Party, in full support of the war effort. The popular front was revived with new passion. Bemused Canadian workers now heard communist labour leaders discouraging strikes and attacking the CCF-dominated unions for fomenting protests. The party publicly threw its support behind the King government, and, in several communities, communists cultivated political alliances with the local Liberal party. In Windsor, Ontario, they helped elect the rising Liberal star Paul Martin. They showed no such willingness to cooperate with the CCF, whose candidates sometimes faced communist challengers in elections. Within the national labour congresses, communists fought for a "nonpartisan" political orientation. They achieved greater success in the Trades and Labor Congress, where the CCF influence was weaker and where the secretary-treasurer was for several years an acknowledged communist. In contrast to the situation during the World War I period, the left in the Canadian labour movement was deeply split, and the far left was trying to keep Canadian workers' aspirations from moving in more radical directions.

As the war came to an end in 1945, the future of the new organizational giant that had emerged in working-class communities across the country remained largely unresolved. The movement's ideological complexion was still undefined, but, more important, its main prop, P.C. 1003, was still only a wartime measure, due to expire with the end of hostilities, when most responsibility for industrial relations eventually returned to the provinces. The federal government extended the life of this and other emergency legislation for two years into the "reconstruction" era and waited to see how power relations between capital and labour would stabilize before introducing new legislation. Both workers and employers held their breath;

the president of the steelworkers' local at Stelco later recalled that the members of his union were so uncertain of the future that not one worker had come forward to process a grievance during the term of the first contract.

The Postwar Compromise

Stakes were high when massive strikes erupted in almost every major industry between 1945 and 1947, often involving thousands of workers, and, in a few cases, spanning the whole country. Both the communist and social democratic union leaders adopted a tough approach to bargaining. In the peak year, 1946, strikers shut down the British Columbia logging industry, the Ontario rubber industry, the central Canadian ports, the Southam newspaper chain, the country's steel industry, and dozens of mass-production plants, in the biggest strike wave Canada had ever seen. The next year's disputes were highlighted by a national strike of packing-house workers, and in 1949 Quebec's asbestos miners fought a bitterly contested battle symbolizing the postwar shift from passive conservatism that had dominated Catholic unionism. The wave ended in 1950 with the first national railway strike on both transcontinental lines. A major social movement had taken shape in these years. In many industrial centres, thousands of workers had maintained mass picket lines for weeks, drawing on wide support in working-class neighbourhoods to feed and entertain them. Their bosses had just as stubbornly refused to budge, hoping to dispense with these young unions or at least to weaken them severely. In the end, most of these workers won significant concessions and consolidated their organizations permanently.

In one sense, this dramatic moment of working-class assertiveness replayed the workers' revolt at the end of the last war: determined industrial wage-earners stood their ground to preserve the gains they had made and to ensure a better life for themselves and their families in postwar society. But there were important differences. Each of these strikes was preceded by lengthy negotiations that were closely monitored and mediated by state officials, in sharp contrast to earlier refusals by employers to talk to union committees and the government's willingness to use force to curb the militancy. As well, these strikes were not isolated local events (neither did they develop into community-based general strikes as in 1918–19). Rather, the focus was on single industries across the country, and the key leadership came not from the local trades and labour councils, as in the past, but from highly centralized bureaucracies of national union officers and staff, who tried to channel and shape the restlessness and anger of the militant membership. These officials developed one package of demands for workers across an industry and tried either to bring all employers to the same bargaining table or to carry that package into negotiations with each employer (soon known as "pattern bargaining"). Several industrial unions were also committed to some form of joint council of business, labour, and the state to develop general policy for each industry. In 1946 the CCL also adopted a coordinated campaign for a common minimum wage across the industrial landscape; although unions were not supposed to settle without consulting a wage committee of the main union leaders, several groups ultimately abandoned this common front in their settlements.

A "living wage" (for male breadwinners) and an eight-hour day were clear priorities, but the central issue was usually the status of workers' organizations after the war, or "union security." The new industrial unions wanted employers to guarantee their stability by requiring all workers to join and by deducting union dues from workers' pay packets — the so-called check-off. Justice Ivan Rand, the arbitrator for a lengthy strike against Ford in Windsor, Ontario, in 1945, conceived of a compromise solution that was eventually adopted in several other major industries. Under the Rand Formula, employees were not required to join a union that had been certified as a bargaining agent, but they were required to pay union dues, since they benefited from the terms of employment that unions negotiated. With these restrictions, most corporate employers adopted the check-off. The unions thus established a firm financial basis to ensure their survival.

By 1948 the federal government recognized that the wartime shift in the balance of power between capital and labour had not been rolled back as it had at the end of World War I and therefore passed the Industrial Relations and Disputes Investigation Act, to establish P.C. 1003 as a permanent framework for industrial relations in Canada. Virtually all the provinces had done the same by 1950. The new industrial regime that had emerged from this decade of intense conflict was thus enshrined in law and would last for the next three decades. However, the new system became decentralized as much more responsibility was shifted back to the provinces than they had exercised in the first half of the twentieth century. As a result, the eleven sets of labour laws had a similar shape but varied widely in crucial details. The Saskatchewan CCF government's legislation was the most supportive of labour, but in the late 1940s the repressive Cold War climate encouraged several other provincial administrations to set up tighter constraints on union organizing and strikes and harsher penalties for violations. The ongoing rulings of the new labour relations boards hamstrung unions further. In both Quebec and Nova Scotia, alleged communist influence actually blocked union certification. It was soon evident that the basic legal framework of labour relations could be fleshed out with administrative detail that could make forming and using unions difficult. Compared to other countries' versions of industrial legality, the postwar Canadian situation found governments keeping a tight leash on unionized workers.

How much, then, had workers actually won? New unions had been consolidated, but what could workers do with them? The greatest victory was the right to negotiate the terms of their employment. As mentioned previously, employers were legally bound to deal with any union that a labour relations board determined had majority support in a workplace. These certified unions soon pressed for wage increases, benefit plans, and relief from the pressures of work, such as an eight-hour day and paid vacations. They also pushed for an end to industrial autocracy ("Hitlerism," as some called it) and for greater fairness in workplace administration. The new labour legislation guaranteed that, after the two parties had signed a contract, they dealt with new disputes through a formal grievance system, which culminated in arbitration in the case of an impasse. The vast network of shop stewards at the base of the industrial union movement became the watchdogs of workers' interests in the grievance system. Unions also invariably entrenched the principle of seniority for promotion and lay-off in their agreements to further guarantee fairness and to undermine the despotism of supervisors. Employers and their supervisory staff were now expected to abandon the arbitrary, unpredictable practices of the past and to administer their enterprises according to the procedures set down in the collective agreements negotiated with their unions. Workers thus added their own bureaucratic constraints to an already bureaucratized workplace. Compared to the uncertainty and unfairness of employment practices before the war, these measures comprised substantial gains for workers, as any veteran who lived through this transformation will still say today.

The price, however, was high. First, while some commentators have called this new system a "rule of law" in the workplace, it should be remembered that workers made few of the rules. During the war, many workers had begun to boldly challenge managerial authority over numerous issues on the shop floor; however, their bosses made sure that the range of issues open to negotiation was narrowed drastically after the war. In exchange for recognizing unions and granting the check-off of union dues, most employers insisted on including a "management rights" clause in each collective agreement. These clauses gave the companies exclusive control over the organization of the work process at the firm; thus, the employer still wielded authority regarding staffing, work routines, and new technology. As a result, some of the most important and contentious issues, which sparked conflict in the workplace every day, were excluded from the new system of collective bargaining. Unions were expected to limit their concerns to wages and benefits. In the first rounds of negotiations in the 1940s, some unions attempted to retain greater flexibility in bargaining demands. In Quebec, for example, the Catholic unions promoted far-reaching ideas such as the co-management of enterprises with employers (this particular concept shocked Canadian Johns Manville at Asbestos, Quebec, in 1949). But by the early 1950s virtually all unions had been compelled to accept the new limitations. Consequently, each new industrial union had to accept the work process (the division of labour, the skill distribution, the technology, the recruitment practices, and so on) that it found in its particular industry. In addition, industrial unions had difficulty eliminating the segregation of women and immigrant workers into low-wage job ghettoes (even if the male unionists' pride had allowed more equity, most men still assumed that women should be at home, supported by a male wage).

The Canadian state had never guaranteed anything more. The new labour legislation, like its predecessors, was primarily concerned with keeping workers on the job and away from picket lines, not with establishing rights that workers deserved and that employers had to accept. Even the new conciliation boards were given no guidelines for judging individual disputes. Pressure from organized labour did result in the statute books' containing several new laws governing employment standards (minimum wages, paid vacations, discrimination, the eight-hour day, and so on), but these laws generally set standards far below those won in unionized industry and were intended for the unorganized. The state's view was that unionized workers were entitled to only whatever their power enabled them to extract from their bosses.

Furthermore, most employers managed to beat back the industrial unions' attempt to create industry-wide bargaining and made the individual plant the most common bargaining unit; this framework was reinforced by the labour relations boards. Canadian capitalists had tried to keep workers' attention focused on their own employer and their own workplace, rather than on working-class solidarity in an industry or a community. In these circumstances, negotiations became highly fragmented, and only pattern bargaining, with its high success rate, helped to maintain cohesion among related workers. The gains workers made thus varied widely across the country.

The new legal and bureaucratic strait-jacket also constrained solidarity. The direct action that workers had used spontaneously to resist management pressure was now replaced by slower, more impersonal procedures. In place of the direct shop-floor confrontation was the grievance slip, which tended to focus the issue on one individual and which quickly passed into the hands of professionals, often lawyers, to be argued before an arbitrator (who was most often legally trained) months, or even years, later. The new legal language of industrial relations mystified most union members. The settlement of important issues in the daily lives of workers thus moved off the shop floor and out of their direct control.

Strikes were also now more controlled. Under the new procedures, unions had to persuade workers individually to pay dues and sign cards (in order to get unions recognized), rather than use mass protests outside plant gates, as in the past. Even more important, once a collective agreement was signed, strikes were illegal until the agreement expired and compulsory conciliation had run its course. Stopping work illegally now became known as a "wildcat" strike, and union officials became the "police officers" responsible for preventing such incidents. Sympathy strikes were clearly out of the question. The eagerness of Canadian workers to support each other's struggles, which had been evident for decades, now had to be curtailed. Unless all contracts could be made to expire at the same time, the Winnipeg General Strike could never be reenacted. It is doubtful that any other legislation constrained class consciousness as effectively among Canadian workers over the next fifty years.

This rigid new framework also helped to shape a new kind of unionism. Bureaucratic tendencies that had existed within the North American labour movement since the late nineteenth century now reached full bloom. By 1950 the Canadian and international headquarters of the major unions were far more preoccupied with negotiating and administering contracts than with mobilizing masses of men and women, as unionists had in the 1930s and early 1940s. The most important skills for effective union leadership were not the ability to inspire a meeting from the back of a pick-up truck or to maintain picket lines of underpaid workers for weeks on end, but rather to engage in closed-door, across-the-table negotiations with management representatives. Most bargaining remained in the hands of the local union executives, but staff from union headquarters were usually present to guide labour's side of the proceedings. The social democratic politics that inspired so many of these labour officials had always emphasized the importance of expertise and centralized bureaucratic administration, rather than direct rank-and-file initiative. First the Canadian Congress of Labour and then several of the individual industrial unions developed impressive research departments to provide data for negotiations. Education departments concentrated on training workers to handle grievances or to negotiate contracts. The new unions were officially committed to a broader political program of social reform, but the daily demands of the new world of industrial relations overshadowed that larger vision. Certainly the close connection that had existed before World War II between industrial unionism and socialist transformation had been lost in most cases.

Of course, the national Liberal government's apparent conversion to stable employment and incomes and a few social security programs took some of the wind out of social democratic sails. Yet, in the late 1940s, these unions also deliberately clipped their own political wings. The hostility between the social democrats and the communists continued into the postwar period despite the Communist Party's renewed efforts to build labour unity. The social democrats seized upon the Cold War mentality that had begun to grip the business community, the state, and the media by 1946, and launched a campaign to drive the communists from the industrial-union movement in Canada. Those unions that could not be manipulated internally were shut out and new organizations were authorized to take their place as the "legitimate" unions. Between 1948 and 1950 the Canadian Congress of Labor expelled the International Union of Mine, Mill, and Smelter Workers, the United Electrical Workers, the International Leather and Fur Workers, and the International Woodworkers of America, the biggest union in British Columbia. Congress organizers, most often from the steelworkers' union, then used highly undemocratic tactics to raid and otherwise destabilize the unions. The miners successfully resisted these attacks until the early 1960s, but only the electrical workers were able to hold on to most of their membership. The more nonpartisan Trades and Labor Congress was slower to respond to the Cold War hysteria, but in 1949 suspended its largest communist-led organization, the Canadian Seamen's Union, allowing the gangster-ridden Seafarers' International Union from the United States to replace it, with the collusion of shipowners and the federal government. Five years later, the West Coast fishers' union was also expelled, though it survived independently. Despite its debilitating deference to Soviet leadership, the communist brand of unionism in Canada had always put greater emphasis on rank-and-file democracy than on the more bureaucratic social democratic form, but, hounded out of the house of labour, the communist alternative had little chance to develop.

Ironically, the social democrats gained little or nothing from these purges (or from their stridently anticommunist resolutions on Canadian foreign policy), since all left-wing political organizations were swept away in the Cold War deluge. Most of the handful of elected communists were defeated in municipal, provincial, and federal elections (the party's most prominent parliamentarian, Fred Rose, an MP from Montreal, was arrested in the aftermath of the famous Gouzenko affair, which uncovered Soviet espionage in Canada). The Communist Party was driven into oblivion, never to exercise the same influence in local politics or the Canadian labour movement. Outside Saskatchewan, the CCF also floundered in the late 1940s, losing most of its seats in Parliament and the provincial legislatures. It all but disappeared in the 1950s.

World War II was a watershed in the history of the Canadian labour movement. Before 1940, workers seldom overcame the stubborn resistance of Canadian capitalists to unions and never managed to convince the state to intervene decisively on labour's behalf. The unusual conditions of wartime society gave unions the chance to recruit a vastly greater number of members and to pose an industrial and political challenge that was serious enough to push the state into enacting new legislation. The general development of the labour movement in Canada paralleled that in the United States, but the timing was quite different. In the second half of the 1930s, U.S. workers created a mass movement and entered the war with a more substantial organizational base that merely expanded in the early 1940s. Their Canadian counterparts were weakly organized at the end of the 1930s and only just found their feet by the end of the war.

Most industrial unions in Canada signed their first contracts in 1944–45. They were therefore not nearly as well prepared as U.S. unions to face the postwar confrontations.

The outcome of the great surge of new unionism in the mid-1940s amounted to a historic compromise between class forces. Labour laws and collective agreements bound employers to important concessions and opened up possibilities for workers to pursue more economic security. But the new working-class movement was tamed in crucial ways. Its traditional tools of direct action and solidarity were severely restricted or taken away. The scope of its power to negotiate the terms of employment was sharply limited so as not to challenge capitalist power in the workplace. And the political threat of a massive workers' movement was undercut by destructive conflict between the social democrats and the communists, neither of whom ultimately won broad support among the postwar Canadian working class. Canada did not need the Draconian Taft-Hartley Act, passed in the United States in 1947, to undermine union strength, since some of the constraints of that act were built into postwar Canadian legislation and since labour leaders made the necessary compromises themselves. The union leaders who emerged at the top of the new unions were probably more comfortable with the new state mechanisms for controlling rank-and-file activism and for channelling labour relations into the hands of full-time officials and experts, since this framework was not so different from the social democratic vision of social planning. Superficially, these developments may seem like a "sell-out." However, the labour movement probably lacked the power to present a more potent challenge to the deeply entrenched capitalist resistance, and its leaders grasped at the restricted recognition offered by the state.

The "compromise" that the unions made has often been called "Fordism," after the major North American manufacturer that set the pace. The argument states that corporations traded off the higher standard of living provided by better wages and benefits, which would fuel consumer spending, for the ability to use Taylorist management and new technology to intensify work in their enterprises and crank up productivity. These employers would be protected by the stability of union contracts (policed by union leaders) and the sanctity of their managerial prerogatives. In fact, few employers accepted this new labour-relations regime willingly; most fought it vigorously in the formative period (sometimes decisively, as in the fishing industry on both coasts). And, as workers discovered at the

Gaspé Copper Mines in Murdochville, Quebec, in 1957, in the Newfoundland woods in 1959, and in other less dramatic confrontations,
many bosses still fought hard to keep unions out.

The expansiveness of the Canadian labour movement that had
swept up so many blue-collar workers in the 1940s was gone by
1950. The organized workers in resource, mass-production, and
transportation industries had dominated these years of union consolidation; the typical union member was now a relatively settled, semiskilled male worker within a large industrial corporation. But
thousands remained outside organized labour. Blue-collar workers in
small-scale industry continued to eke out a living at wages far below
those in the unionized sector and with far less job security. Moreover,
the labour movement included few white-collar workers. Private-
sector employers had defeated the scattered efforts of unions to
recruit bank clerks or retail store employees, most dramatically at
Eaton's department store in Toronto between 1948 and 1952. Federal
and provincial governments had also deflected the organizing efforts
of public-sector employees into nonconfrontational consultative bodies
without power. In addition, outside Saskatchewan, the new collective-
bargaining legislation excluded civil servants. Teachers in several
provinces had created much stronger organizations, but, by law and
by professional inclination, were hived off into narrow bargaining
channels far from the unions, where militancy and strikes were generally unknown (in a rare act of defiance, Montreal's Catholic teachers broke this mould briefly in an illegal strike in 1949). There were
also sharply etched regional differences resulting from the unevenness of the postwar prosperity, the constraints of specific provincial
labour legislation, and the animosity of antilabour politicians such as
Quebec premier Maurice Duplessis, Alberta's Ernest Manning, and
Newfoundland's Joey Smallwood.

Overall, postwar unions were also primarily men's domain, which
enrolled few of the thousands of women outside the big industries
and which, as in the past, drew few female members into leadership
roles. Occasional, halting efforts surfaced in unions with large female
memberships; for example, the United Electrical Workers allowed
women activists to organize their own conferences. However, the
many "Rosie the Riveters" who had helped build unions in auto,
aircraft, or munitions plants were forgotten or ignored after the war,
especially if they were married. Similarly, although many workers
with mother tongues other than English or French in large-scale
industry had found a place for themselves inside the new industrial

unions, many more immigrants in sectors that were harder to organize remained outside the gates of the house of labour. For all these reasons, it was inevitable that, however long its shadow over Canadian industrial life, the labour movement would remain a restricted segment of the Canadian working class for the next twenty years.

4

The New Resistance

By the 1950s, it seemed that many Canadian workers had never had it so good. Their national government had declared its commitment to steady employment and incomes. The government accomplished that goal not by creating an extensive welfare state (the move toward social security had stopped abruptly in the late 1940s), but by actively supporting and stimulating private capitalist development and by smoothing out the economic cycles of boom and bust that had often threatened working-class living standards. With strong new unions to promote and defend labour interests within a state-supervised system of collective bargaining, workers could push for greater improvements in their living standards, limited only by the intransigence of the corporations they faced across the negotiating table. And consumerism might compensate for their limited control over the workplace. Yet if many workers seemed to have found their feet by the 1950s, the earth was moving underneath. The social and economic structures of daily life and work were changing rapidly and profoundly. By the 1970s these workers were once again reeling from the shocks and striking back to regain some stability.

The structures of capital accumulation were again being transformed. The concept of an independent national economy that had guided business and state policy for half a century before the 1930s no longer existed. International free trade was the new capitalist orthodoxy. Tariffs in long-protected Canadian industries slowly came down. By the 1970s the "new international division of labour" had shifted much of the production of clothing, shoes, textiles, appliances, and other light consumer goods to the Third World. At the same time, Canada was filling a much more important role as a resource hinterland for the United States. The transnational corporation dominated this increasingly open economy. A few Canadian corporations made the leap to the world stage, but far more sold out to U.S. companies or left new development to these outsiders. By the 1960s foreign ownership of the manufacturing and resource sectors of the Canadian economy had reached staggering proportions. The national capitalist class, still strong, was content to hold on to its bastion in finance and transportation and to cooperate with the new foreign-controlled transnationals. The Canadian economy was thus becoming less internally cohesive and less easily regulated by the state. Under U.S. leadership, this new international economy enjoyed unparalleled prosperity in the 1950s and 1960s as a result of huge productivity increases and markets that expanded — domestically, feeding the voracious appetite of the arms race, and, internationally, penetrating deeper into the Third World. But the bloody quagmire of the Vietnam War and the rise of new international competitors led to an international economic crisis by the early 1970s.

The new Canadian economy also underwent important internal shifts. Hundreds of thousands of rural Canadians abandoned farming as a livelihood (and a way of life) and moved to the city. A country that had always prided itself on its agricultural economy saw farm employment shrink from nearly 16 per cent of the workforce in 1951 to less than 6 per cent in 1971 and 4 per cent in 1981. More significant for the labour movement, the unionized sectors of the economy were not growing. The proportion of workers employed in factories levelled off, while the number of workers in mining and logging dwindled. By the 1970s many commentators were talking, mistakenly, about a "postindustrial" society. The major growth sector was services, especially those designed to facilitate capital accumulation (financial services, data processing, communications systems, and so on) and those that absorbed the much larger disposable income of Canadian consumers (from McDonald's to Speedy Muffler to the Bay). Most of the postwar jobs were being created in this sector. White and pink collars were overwhelming the former blue-collar majority.

The Canadian state contributed to this shift in employment patterns, in expanding the civil service enormously. Starting in the 1940s, federal and provincial governments and their many agencies and employees assumed a much more active role in Canadian economic and social life. The state continued to promote and regulate capitalist expansion as it had done during World War II; it granted tax concessions, built roads and highways, opened industrial parks, and aggressively promoted trade and commerce. But it also undertook huge new expenditures on schools and colleges, hospitals, and cultural facilities, as well as on a small number of social welfare programs — unemployment insurance, public housing, health insurance, and old-age pensions. In addition, the federal government had undertaken a commitment in the 1940s to use fiscal and monetary tools to stabilize the economy and maintain a reasonably high level of employment.

Canadian capitalists remade the world of work within this new context. They concentrated more of their operations in or near major metropolitan centres and thus contributed to the huge growth in urban congestion. They experimented with new technology, especially in the resource and transportation industries, on a scale not seen for nearly half a century. They sought new pools of labour, looking to Canadian farm boys and girls, immigrants from southern Europe, Asia, and the Caribbean for the least-skilled work and to workers from Britain, eastern Europe, and Asia for jobs requiring greater expertise. They also drew more married women out of their homes, usually on a full-time basis. And they began to demand higher educational qualifications for workers in more technically sophisticated production processes. By the 1960s that demand had spurred the growth of many more universities and community colleges. Once again, the Canadian working class was being recomposed to meet the demands of the constantly evolving capitalist economy. By the late 1960s and early 1970s, many workers were clearly unhappy about some of these developments.

Revolt from Below

Compared to the turbulence of the preceding decade, the 1950s seemed tranquil, even complacent. Within unions, membership, structure, and ideology had stabilized. In search of recruits, affiliates of the two rival national unions, the Trades and Labor Congress and the Canadian Congress of Labor, began to infringe on each other's membership. To end this raiding and to confirm the ideological harmony of the labour movement, the two congresses merged in 1956, a year after a similar merger in the United States, to create the Canadian Labour Congress (CLC). City labour councils and provincial federations across the country were similarly unified. The Catholic unions in Quebec continued to become more like other unions in the country, finally shedding their religious trappings and ideology in 1960, and reorganizing as the Confederation of National Trade Unions (CNTU). An abiding sense of cultural distinctiveness nonetheless kept this union centre outside the CLC.

At the same time, the new industrial regime of state-sanctioned collective bargaining was tested well, as unions settled down to negotiate better wages and benefits, especially new pensions, insurance plans, and job-security measures. Employers were developing more sophisticated personnel departments in response to these pressures. Strikes were less common, more ritualistic, and less a part of national strategies than in the recent past.

By far the most important units in the labour movement were the individual international and national unions (steelworkers, autoworkers, carpenters, and so on), which remained great blocks of independent, jealously guarded power. The smaller Canadian membership in the international unions gave the Canadian labour movement a highly fragmented appearance. Yet these organizations refused to grant central federations at any level the power to coordinate labour activity beyond lobbying, backing a political party, or settling jurisdictional battles. Each union had its own, often extensive educational programs, research facilities, and communication media, which together dwarfed the staff and programs of the labour councils, provincial federations, and the CLC.

At the top of the old craft unions and the large industrial unions sat a full-time bureaucracy made up of elected officials and salaried staff, who exercised considerable power within their organizations. The pattern of decentralized collective bargaining in Canada, rather than centralized, industry-wide negotiations, probably gave these bureaucrats somewhat less power than their European counterparts, but Canadian officials nonetheless kept a tight control on their unions. Union officials still exercised veto power over some local decisions and, when necessary, were prepared to place a local in "trusteeship" (that is, dismiss the local's officers and administer its affairs directly from union headquarters). They guarded their organizations' financial stability, public image, and internal cohesion cautiously and suspiciously. The term "labour bosses," however, distorts their role. Because of the formally democratic structures of the unions (with elections, conventions, and a large army of unpaid, part-time officers spread through the locals), these bureaucrats were more similar to politicians who had to make some effort to meet membership concerns, especially when negotiating collective agreements, if they wanted to hold on to office. Some officials undoubtedly followed opportunistic career paths to power within the labour movement. Others used their wide powers of appointment to build almost impregnable personal empires and demanded unquestioning loyalty from staff and local officials. Challenges to these empires by other ambitious officials or, later, by rank-and-file reform movements (which began to appear in the 1960s) led to power struggles inside a national or international union. Yet, outside a few pockets of corruption in the union offices of teamsters, sailors, longshoremen, and construction workers, Canada saw far less blatant misuse of bureaucratic power than the United States experienced. With few exceptions, union leaders kept their sights on what they believed to be the needs of the membership. Their toughness and organizational abilities had helped to nail down many of the improvements in living standards that unionized workers were enjoying by the 1960s.

The behaviour of these union leaders was shaped much less by personal ambition than by the structural restraints of the postwar industrial regime, especially the legal restrictions on the right to strike and the imposition of a grievance-arbitration system. Much union administration, collective bargaining, and grievance work was carried out in an orderly fashion from behind a desk or across a table. Working regularly with labour lawyers, union leaders became intensely legalistic, constantly enforcing on their membership the rigid rules of industrial conflict that postwar labour legislation imposed. Direct action in the form of strikes made many union leaders uneasy, and, in some cases, leaders learned to manipulate these events to allow their members to let off steam before tying them down with a new collective agreement. Aside from training shop stewards and local executive officers in bargaining and grievance skills, union officials did not encourage activism among their members. In fact, most unionists became fairly passive members, viewing their unions as useful but somewhat distant service organizations. Few members attended union meetings except before contract negotiations. Successful union leaders within this framework had the skills to negotiate with employers, to lobby with state officials and politicians, and to manage the politics within their own organizations.

Union leaders saw their main business as the narrow range of issues covered by collective bargaining (and not excluded by management rights clauses); these issues usually concerned wages and benefits. Larger political and social questions had little place in union affairs. Occasionally, quiet political lobbying in Ottawa or the provincial capitals was necessary — to have amendments made to labour legislation or to obtain government protection for a specific industry, for example. The more politically conscious leaders were generally social democrats, still animated by vigorous red-baiting anticommunism. But even these men and women believed in a rigid division between the economic and political struggles, and tried to direct their membership's frustrations with an industrial capitalist society into votes for a social democratic party, rather than into union actions. They envisioned social change coming gradually, through break-throughs in collective bargaining and through progressive legislation passed by social democratic governments. These labour leaders were, above all, cautious — about the organizations they led (which paid their salaries), about union tactics, and about political possibilities.

The appearance of calm can be deceptive in industrial relations. Some large corporations began to acknowledge unions as a useful stabilizing influence in their operations, but most accepted them reluctantly and were always ready to batter them, if the opportunity arose. Even the largest, most powerful unions had to wage long, determined strikes during the 1950s to win concessions. By the end of the decade, some corporate employers, notably in the electrical-parts industry, had adopted a much more aggressive posture in ne-gotiations, stonewalling unions and attempting to limit or roll back their gains. Furthermore, some provincial governments were tight-ening the postwar labour legislation to make certification of unions more difficult and to penalize wildcat strikes more heavily. Mean-while, in more isolated resource communities, some workers were still struggling to win the protection that unionized workers had already gained. Quebec copper miners and Newfoundland loggers, for example, were drawn into bitter, violent strikes in 1957 and 1959 respectively; the provincial governments helped to break these strikes. The percentage of unionized workers actually fell from 34 in 1955 to 30 in 1965.

More important, the seeds of deeper problems were germinating and would blossom by the mid-1960s. First, clouds loomed on the economic horizon. The boom in the 1950s translated into prosperity for organized workers, as unions extracted dramatic wage hikes from the leading corporate employers (and thus set the pattern for the rest of the workforce). A Canadian working-class family could now more easily afford a car, a suburban home, basic home appliances, and even a television set. These consumerist aspirations continued to expand as aggressive advertisers constantly drove up the level of the requirements for a comfortable, respectable lifestyle. Yet growing economic instability within this boom raised concerns among work-ers that this new lifestyle would be unaffordable. Unemployment was certainly not the problem it had been in the 1930s, but there were still periodic slumps, notably at the end of the 1950s and the beginning of the 1960s, when rates climbed as high as they had been in 1939. By the late 1960s, after another spell of fuller employment, jobless rates were slowly rising again. Unemployment insurance made a major difference, but could not dispel all workers' anxieties. Economic prosperity was uneven across industrial sectors, with the result that, in the highly fragmented system of bargaining, some groups of workers fell behind others and struggled to catch up. This pattern was particularly noticeable in the busy urban construction industry, where a multiplicity of craft unions bargained individually in each city. More disturbing was the possible erosion of the purchasing power of wages, as the cost of living began to rise quickly at the end of the 1950s and took off in the 1960s. Inflation put even more pressure on union negotiators to win heftier wage gains. By the early 1970s, unionists were also insisting on one-year contracts and cost-of-living allowances, so that workers' real wages did not deteriorate further.

A second destabilizing factor within the new industrial regime was the rapid, disruptive change that workers faced on the job and that collective agreements could scarcely touch. In many industries, including auto production, the problem was a rapid speed-up of the work to an unprecedented pace. By the 1960s new technology added a more serious threat to both the work experience and job security. In transportation, the railways abandoned their steam engines for diesel and numerous mechanized processes in handling cars, and the maritime shipping companies began a rapid conversion to containers that did not have to be unloaded on the docks. In the resource industries, miners faced more mechanization of hewing and hauling, loggers confronted new machines for harvesting and transporting trees, and fishers encountered better equipped trawlers (and eventually monster "factory" trawlers). In many cases, mechanization was being surpassed by automation. From the 1950s onward, thousands of workers, especially white-collar workers, started to find computers installed in the workplace; the goals of computerization included replacing manual skills, speeding up work, and coordinating and monitoring workers more closely than F.W. Taylor could ever have dreamed. This new technology opened up job opportunities for some workers, but it frequently displaced many more. Thousands of railway workers caught the public's attention in the late 1950s and early 1960s when they went on strike across the country for more job security or compensation in the face of technological change. But, in fact, the old, craft-based, running-trades unions actually had more protection in their long-standing contracts with the railways than most other workers in this period. Printers, for example, were shut out of the new computerized typesetting operations. The postwar compromise that left most of these matters exclusively within employers' control was coming home to roost. The issues of technological and managerial change remained a source of recurrent friction and contributed to many workers' smouldering resentment and bitterness into the 1980s and 1990s.

Yet another threat to the equilibrium of the postwar industrial regime came from the attitudes and experience of many new workers. In the 1950s and 1960s, huge numbers of new immigrants from southern European peasant villages entered the Canadian labour market. As wage-earners, they were initially too vulnerable and culturally isolated to pose a challenge to their employers, especially in the highly fragmented construction industry, where many Italians worked. But by the early 1960s the pride of artisans and peasants in their abilities as producers and resentment over their treatment by Canadian employers were fuelling their growing resistance. In Toronto, in particular, Italian construction workers swarmed into new unions and threw down the gauntlet to building contractors. The labourers' union eventually became a bastion of their organizational power. These workers were not the supposedly docile sojourners of the past. Moreover, by the late 1960s, many immigrants were arriving from more industrialized backgrounds and with recent experience in labour militancy back home.

Women, too, were contributing to the ferment. After World War II, Canadian working-class teenagers stayed in school longer and wives and mothers entered the labour market as secondary wage-earners. By the 1960s thousands of Canadian women were working for wages after marriage and returning to the paid workforce once their children were in school on a full-time basis. In short, they were becoming more committed wage-earners who, by the late 1960s and early 1970s, were beginning to show toughness as unionists. Women were also figuring more prominently on picket lines. By this point, some of the larger unions were responding to this new interest by launching organizing campaigns in the small firms where many women and immigrants worked.

Moreover, a new generation of workers was entering the Canadian labour force in large numbers by the mid-1960s. These so-called baby boomers had grown up in a period of relative prosperity and, therefore, had high expectations of their opportunities in Canadian society. Probably no generation of workers had felt as lightly the disciplinary power of poverty, potential or actual. On the average, this generation also had more schooling. In this prolonged adolescence, they developed a vibrant youth culture that celebrated self-expression and contested authoritarianism. They wore distinctive clothing and hairstyles, listened to new music, broke sexual taboos, and experimented openly with illegal drugs. By the late 1960s, the young workers that emerged from this culture were chafing under the traditional management practices of most firms. They also held different attitudes toward the unions, which they joined automatically when they started a new job in a unionized industry. Not having helped to build these organizations from scratch, they grew impatient with the bureaucratic constraints and cautious leadership, which almost universally consisted of the union pioneers of the 1930s and 1940s. Not surprisingly, workers in the 1960s more regularly rejected contract settlements and ignored their leaders' advice against wildcat strikes. The ever present distance between union leaders and the rank-and-file widened.

By the mid-1960s, then, a new workforce was facing new threats to its living standards and working conditions. But the existing industrial relations system was ill-adapted to cope with these pressures. The grievance-arbitration system, in particular, was proving far too slow and cumbersome. Most of the thousands of grievances that were filed were simply abandoned or negotiated away as part of a larger bargaining strategy. Frustrated workers still called wildcat strikes to voice their anger. But judges liberally granted injunctions to stop such actions, and many employers sharply increased the disciplinary penalty for these breaches of the industrial peace, often firing or suspending workers. A lot of pressure thus centred on contract negotiations. After 1960, far more of these negotiations ended in strikes, often against the recommendations of union leaders. In 1966 the number of strikes and strikers far surpassed the previous peak in 1946 (though each strike was much shorter). In contrast to earlier strike waves, these protests involved unionized workers in well-established collective-bargaining relationships with their employers. Yet an unprecedented one-third of the 617 strikes in 1966 were wildcats. And picketers engaged in more violent tussles with scabs and police. Many employers rushed to the courts to obtain injunctions, and, despite the Canadian Labour Congress's concerted campaign against this legal weapon in 1966, the state threw prominent union officials in Ontario and British Columbia behind bars for contempt of court. That year, a worried federal government appointed a task force on labour relations, which three years later submitted recommendations for fine-tuning the existing system (the Ontario and British governments heard more Draconian advice from their commissions at the same time). In response to this conflict, the federal government overhauled its labour legislation in 1971 to produce a new Canada Labour Code, which broadened the legislation and added some protection from the consequences of technological change (the code was rarely used in subsequent years). But the strike wave rolled on. One-quarter of the industrial disputes recorded after 1900 erupted between 1971 and 1975. At the peak, in 1976, a record one and a half million strikers marched in more than a thousand picket lines and stopped production for 11.6 million person-days. Three out of ten strikes in the 1970s were wildcats. Italy was allegedly the only country in the Western World to match Canada in terms of militancy. The country was witnessing a full-scale, rank-and-file revolt.

By that point, new groups of workers were venturing into the turbulence. In 1970–71 Nova Scotia fishers rose up again to challenge the legal nonsense that they were "co-adventurers" with sea-products corporations, and established a beachhead of unionism in the industry. At the same time, Newfoundland fishers joined an even more impressive organizing campaign that soon brought workers in all branches of the industry into the same union. But the most astonishing addition to the Canadian labour movement in the decade after 1965 was the hundreds of thousands of state employees who won collective-bargaining rights and who entered the battle with as much determination as blue-collar workers.

Uncivil Servants

The only public-sector workers who had a long history of affiliation with the mainstream of the labour movement were blue-collar municipal employees, who since the 1940s had been covered by private-sector labour legislation. There were many compelling reasons why so few others had embraced unions. State workers usually fared well without union cards. They often had more job security than most other workers, thanks to either the civil-service promotion system or old-fashioned patronage, which implanted many workers in provincial governments until well after World War II. The white-collar workers among them, like their counterparts in private industry, felt smugly superior to blue-collar unionists because of the clean respectability of their work and their generally higher salaries. Whatever the inclinations of these workers, employers held the ultimate power of the law over them and, except for the CCF government in Saskatchewan, expressly denied them the right to join unions and to bargain collectively. In the words of Quebec premier Jean Lesage, "the Queen does not negotiate."

Since the early 1900s civil servants at the federal and provincial levels had organized departmental associations among themselves. For the most part, these groups were morale-boosting, tea-and-crumpets societies that included anyone, from janitor to deputy minister, who cared to join. Occasionally, however, they became polite vehicles for requesting improvements in salaries and working conditions, in a rarely successful form of collective begging. By the end of World War I, many of these societies had coalesced into loose provincial and national federations. At that point, and again in the early 1940s, a more militant spirit percolated through the ranks of these organizations as members realized that blue-collar unionists were making great gains and closing the income gap that assured their superior social status. British Columbia's civil-service organization came closest of all such groups to full-fledged unionism in the 1940s. But federal and provincial governments erected an alternative known as "joint councils," in which equal numbers of employee and management representatives could discuss issues of industrial relations. The councils were purely advisory, however, and the government frequently ignored their advice.

In the 1950s and 1960s new working conditions in the public sector contributed to discontent that could not be contained by consultative structures. Public-sector wages were not keeping pace with those in the unionized private sector, and by the 1960s some clerical salaries were actually falling below blue-collar wages. The public sector was also growing so large that the intimacy of government offices was being replaced by extensive, impersonal bureaucratic structures. Private-sector management practices were put in place to impose capitalist principles of efficiency on public workers. The post office's reorganization, announced in 1968, was one of the most publicized examples. Few departments escaped these efforts to tighten control over labour costs as business people, politicians, and state mandarins began to question mounting public expenditures.

By the early 1960s, civil servants across the country were seething. During the preceding decade, they had rapidly transformed their associations into organizations that looked and acted more like unions, with full-time staff, research facilities, and tighter structures at the local level. Virtually all of these employees' associations were demanding legal collective-bargaining rights. In deference to white-collar sensibilities, these workers generally proposed settlement of disputes through arbitration rather than strikes. Federal and provincial governments resisted this pressure as long as possible. The federal Conservative and Liberal governments appointed a series of special inquiries, before finally introducing legislation in 1965. The minority Liberals were anxious to steal more thunder from the social democrats, but were pressed further than they had planned to go when the country's postal workers walked out later that year in the first national strike since the 1920s. The Public Service Staff Relations Act, which was finally passed in 1967, thus gave federal employees the option of arbitration or strike action to settle disputes. The unusual political context had pushed the Canadian government further than the U.S. government, which granted federal civil-service unions less power and which denied them the right to strike. At the provincial level, Saskatchewan was the first to legalize public-sector collective bargaining in 1944; the other provinces followed much more slowly and cautiously. Between 1965 and 1975, all provincial employees were eventually granted some bargaining rights. This legislation varied, ranging from that in Quebec, where state workers won the full rights of private-sector workers, to that in Ontario, where civil servants were denied the right to strike.

A general pattern emerged at both the federal and provincial levels. Recognition was granted to the highly centralized unions, the Public Service Alliance of Canada (PSAC) and its provincial counterparts, which took in virtually all workers in each jurisdiction. A provincial convention of government employees typically included a diversity of representatives, such as secretaries, social workers, prison guards, and road crews. Negotiations usually involved a single occupational group (for example, all clerks, custom officials, or inside postal workers across the province or country); representatives of this group sat down across the table from officials from the federal or provincial treasury boards. Numerous important issues, such as job classification and pensions, were nonnegotiable, since they were left in the hands of civil-service commissions. The system was a cumbersome adaptation of the 1940s model, which had been developed for blue-collar workers, although with more frequent use of arbitration. By the early 1970s the new unions were making full use of these new collective-bargaining structures, and were contributing new vigour to the widespread militancy. Strikes by public-sector workers caught the public eye much more often in this period; in particular, the series of militant postal workers' strikes that erupted in response to managerial and technological shake-ups was highly publicized.

During these years, workers in the so-called para-public sector joined those directly employed by the federal and provincial governments in organizing unions. These workers fell into two categories: less skilled clerical and manual workers, and professionals. Unions attracted large numbers of clerical workers in municipal government offices for the same reasons as those at the federal and provincial levels. Outside Quebec, these workers most often joined blue-collar municipal employees in the rapidly growing Canadian Union of Public Employees (CUPE). This organization was also recruiting heavily among manual workers in hospitals and schools, which, by the early 1970s, were feeling the pinch of cuts in government spending in the social-service sectors. Workers at these institutions were both resentful of their shrinking incomes and deteriorating working conditions and inspired by the other organized workers who were rising up to defend their interests.

In contrast, professionals such as teachers, nurses, social workers, professors, and librarians were annoyed that their relative prestige in the labour force was being eroded, and that the more rigid, bureaucratic managerial style was insensitive to their professional judgement and independent modes of work. Their dilemma bore striking similarities to that of the outraged craftworkers of the late nineteenth century. While some professional workers joined branches of CUPE or the provincial employees unions, most turned their professional associations into unions (or, like the nurses, created new unions), which won certification as bargaining agents under private-sector legislation. But teachers, nurses, and professors, still not comfortable rubbing shoulders with blue-collar unionists at labour conventions, held back from the larger labour movement, nurturing their long-standing self-image as "above all that." These professionals were nonetheless prepared to turn to picket lines if sufficiently agitated. One of the most dramatic examples of the new militancy in their ranks was the Metropolitan Toronto secondary school teachers' strike, which dragged on for two months in 1975.

Civil servants had thus become decidedly uncivil. In fact, they injected into the wave of militancy new energy and dynamism, which probably helped to sustain it. Certainly their restlessness helped to revitalize the whole labour movement; no such revitalization concurred in the United States. Union membership in Canada rose from below 30 per cent of the nonagricultural workforce in 1961 to nearly 37 per cent by the mid-1970s. By 1975 the Canadian Union of Public Employees was the largest union in the country, and the Public Service Alliance of Canada was not far behind. Nearly half the union members in the country worked in the public sector. The image of the union member as a burly man from a blue-collar job had shifted dramatically, as secretaries and librarians lined up with steelworkers and plumbers at the microphones at union conventions and showed just as much fervour in their singing of "Solidarity Forever."

However, public-sector strikes generated a vigorous public backlash, since the disruption of mail service or the closing of schools or hospitals affected consumers more directly than the implications of most private-sector strikes. While public-sector protests made much more visible the weakness of the local-by-local negotiations of workers' demands through individual collective agreements, that structural problem in the collective-bargaining system was buried by a rising chorus of criticism that scapegoated the allegedly greedy civil servants.

New Politics

In the past, working-class militancy on the job had invariably spilled over into politics, while radicalism had also inspired and shaped militancy. This time was no exception. Not only was there a revival of mainstream social democracy, but there were also new political currents that were helping to stiffen the overall spirit of confrontation. In contrast to the past, however, the structures of the collective-bargaining regime helped to limit that politicization.

The Co-operative Commonwealth Federation may have inherited the mantle of the left after it helped to destroy the communist movement in Canada, but during the 1950s social democracy seemed to be a spent force. Saskatchewan was the only toehold on power for social democrats; elsewhere they suffered repeated humiliations at the polls. After the merger that created the Canadian Labour Congress, quiet discussions began between the congress and CCF leaders about the organization of a new party, based on the model of the British Labour Party, with greater labour movement participation. The outcome of those discussions was the 1961 "New Party" convention, out of which emerged the New Democratic Party (NDP). Aside from some organizational tinkering, the most important change was ideological: the party consciously took a step away from the socialist vision that had formally guided the CCF since the 1930s, towards a vaguer reformism that deemphasized public ownership. The party thereby hoped to attract much more middle-class support. Its inner circles clearly consisted of a coalition of professionals and intellectuals on the one hand and labour-movement bureaucrats on the other, although, as in the postwar CCF, many rank-and-file workers were active at the riding level. Large industrial unions, especially those in steel and auto, were the backbone of labour support; the traditionally "nonpartisan" craft unions took no part whatsoever. Most of the leadership and electoral candidates were lawyers, teachers, social workers, clergy, and other professionals, but most of the crucial funding and much of the ideological caution came from the labour leaders. The social democratic alliance created an unresolved tension between the rule of experts, who used the state to improve working-class living standards, and workers, who used tactics such as collective bargaining and strikes to improve their lot. But, as working-class militancy mushroomed, union leaders hoped to be able to deflect some of the members' anger from the picket lines to the ballot box.

Under the leadership of Tommy Douglas in the 1960s and David Lewis in the early 1970s, the party set out to recapture the voters' imagination. Nonetheless, the NDP remained a distant third in national politics. The social democratic caucus in Ottawa slowly grew, peaked at thirty-one members in 1972, and then slumped back to sixteen in 1974. During two crucial interludes, however, the NDP's federal members wielded more influence than their meagre numbers might otherwise have allowed. Between 1963 and 1968 and again from 1972 to 1974, the Liberals ruled with a minority government and moved leftward to appease the New Democrats and, they hoped, to undercut the NDP's standing as the reform party. In that first period, the Liberals pressed ahead with missing pieces of the welfare state, such as contributory old-age pensions, state health insurance, and the Canada Assistance Plan, which they had promised twenty years earlier. It was in this context, too, that the Liberals enacted the new legislation for public-sector collective bargaining. Who won the credit for these measures is less important than the fact that a bloc of social democrats, supported by the Canadian labour movement, sat in the House of Commons and helped to bring some measures of benefit to Canadian workers onto the statute books.

The NDP's real triumphs, however, appeared at the provincial level. First in Manitoba in 1969, then in Saskatchewan in 1971 and in British Columbia in 1972, some of the working-class anger from the militancy on the picket line carried over into provincial elections and gave the New Democrats control of the legislatures. In all three cases, unionized workers had built up plenty of hostility towards decidedly unfriendly provincial goverments. As a result, high on the legislative agenda of the new NDP administrations were reforms to labour laws and initiatives on such matters as occupational health and safety and technological change. In fact, these administrations set the pace for progressive labour legislation over the next two decades. Relations between organized labour and these social democratic regimes, however, were often tense. Both the Manitoba and British Columbia New Democrats met defeat after only one term in part because they had legislated public-sector and other strikers back to work shortly before the elections. Social democrats had always maintained a clear split between industrial and political battles, and kept some distance from picket-line confrontations. So, while working-class anger may have given the NDP crucial support, the favour was not always returned.

Other political currents fed into the Canadian labour movement during these years. By the mid-1960s a New Left was taking shape in Canada, just as it was in the United States and in the rest of the Western World. This new brand of politics was based on a set of ideas and strategies that put much less faith in electoral politics than in "participatory democracy" (that is, the power of people to influence directly the decisions that affect their lives). Bringing about social change meant direct action through demonstrations, sit-ins, and other forms of extraparliamentary confrontation. A movement began to emerge after 1960 in a series of campaigns against nuclear weapons, racial discrimination, and poverty, and gathered steam later that decade in reaction to the Vietnam War. It was youth who were most caught up in this new politics, and university and high-school students were soon demanding democracy within the country's educational institutions. Radical politics and the broader youth culture melded into a bold, flamboyant political alternative to the cautious reformism of social democracy and to the old-line marxism of the small Communist Party. The New Left became a countercultural lifestyle of self-expression, communal living, and community solidarity, as much as it was a swirling vortex of new ideas. Despite the small size of the movement, society as a whole felt its influence.

There was no central organization for all this activity. Nor was there clear ideological unity. Individualism and collectivism coexisted in an often uneasy balance. But the more intellectually inclined found new inspiration in marxism, which they began to adapt to new conditions and struggles. Thus, many New Left activists became more sensitive to the situation of the postwar working class. In fact, by the early 1970s, many were becoming impatient with the looseness of the movement and, inspired by the example of Leon Trotsky or Mao Tse Tung (Zedong), they regrouped in small socialist or neocommunist organizations that put the working class at the centre of revolutionary struggle. Although many of these activists had middle-class and university backgrounds, most chose to move into the blue-collar work world to help organize workers. By 1975 some left-wing activists were appearing as rank-and-file leaders in the hot spots of industrial militancy, notably the post office. The labour movement consequently felt the direct effects of this new politics.

The women in the New Left had their own struggle. Within the movement, they were most often crushed beneath the weight of male egos and left on the margins to cook and clean while the men did the "serious" political work. Seizing the New Left rhetoric of democracy, the women rebelled. They assembled in small consciousness-raising groups that quickly developed an activist orientation to challenge the sexism that confronted them. They also began to analyze the oppression and exploitation of all women in society. A new women's movement and a new brand of feminism were thus born. Campaigns for adequate day care, reproductive rights (especially the choice to terminate a pregnancy), and equal access to the opportunities of late-twentieth-century industrial society sent seismic waves through the population. Politicians had to take heed, especially after a royal commission report in 1970 set out an extensive agenda for establishing equality for women in Canadian society. The mass media kept the nation's attention riveted on the most colourful feminists and their unprecedented feistiness. Thousands of women who found themselves in the workforce more or less for life began to ponder the implications of this new challenge to gender relations. By the mid-

1970s, as we will see, the reverberations were felt within the labour movement, too.

In Canada, imperialism was also a particularly hot issue for the New Left, as well as for many social democrats and conservatives. In English Canada the rapid Americanization of the economy provoked widespread discussion. The ugly militarism of the Vietnam War made many Canadians uneasy about closer integration with the United States. By 1970 a vibrant nationalism was percolating through political and cultural circles. The New Left's neomarxists drew inspiration from the dramatic struggles of Third World revolutionaries against U.S. imperialism, and posters of Che Guevara proliferated in scores of Canadian households. In 1969 the New Democrats felt the challenge of this new anti-imperialist nationalism when, at the party's national convention, a group of left-wing intellectuals introduced a manifesto calling for a return to a stronger socialist response to U.S. domination. The document was rejected, but a lively "Waffle" movement flourished within the party until its expulsion in 1972.

In the same period, the labour movement itself came under attack from many of these nationalists for its integration with U.S. organizations (whose commitment to the Vietnam War effort made them doubly suspect). Unions had been required to submit annual reports on revenues and expenditures in Canada to the federal government since 1962; these reports gave the nationalists more ammunition for the argument that international unions did not serve Canadian workers adequately (although the information demanded by the government was inadequate to settle the debate conclusively). In 1969 Kent Rowley and Madeleine Parent, two outcasts from the purges of the 1950s, rallied a handful of unions outside the international labour movement to create the first significant nationalist centre in three decades. The Council of Canadian Unions (CCU) (rechristened a Confederation in 1973) attracted several breakaway locals from international unions (including the large membership of the steelworkers' union in Kitimat, British Columbia), most often because of poor servicing or undemocratic practices in the international unions. In the early 1970s CCU affiliates led small, prolonged, and highly publicized strikes that attracted considerable attention to the organization. For many left-wing nationalists in southern Ontario, Manitoba, and British Columbia, this new organization provided the inspiration for a revitalized, independent labour movement. Although its ultimate success was limited, this nationalist challenge pressured the Canadian Labour Congress and its affiliates to respond by the early 1970s.

The relationship between this new political ferment and the much greater working-class militancy is complex. The start of the revolt cannot be attributed to neomarxists, feminists, nationalists, or New Leftists. Nor does the evidence suggest that thousands of Canadian workers were suddenly signing on for the revolutionary struggle. The limited success of the New Democrats outside three western provinces underlines the fact that the political consciousness of most workers still moved along different channels. The fragmented structure of labour relations prevented most workers from uniting with others outside their legally recognized bargaining units. This legal prohibition of sympathy strikes kept the militancy from mushrooming into the working-class consciousness of the World War I era. But the energy and imagination of the new politics undoubtedly influenced many workers.

Quebec Explodes

These social and political developments reached a pinnacle of intensity in Quebec. A distinctive labour movement based on the European model of Catholic unionism had existed in that province since the World War I era. In the 1940s the clerical influence faded rapidly, as a new generation of labour leaders united with liberal intellectuals to challenge the traditional forms of worker subordination by capital, state, and church in Quebec society. In the 1950s this labour movement played an important role in the rising resistance to the repressive administration of Premier Duplessis. The election of a new Liberal government in 1961 unleashed a wave of activity to modernize Quebec society and to make Quebeckers "masters in their own house," soon known as the Quiet Revolution. Even within this tame nationalist variant, the consciousness of being a colony within English Canada was strong. Poets, musicians, and journalists celebrated French Canadian aspirations in a blossoming cultural renaissance in the province. Hard-nosed neomarxist intellectuals developed an anti-imperialist theoretical perspective on Quebec's situation. By the late 1960s the yearning of many of these Quebeckers for self-expression had crystallized into a desire for a fully independent society. The separatist movements ranged from the insurrectionary Front de libération du Québec (FLQ) to the social democratic Parti Québécois headed by René Lévesque.

The Quebec labour movement was infused with this new spirit of resistance. The Confederation of National Trade Unions, which had shed all religious trappings in 1960 and embraced a secular liberalism, had taken a new lease on life as a result of its close association with the provincial Liberals in the early 1960s; the relationship was especially close after the Quebec government reformed the province's labour law and extended full collective-bargaining rights to civil servants in 1965. By 1970 the CNTU had expanded its membership, largely in the public and para-public sectors (though its size never reached that of the Quebec Federation of Labour (QFL), the provincial organization with links to the international unions and the Canadian Labour Congress). However, the CNTU's warm relationship with the Quebec state had cooled by the late 1960s, as the unions more regularly confronted each successive government through collective-bargaining structures. The militancy that was exploding in other parts of the country in this period found support in Quebec from the nationalist and marxist intellectuals who were employees at the two provincial labour federations and the Quebec teachers' union (Centrale de l'enseignement du Québec, CEQ) and from the country's largest groups of neomarxist activists at the local level. The radicalization of the CNTU was clear in 1968 when the organization announced its commitment to struggles on a Second Front outside collective bargaining (such as consumer protection) in alliance with other institutions and movements (tenants, the unemployed, credit unions, and so on) in local "political action committees," most notably le Front d'action politique des salariés de Montréal (FRAP).

In fact, Quebec union leaders were soon calling for fundamental changes in Quebec society. In 1971 the three Quebec labour organizations published the most radical documents seen in North American labour circles in decades; these papers analyzed the exploitation of Quebec workers and made a strong case for a socialist alternative in an independent Quebec. In contrast to social democratic policy statements, these manifestoes emphasized the active role for workers in creating and running a socialist society (some commentators have even called them "syndicalist" in tone, though these unionists were often heavily involved in alternative electoral campaigns in individual communities). This radicalism was not simply imposed from the top; much was flowing up from the rank-and-file activists in communities across the province, particularly in Montreal. And it was closely connected to the growing movement for Quebec's self-determination. The voice of Quebec labour was thus far outside the North American mainstream.

At this time, the three federations agreed to form the Common Front, an organization for bargaining with the provincial government (the unique Quebec labour legislation allowed such a formation). They demanded a uniform wage increase and a common minimum wage for the 250,000 workers they represented, and in 1972, after months of fruitless negotiation with Robert Bourassa's Liberal government, they led their membership in the province's first general strike of public-sector workers and the biggest strike in Canadian history. Schools, hospitals, hydroelectric facilities, and all other branches of the Quebec state felt the ramifications. When the strike leaders, Marcel Pepin, Louis Laberge, and Yvon Charbonneau, were jailed for defying back-to-work orders, the strike spread spontaneously to large parts of the private sector. In some towns, general strikes erupted, and workers took over radio and television stations. Lacking coordination and effective leadership, the strike petered out within a week. The aftermath was less glorious, as a large chunk of the CNTU membership withdrew to form a new, less radical organization, and the three members of the Common Front reverted to unfriendly competition for recruits. But Quebec's pattern of class confrontation, symbolized by the tumultuous, twenty-month strike at United Aircraft in 1974–75, had been set and would resurface at regular intervals in the 1970s and 1980s. In addition, Quebec's unionists had established that their workers' movement was distinct from that in English Canada.

By 1975 the industrial regime that had been laid down in Canada in the 1940s was coming unstuck. A keen observer in the 1940s might have predicted this breakdown of the postwar compromise. The system of collective bargaining was open ended enough to encourage unionized workers to try to improve their living standards, but fragmented enough that those improvements would vary widely across the working class and disrupt traditional status relationships between groups of workers, particularly white- and blue-collar employees. The relative weakness of the Canadian state's social welfare provisions also put much more pressure on the factory-by-factory negotiations. As the prosperity of the 1950s turned into the economic uncertainty, and especially the spiralling inflation, of the 1960s and 1970s, a great turbulence of "whipsawing," "leap-frogging," and catch-up pushed up wage demands and precipitated strikes. Behind the wage demands lay cultural and political challenges that never coalesced into an overt threat to the social order, but were nonetheless disturbing to capitalists and the state. By the early 1970s far too many workers were beyond the control of their bosses, the law, and even their own union leaders, and were demanding concessions that business people and politicians thought were excessive in a healthy capitalist economy. Capitalists and the state were convinced that something had to be done to curb working-class power.

5

Counterattack

A sense of crisis was hovering over Canadian corporate boardrooms and cabinet chambers by 1975. This anxiety was shared throughout the capitalist world. An unprecedented combination of rising unemployment and inflation ("stagflation") was throwing the international economy into chaos. The U.S. economic empire was also in deep trouble, as upstart contenders, especially West Germany and Japan, set the new pace of capitalist growth. Ambitious Third World countries such as Brazil, Taiwan, and Korea were emerging as major industrial competitors on the basis of cheap labour and repressive military regimes. In the face of increasingly uncertain markets and stiffer competition, Canadian capitalists were beginning the desperate search for a secure place in the reconstructed world economy. Inflation and aggressive union demands, they believed, squeezed profit margins and introduced too much insecurity into capitalist planning.

Initially, public debate about this crisis had a narrower focus. By the mid-1970s, instead of wondering how the economy had become so disjointed and chaotic, business people, politicians, civil servants, newspaper editors, and talk-show hosts simply wanted to know what could be done about labour. Workers' wage and salary demands seemed to be the most visible cause of retail price inflation, (if the sudden jump in oil prices set by the Organization of Petroleum Exporting Countries and rampant real-estate speculation in metropolitan areas were overlooked). But, in a broader, more menacing way, the contented, deferential worker seemed to be disappearing. School and hospital workers and even the once-staid civil servants were aggressively demanding higher wages and enforcing their demands by marching out of so-called essential services. The crime attributed to organized workers was simply that they were using the structures of collective bargaining as the system had been designed, for maintaining living and working standards in the face of inflation, technological change, and other disruptions. By the mid-1970s these workers' efforts were being painted as motivated by simple greed and selfishness.

Proponents of the counterattack against working-class power and income redistribution justified their offensive as a necessary means of compelling workers to make sacrifices to help their bosses save the capitalist system in Canada. The Canadian state led the assault on the labour movement, but by the early 1980s corporate capitalists and the state élite were working closely together on a common agenda to restructure the industrial regime. At the start of the 1980s, the emphasis was on cutting labour costs through wage freezes or roll-backs. By the end of the decade, however, "restructuring" had become a buzz-word for extensive disruption of the economy and the workplaces within it and for grand new strategies for coping with "globalization." The gains that unionized and non-unionized workers had made in the thirty years after World War II were now at risk.

The State Offensive

The state's main goal was to curtail workers' power to bargain collectively and to strike, without completely dismantling the postwar system of carefully managed industrial conflict. The first initiatives came from the federal government, mainly because for thirty years it had assumed responsibility for regulating economic swings. Its Keynesian tools seemed poorly adapted to the crisis of the early 1970s, while curbing inflation with higher taxes and tighter money policies would only have raised unemployment unacceptably. Instead, federal policymakers took a closer look at the European approach of incomes policies.

The first step was to try to persuade employers and unions to agree voluntarily to restrain increases in incomes. In 1969 the Liberal government appointed the Prices and Incomes Commission to monitor the economy and to advise capital, labour, and the state on the appropriate level of increases in wages and prices. The commission met resistance to its proposed wage-restraint program and was quietly scrapped three years later. Wage and price controls surfaced again as a central public issue in the 1974 federal election, when the Conservatives promised to introduce mandatory controls, including a wage freeze. The Trudeau Liberals, fighting for a new majority government on a reformist platform, vigorously opposed the Tory proposal and romped back to power. Finance Minister John Turner promptly began a new round of consultations with business and labour to work out a voluntary restraint program. As in the past, the initiative floundered on the Canadian Labour Congress's concern that workers would be the only Canadians to feel the pinch unless the plan included prices, rents, and profits. Voluntary income policies seemed doomed.

The political pressure for state action was unrelenting. A few highly publicized wage increases won by public-sector workers in 1974 and 1975 elicited howls of outrage from business and the media. On Thanksgiving Day in 1975, Trudeau appeared on national television to announce the first peacetime compulsory wage and price controls in Canadian history. The program was to last for three years. Provincial governments were invited to opt in, and they did: three New Democratic Party administrations were among these governments. (The Supreme Court dispensed with the constitutional difficulties of such federal action by agreeing that inflation constituted a national emergency.) The obvious targets of the new program were the well-organized workers who had made the biggest gains in recent years. Controls on increases in income were clamped on workers in companies with more than five hundred employees, construction firms with more than twenty, the entire federal public-sector workforce, and self-employed professionals. The formula became complicated in specific cases, but basically increases in all forms of compensation were not to exceed 8 per cent in the first year, 6 per cent in the second, and 4 per cent in the third. Employers had to send notice of all increases to the Anti-Inflation Board in Ottawa, where a growing staff of bureaucrats determined whether the settlement violated the guidelines. In the case of overpayment, the employer was required to collect the excess wages or salaries. The board's staff also monitored prices, though far less rigorously, and excessive price increases (determined much more loosely on the basis of estimated increases in costs) were much harder to undo. The inevitable conclusion was that the program was fundamentally a wage-restraint measure and that toothless price control was inserted primarily to ensure labour's compliance.

Canadian labour leaders were furious. The largest unions announced that they would bargain as though the controls did not exist. The autoworkers' union became particularly adept at dodging the board's rulings. The union convinced the auto manufacturers to implement any compensation packages in their new collective agreements before submitting them to the Anti-Inflation Board and then used every loophole and appeal process in the guidelines to delay roll-backs. Not all unions achieved the same success, however. The administration of the program soon revealed that public-sector workers would be hit hardest. Some of the biggest roll-backs that the board ordered affected traditionally low-paid workers in hospitals, schools, and municipal governments organized by the Canadian Union of Public Employees. At the national level the CLC immediately pulled labour representatives off all consultative bodies. At the congress convention the next spring, the executive presented a manifesto that denounced the controls and, in response to the anger that was bubbling up from locals across the country, uneasily called a one-day general strike. The Canadian Union of Postal Workers spearheaded the forces within the congress that wanted a militant campaign of resistance to the wage-restraint policy.

On the first anniversary of the implementation of controls, October 14, 1976, more than a million workers walked out in Canada's first national general strike, modestly called a Day of Protest. Participation was uneven across the country. In towns with weak labour movements, it was more or less business as usual. In other towns, corporations had secured court orders threatening unions with suits for damages and promised stiff penalties for workers who took part in the strike. In many communities with strong labour movements, however, most workers were off the job. Unions held rallies and marches in most major centres. The national labour leaders were generally uncomfortable with such mass action and were relieved that the rank and file had been able to blow off some steam in a weakly coordinated, one-shot affair. But they also hoped to use this show of anger to persuade the government of the need for some kind of agency for ongoing social and economic planning involving capital, labour, and the state (a proposal that was loudly criticized by ever larger numbers of delegates at succeeding CLC conventions). Those negotiations dragged on inconclusively into 1978 as the controls program wound down.

The long-term implications of the wage-control program were not immediately obvious and remain controversial. Wage increases dropped off precipitously, but, by the third year of the program, prices were again surging upward. Clearly it was hard to blame labour for all or even most price inflation. The transnational structures of the new international capitalist economy did not allow an individual national government such as Canada's to control inflation effectively, but such a government could restrict the incomes of the weakest social force, the working class. The controls had a more important effect, however: workers lowered their expectations, and the number of strikes plummeted. The wave of militancy had been broken, at least temporarily. Employers in the private sector also learned a lesson: they did not like to have their operations scrutinized by Ottawa bureaucrats. Other means would have to be found to restrain workers' demands.

By the end of the 1970s, double-digit inflation had returned, workers were once again pressing for higher wages to catch up, and strikes were erupting. The state responded in a variety of ways. In 1975 the federal government had already made a decisive turn against Keynesian economic policies and launched the tighter money policy that would become known throughout the Western World as "monetarism." At both the federal and provincial levels there was also a new effort to reduce government spending, especially on social services. Basically, the Canadian state abandoned its thirty-year-old policy of maintaining relatively full employment and steady incomes, in favour of severe checks on the expansion of workers' income. In the early 1980s the Bank of Canada used extremely high interest rates to slow down the economy, and from 1981 to 1984 the country was thrown into the worst recession since the 1930s. Most regions never pulled far out of this slump during the 1980s, but southern Ontario bounced back by the middle of the decade, pushing national inflation rates upward again. Therefore in 1989, in a general context of international economic crisis and decline, the Bank of Canada administered another dose of high interest rates, which once more dragged economic activity down and sent unemployment levels soaring. Over the tumultuous years after 1980, some industrial sectors never recovered, and most new jobs appeared in low-wage private-sector service work.

In the recessions that buffeted Canada in the early 1980s and early 1990s, plant closings and lay-offs of thousands of workers had devastating effects on Canadian workers, especially in construction and in the core manufacturing and resource industries, where many workers had come to expect regular employment for most of their lifetime. In both periods official unemployment hit 12 per cent, and, if "discouraged" workers (who had given up looking for work) and part-time workers wanting full-time work were included, the national figure would probably have reached 16 to 20 per cent. Even in 1988, a boom year, the national unemployment rate still hovered around 8 per cent (lower in Ontario, much higher in the East and West), which was still above prerecession levels. Longer-term unemployment became a chronic problem for many Canadian workers, especially the young. Governments' weak response suggested that higher levels of joblessness had become a permanent feature of the Canadian labour market. As we will see, the effect of these conditions on working-class expectations was more profound than that of the controls program, and employers came to the bargaining table with new-found strength.

After 1975, Canada's federal and provincial governments also began to weaken the "safety net" that the country's limited welfare state had provided. One of the great changes of the postwar era had been the "social wage" that the state had provided as a result of agitation by the labour movement and pressure from the social democratic party; with this legislation, workers did not rely solely on their own wages during personal or family crises. The state had embellished the old, parsimonious welfare system (now generally known as social assistance) with newer universal programs such as unemployment insurance, old-age pensions, and health insurance. In the 1970s, many Canadian employers openly criticized these programs for supposedly undermining the work ethic. Of course, what they meant was that, with unemployment insurance or other payments to fall back on, workers were too independent of their bosses. Business organizations therefore began demanding the dismantling or weakening of these programs. The assault on the unemployment insurance system began with severe tightening of eligibility criteria in 1978. A new wave of restrictions and cuts in benefits hit in 1990 and continued through the first half of the decade. The family allowance program was also scrapped in 1992, public pensions were undermined by a "claw-back" from higher-income groups, and in 1995 the federal government announced massive cuts in transfer payments for these social programs. The trend in the mid-1990s is toward means-tested programs for only the most "deserving" poor. At the provincial level, various social assistance programs had their budgets trimmed and their eligibility restricted. The Canadian welfare state was in tatters. A 1990 study conducted by the OECD (Organization for Economic Cooperation and Development) revealed that, among the major nations, only Japan, Australia, the United States, and Spain spent less per capita on social programs than Canada. By 1995 public debate ignored these comparisons and focused on how to turn social assistance programs into job training exercises. The tone of the debate turned neo-Victorian. The problem of poverty was defined as how to reform the poor.

Simultaneously, the Canadian state has become a more tough-minded employer of its own workers. These workers have tradition-ally been protected from the effects of an economic downturn since their jobs were more secure. Not only have federal, provincial, and municipal governments cut back in the 1980s and 1990s on public employment through lay-offs and privatization of government serv-ices, but they have also launched two separate assaults on public-sector unionists. No longer was the state willing to rely on toughening up collective-bargaining legislation to weaken the pow-ers of public-sector unions and thus contain these workers' aspira-tions. Now there were regular interventions to disrupt and override those procedures and to snap workers into line. First, from the mid-1970s onward, the state brought down an iron heel on public-sector strikes. Federal and provincial governments had resorted to back-to-work legislation with increasing regularity after 1965, but the fre-quency increased abruptly following 1975: after only six such orders between 1950 and 1964, there were twenty-six from 1965 to 1974 and then seventy-nine between 1975 and 1992. Violations of these measures resulted in stiff fines and jail terms for labour leaders, and even threats of decertification of unions. The federal government used its frequent confrontations with the militant Canadian Union of Postal Workers to sound the alarm. In 1978 the state threatened coercive legislation before a strike even began, and then arrested the union's leader, Jean-Claude Parrot, for not ordering the postal work-ers back to their jobs (that is, for remaining silent). By 1987 the government's responses to national postal strikes of both letter car-riers and inside workers included stonewalling negotiations and or-ganizing armies of strikebreakers to break through picket lines. Back-to-work legislation threatened to bar any violators from a job at Canada Post and from any union office for five years. The gov-ernment also intervened in the 1991 postal strike. Provincial govern-ments were as heavy-handed, as in the 1980 Ontario hospital employees' wildcat strike and in the legal strike of Alberta nurses in 1982.

Second, in the early 1980s, the state drastically curtailed its em-ployees' right to collective bargaining; this measure was effective only for a specified term of two or three years, but it constituted a permanent threat to unions. Wage controls were reinstated for these workers alone. In 1982 the federal government suspended collective-bargaining rights by extending civil servants' existing contracts for two years, and announced that salary increases would not exceed 6 per cent in the first year and 5 per cent in the second. These public-sector restraints were intended to inspire private-sector bosses to show the same restraint without using the legislated coercion of the late 1970s. Most provincial governments introduced their own versions of the "6-and-5" controls between 1982 and 1984, often with even more destructive consequences for collective bargaining in the public sector. In Quebec, despite its social democratic aura and support from many labour leaders, the government sparked another short-lived general strike of state workers when in 1982 it suspended the right to strike, froze existing contracts, and demanded wage roll-backs averaging 19.5 per cent. It then passed another bill stripping thousands of state workers of existing protection for job security and working conditions. Some of these measures brought condemnation from the International Labor Organization in Geneva and resulted in the appointment in 1985 of an ILO fact-finding investigation (the first being the one that led to denunciation of the Polish government's treatment of the Solidarity movement a few years earlier).

With the return of a deep recession in 1990, a new round of public-sector wage controls began in Ottawa and most provincial capitals. In 1993 Ontario's new NDP government introduced its own version, the misnamed Social Contract, which gave nothing in return for what it took away. Roughly 900,000 workers in government offices, schools, hospitals, universities, and the like were stuck with a three-year wage freeze, which in many cases was imposed through unpaid days off, popularly known as "Rae Days" in honour of Premier Bob Rae.

Over the long term, the Canadian state appears committed to reducing to insignificance the right to strike for its employees and to compelling arbitrators to use "ability to pay" as the overriding criterion in wage settlements. The federal Treasury Board also won a Supreme Court decision that allowed it more freedom in designating an employee as essential and therefore in forbidding that worker from going on strike; the numbers of such restricted workers immediately shot up. Federal and provincial governments are also determined to prevent unionized state employees from blocking plans to deregulate private enterprise and to privatize state operations. Major confrontations in 1988 between the federal government and seaway, railway, and postal workers centred on this issue.

At the provincial level, British Columbia's government set the pace in a general anti-union offensive aimed at permanently weakening the organizing and bargaining power of workers in both the public and private sectors. In 1983 it introduced a package of bills that not only suspended normal collective bargaining but also aimed to change the provincial rules of industrial relations for all time. British Columbia's unions and other social movements quickly formed the Solidarity Coalition, which mobilized a strong campaign of resistance to these measures and to other legislation aimed at slashing social expenditures. The government subsequently softened the impact of some of this package, but, until its defeat in 1991, it continued to set the standard in new legislation to weaken the labour movement. In 1987 it passed the most heavy-handed labour legislation of the decade. These new measures allowed employers to escape from collective bargaining more easily and granted sweeping powers to an industrial relations commissioner, who was permitted to intervene in union affairs, to prevent strikes, and to impose settlements. Alberta, Saskatchewan, Manitoba, Quebec, and Newfoundland soon announced their own permanent legislative restrictions on unions' organizing and bargaining rights. The amendments to their labour acts typically gave employers more rights in organizing campaigns, weakened public-sector unions' power to negotiate and strike, and interfered in internal union procedures (for example, regarding strikebreaking and strike votes). Penalties for violating these new measures were Draconian. The International Labor Organization has formally condemned much of this legislation repeatedly since the mid-1980s.

There was an alternative to this blunt coercion of unions. It appeared most often in provinces with social democratic governments; thus, it surfaced in Quebec in the late 1970s, in Manitoba from 1981 to 1988, and in British Columbia, Saskatchewan, and Ontario after 1990. The goal of this approach was to make collective bargaining work more smoothly without fundamental changes to the industrial-relations regime. The reforms, which were usually pushed by the provincial labour movements, consisted of measures to enhance unions' bargaining strength, and ranged from arbitration of first-contract negotiations to compulsory union check-off to bans on strikebreaking (in Quebec and Ontario). These interventions paralleled new legislation to improve occupational health and safety and to introduce procedures for pay equity. Each piece of this reformist legislation, however, was a watered-down version of what the provincial labour movements had wanted; business had threatened the flight of capital from the province and politicians had listened. None of these changes broadened the postwar legislative framework to make it easier to include rapidly growing numbers of underemployed workers in small-scale, low-wage sectors of the late-twentieth-century economy, especially in the private-service sector. Each reform package was also attacked by the right-wing governments that succeeded the social democrats in office.

By the late 1980s, a new threat to workers' collective power emanated from the courts. Anti-union forces turned to the new Charter of Rights and Freedoms and its protection of individual rights to challenge Canadian unions. In April 1987, after a series of contradictory rulings in the lower courts, the Supreme Court of Canada refused to extend the Charter's protection of freedom of association to the right to bargain collectively and the right to strike. In 1991, however, the Supreme Court deflected another ominous challenge. An Ontario community-college teacher, backed by the right-wing National Citizens' Coalition, objected to paying the portion of compulsory union dues to the Ontario Public Service Employees' Union that supported progressive political causes, including the New Democratic Party. Lower courts had supported him, but the Supreme Court ruled that the Rand Formula of compulsory union dues (entrenched in Ontario legislation) was legitimate. No new legal rights emerged from the case, however, and union activities remained vulnerable under the 1987 ruling.

In 1975, then, the Canadian state had begun to recast the country's industrial-relations regime. Politicians and state officials were no longer willing to let collective bargaining between unions and employers take its own course. State policies first limited how much workers could demand from their employers and then cut the ground out from under union negotiators by deliberately stimulating mass unemployment. In addition legislatures sent strikers back to work with increasing regularity, and in many cases altered their labour codes to weaken union organizing and bargaining permanently. Workers' already limited room to manoeuvre within the constraints of postwar labour legislation was reduced drastically.

Unquestionably, the Canadian state relied primarily on coercive mechanisms to undermine and eliminate workers' collective power in the post-1975 period. But there were parallel, if much more modest, efforts to co-opt labour leaders, and even some of the rank and file, into formal "tripartite" structures of capital, labour, and state representatives. In these organizations, labour leaders could be coaxed into supporting the capitalist campaigns for wage restraint and economic restructuring in return for what in Europe is called a "social contract" (that is, a guarantee of certain social and economic benefits other than wages). Several national labour leaders responded favourably to these initiatives. But the intensity of ongoing industrial conflict and repression severely restricted the effectiveness of these weak "corporatist" experiments.

In the mid-1970s, the federal labour department and the national office of the Canadian Labour Congress had converging interests in tripartism. The labour department officials were attempting to develop a forum for promoting industrial peace and consensus among business and labour leaders. Meanwhile, the congress leaders were inspired by the social democratic tripartite structures that they had discovered through regular contact with the western European labour movements; these structures seemed to offer the power that the CLC was denied as long as the New Democrats remained so far from forming a national government. In 1975 the federally sponsored, tripartite Canadian Labour Relations Council had barely begun to function when the labour representatives withdrew in protest over wage and price controls. In their spring 1976 manifesto, the labour congress leaders nonetheless included a call for "social corporatism" in the form of a powerful tripartite agency will full decision-making authority for social and economic planning. The government deflected the proposal as too radical, but kept an informal dialogue going during the controls period.

The agenda for these discussions shifted subtly after the creation of the Business Council on National Issues in 1976. This immensely powerful, new lobby group of Canada's corporate leaders hoped to convince the country's "responsible" labour leaders that future prosperity depended on clearing away obstacles to enhanced productivity growth. The council preferred a "bipartite" project with less state involvement. By the end of the 1970s, the handful of labour leaders involved in this quiet process was publicly playing down corporatism as a strategy for the labour movement. Yet they agreed to participate in consultative roles in twenty-three sectoral task forces on industrial policy, the cross-industry Second-Tier Committee, and the elaborately structured Major Projects Task Force, which involved seventy business and labour leaders engaging in long-range economic forecasting and planning, within the Department of Industry, Trade, and Commerce. By the early 1980s, the Liberal government was proposing to broaden this consultative network in a new "partnership for recovery." Soon after Brian Mulroney's Conservative government took office in 1984, the prime minister tried to use his reputation as a peacemaker in industrial relations to coax labour into conciliatory talks with business leaders. His highly publicized Economic Summit that year produced only mutual recriminations, and, after those first months, the Tories never returned to such consensus-building projects. This joint economic strategizing nonetheless continued quietly in several major industries, at the federal and provincial levels. At the same time, discussions with the Business Council on National Issues inched toward an agreement, announced in January 1984, to launch the Canadian Labour Market and Productivity Centre, which would be officially funded by the federal government but effectively run by representatives of the two leading organizations of capital and labour. As its name suggests, the centre was intended to combine the labour movement's concerns about unemployment and effective human resource planning with the business community's interest in productivity. After several years of invisibility, the centre became, in the early 1990s, much more active in promoting union-management consultation and helped to create the Canadian Labour Force Development Board for producing joint proposals on training.

In retrospect it is clear that these corporatist projects were unlikely to make a major dent in labour relations in the Canadian context. The constitutional power over industrial relations is too spread out through the provinces for national structures to have an effect. Moreover, neither capital nor labour has a central organization with the mandate to carry out the national negotiations that would be necessary to make such a system work. In any case, most capitalists seemed much more interested in a get-tough approach to weakening organized labour, rather than polite dialogue with union bureaucrats. (Even in western Europe, where the corporatist models had been developed, employers were abandoning these strategies in the 1980s in favour of more confrontational relations with their respective labour movements.) And, in an era of restraint, cut-backs, and slashing of social expenditures, there were few concessions that could cement union leaders' commitment to a social contract. Meeting the challenge of repressive state legislation and belligerent bosses was a much more pressing concern for Canadian unionists.

During the 1980s, however, the spirit of corporatism also entered individual workplaces. The state had again helped by encouraging the settlement of industrial conflict through dialogue and consensus.

The important new occupational health and safety legislation, which the Saskatchewan government introduced in 1972 and which quickly spread to other jurisdictions, brought to life joint labour-management committees on health and safety in every workplace. Although they worked with state inspectors, these committees were outside the collective-bargaining structure and had no power unless the employer agreed to implement their advice. The Ontario government went one step further by establishing a provincial occupational health and safety agency that was jointly administered by management and labour, but the agency became unpopular with business and was dismantled in 1995. In the same vein, the federal labour department tried to encourage the creation of workplace committees to buffer the effects of technological change, but these bodies were incorporated into only a small number of collective agreements and usually had no power.

A far more sophisticated approach to promoting harmony between workers and bosses was launched in Ottawa and Toronto in 1976. In these initiatives, consultants at small centres helped individual employers set up programs to transform industrial relations on the shop floor and to enhance the "Quality of Working Life" (QWL). Workers participated in redefining their jobs to incorporate more responsibility, independence, and group decision making (and often more work) and, in theory, thus became more content and productive. The initial inspiration for these QWL programs was the codetermination experiments in the Swedish auto plants, but, by the end of the 1970s, Japanese industry had become a more compelling model. Japanese companies use "quality circles," small productivity study groups of workers and supervisors. Why not copy or adapt the Japanese secret for profitability? Although difficult to measure, the success of the Canadian state in promoting QWL experiments was probably quite limited. Labour leaders agreed to participate in advisory bodies but remained suspicious. Some companies used the new methods as their forebears had used company welfare programs more than half a century earlier — to avoid unionization. As we will see, many companies were far less interested in promoting industrial democracy than in using these procedures to circumvent their unions and increase productivity. In 1988 the Ontario government closed its QWL Centre. Once again, corporations showed that they preferred to operate unilaterally, rather than to immerse themselves in discussion and negotiation.

Capital Strikes Back

After 1975, Canadian capitalists sought their own cures for their headaches. International competitiveness was their goal, "restructuring" was the remedy, and greater flexibility in corporate operations was the main ingredient. In the late 1970s and early 1980s Canadian businesses concentrated on the simple, old-fashioned method of curbing wages, but through the 1980s companies engaged in thorough economic restructuring. Probably the most coherent statement of the new economic order that they were pursuing appeared in 1985 as the report of the royal commission on the Canadian economy chaired by Donald Macdonald. Canada's leading corporations were preparing to be prominent contenders in world markets, with operations and investments spread around the globe. Labour-intensive industries would probably not survive competition from low-wage, Third World producers, but "lean" high-tech operations might flourish, provided Canadian workers could be brought into line.

Mergers proliferated. Across corporate empires, campaigns of "rationalization" led to drastic reductions in staff and increases in plant closings. Transnational firms globalized their operations, organizing the production of component parts on a worldwide basis. Inside their Canadian operations, corporations set three closely related processes in motion to cut costs. First came the rapid installation of microtechnology. With active government support, computerized equipment quickly replaced thousands of telephone operators, bank tellers, file clerks, autoworkers, and countless others. Computers (and robots) have certainly not been installed everywhere, and their implications for the economy are easily exaggerated. Yet work processes in most clerical, service, and manufacturing jobs have been transformed over the past twenty years. The most important changes involve information technology that connects, coordinates, and integrates. In 1985 only 15 per cent of Canadian workers used computers, but by 1994 that proportion had risen to nearly one-half. This new technology has enabled employers to reduce the number of workers required, to monitor employees more closely, and, wherever possible, to eliminate manual skills. Computers are expected to provide more flexibility in communication, design, production, and marketing; moreover, they have allowed firms to scale down operations to produce steel or meat products or pulp and paper in so-called minimills, located on "greenfield" sites outside industrial centres. This complex, new technology demanded a skilled workforce, but of much smaller size. It also widened the gap between highly trained specialists and those who were restricted to simple, often repetitive input, and who had more limited access to the better jobs.

The second managerial innovation, then, was to encourage the development of the "smart" worker to run this equipment most effectively. For employers such as auto manufacturers, the ideal worker was dedicated to the firm and willing to show initiative in improving the quality of the product. That worker cooperation, Canadian business believed, was the Japanese secret. These employers were thus quite interested in some version of quality circles. The first Japanese auto plants in Canada, including the Honda and Toyota operations in Alliston and Cambridge, Ontario, respectively, became showcases of this new technological and managerial model. Interest has spread much more widely. By the early 1990s the field of "human resource management" was awash in an alphabet soup of new programs: JPM (Japanese production management), TQM (total quality management), EI (employee involvement), STS (sociotechnical systems), and so on. These programs aimed at pushing up productivity by penetrating work groups in industry and office and by harnessing workers' creativity and solidarity. When combined with the new technology, these schemes made possible production innovations such as the "just in time" (JIT) system, which allows companies to fill orders quickly without building up inventory. By the mid-1990s, a relatively small percentage of Canadian firms had actually introduced these new managerial programs, especially compared to the United States, and most of this restructuring involved only part of the employer's operations. Yet, as with the older scientific management, the ideological impact on the business community was much more widespread.

Like the corporate welfarism of the 1920s, this model left little room for workers to voice independent concerns that were not identical with the company's interests, such as the purchasing power of their wages — concerns that were stoutly defended by unions. Many of these employers strained every nerve to keep unions out of their operations. New manufacturers tended to locate far from unionized settings. Honda, for example, was pleased with its largely rural, allegedly malleable workforce. In the East, Michelin moved into three small Nova Scotia towns and hired high-priced management consultants to keep its tire plants "union-free." (Largely thanks to special provincial legislation known as the Michelin Bill, which required the simultaneous unionization of all of one company's plants, three separate unionizing drives at these plants failed in the

1970s and 1980s.) In a similar move, Goodyear left the Toronto suburb of Etobicoke and set up shop in Napanee, in eastern Ontario, in 1990. In the United States, the shift of production from the northeast industrial heartland into the southern sunbelt was one of the most important weapons in capitalist attacks on the U.S. labour movement. Escaping to a non-union nirvana (other than the Third World) has been more difficult for most Canadian employers, however. Most large-scale industrial operations in Canada have remained in or near established industrial centres, where unions have been entrenched for many years and where provincial legislation, however limited, generally still provides protection for workers and their organizations to a degree greater than that in Mississippi or Alabama.

A new approach to collective bargaining became the third arrow in the managerial quiver. As unemployment deepened in the late 1970s and early 1980s, Canadian capitalists began to turn the tables. Instead of simply reacting to union concerns, they followed the lead of U.S. employers and marched into negotiations with their own long list of demands. In addition, they much more often dug in their heels in bargaining sessions until a strike was inevitable, and then resorted to lock-outs, particularly to prevent rotating strikes, rather than letting workers set the schedule of industrial conflict. To extract concessions, some companies threatened to close down or move elsewhere (Burns, for example, announced the closing of its meat-packing plant in Kitchener, Ontario, in the middle of a strike, and the Black and Decker Company in Barrie, Ontario, moved across the province to Brockville when workers refused to accept concessions). Sometimes workers in the same industry or the same union were forced into a bidding war of concessions to see which plants would stay open and which would become "runaways."

This new capitalist strategy of confrontation varied in intensity across the country, with the most bellicose spirit arising in the three westernmost provinces. In Alberta, construction contractors destroyed the building trades unions in 1984 by locking them out for twenty-four hours (in order to legally break an expired collective agreement) and rehiring the workers individually, sometimes through spin-off firms, at much lower wages. Between 1982 and 1987, the unionized sector of the province's construction workforce shrivelled from 80 to 10 per cent. In 1986, the long, bitter strike at Gainers meat-packing operation in Edmonton, owned by Peter Pocklington, became a national symbol of union-busting and sounded a dire warning to unionists and a rallying cry to antilabour employers. This fighting spirit was not limited to the West. In 1987 managers at the Montreal *Gazette* locked out press operators, mail-room workers, and cleaners and ran the paper themselves for months to wrench concessions from the union. Similarly, the next year, the Toronto flagship of the CTV Television Network, CFTO, followed the Pocklington model and used a three-month lock-out to force broadcast employees to accept contract terms that allowed the company to transfer many workers to a non-union subsidiary. On the whole, however, the capitalists' goal seemed to be to weaken the Canadian labour movement, not to destroy it; this situation again contrasts with the union-busting fervour of U.S. employers in the 1980s.

The new capitalist agenda for collective bargaining closely resembled that of capital in other Western nations, especially the United States (the 1979 Chrysler negotiations might be seen as the turning point). Canadians were a bit slower off the mark and more cautious undoubtedly because the existing legal regime and the political clout of labour in some provinces acted as constraints. In the new era of international economic uncertainty, Canadian employers had two priorities in collective bargaining: reducing labour costs and creating more flexibility in their workers' labour power to boost productivity. In both cases workers were asked to give up hard-won gains in living standards, job security, and shop-floor protection. Labour costs were a preeminent concern. Typically employers argued that these costs must be decreased to meet the challenge of international low-wage competitors. Not content to limit wage and salary increases, many employers, especially in construction and manufacturing, insisted on wage freezes and roll-backs. As well, they set out to reduce overtime rates, the number of paid holidays won in previous contracts, and contributions to medical, dental, and pension plans. By the mid-1980s a two-tiered wage system, first tested in the United States, had become popular; in this system new employees started at an hourly wage well below existing rates (for example, five dollars per hour less than the regular wage). Airlines, meat-packing firms, and super-markets all pushed their employees into strikes over these issues. Many large corporations that had long-standing collective agreements with strong unions also demanded the elimination of cost-of-living clauses; these companies preferred to pay lump-sum increases that were not connected to retail-price indices and that left the hourly wages unchanged. In an even better arrangement, management negotiators tried to persuade workers to accept wage increases tied to the company's economic fortunes, as measured in either poductivity or profit levels. Profit-sharing became a prominent part of collective agreements in the United States, notably in the auto industry, but, despite encouragement from federal and provincial governments, remained more limited in Canada as a result of union resistance. The autoworkers' union was especially intransigent on this issue.

Flexibility was the second priority in collective bargaining. Employers began to move away from centralized, industry-wide bargaining, and insisted on longer contracts to permit more stable planning. They also tried to reduce the constraints in collective agreements on their freedom to marshal their workforce. With the spread of computer technology, many companies succeeded in having technicians excluded from the union's bargaining unit. Some major firms compressed all the carefully worded job classifications into a handful of general job descriptions, which covered all employees and made it easier to reassign workers. Even more widespread was the trend toward part-time and temporary employment; companies began to schedule workers only for the peak periods in the day or week. Of course, part-time workers were usually paid less (both by the hour and in their total pay cheque), received few benefits, were often exempt from labour standards legislation, and frequently did not qualify as part of the union's bargaining unit. Many employers turned to contracting out for similar flexibility. They could thereby move some of their workers outside the coverage of the collective agreement and ultimately pay less for their labour power, since subcontractors were typically not unionized and paid much lower wages (in 1986, for example, unionists claimed that cleaners at Toronto's Pearson International Airport earned $4.50 per hour from a contracting company, compared to the $10.00 per hour paid to those on the government payroll). Municipal employees across the country faced pressure to contract out garbage collection, snow removal, road maintenance, and much more. The CBC also turned to this method of developing its programming. In 1986 British Columbia loggers fought a four-and-a-half-month strike to block subcontracting, and pulp-and-paper workers in the East made a similar stand a year later. Increasingly, employers also wanted to be released from collective-agreement provisions that restricted their ability to lay off workers. Strikes at Canada Post in 1987 and 1988 and on the railways in 1995 reflected efforts to resist such changes. Workers were often provoked to strike simply to block all these initiatives and to hold on to what they had.

Canadian business people were not content simply to engage in hard bargaining. They also intervened aggressively in setting the agendas for politics and public policy. Through lobbying organizations and intimate connections with the ruling parties in Ottawa and several provincial capitals, they determined the goals for state activity in labour relations. The most rabid anti-union voices have emanated from western Canada, where governments in those economically hard-pressed regions have been guided by small-business anxieties and by advisors from the right-wing Fraser Institute. The Canadian Federation of Independent Business and the National Citizens' Coalition have carried the same message across the country. These groups became the Canadian standard-bearers for the harsh neoconservatism that Margaret Thatcher and Ronald Reagan made famous. A less confrontational, more sophisticated, and more influential voice belongs to the Business Council on National Issues, which is the mouthpiece of Canada's most important corporate leaders; the council represents $1.2 trillion in assets in 150 dominant corporations, and is modelled on the Business Roundtable in the United States. By donning the mantle of sober, concerned corporate statesmen and by soft-peddling their program to avoid an ugly backlash from workers or the disadvantaged, the council's leaders have played a central role since 1982 in shaping the priorities of the federal government.

Despite their different tactics, capitalist activists of the 1980s and 1990s maintained a broad consensus. Public-sector unionism should be restrained. Government spending should be cut, especially for state-supported social-security programs. Taxation should be shifted onto the shoulders of consumers. Many government services should be privatized. And business activity should operate with much less regulation (whether pay equity, health and safety measures, or environmental controls). At the centre of this vision was the dominance of the "market" in shaping economic, social, and political life. The symbol of capitalist aspirations in Canada became the free-trade pact with the United States, which was spearheaded by the Business Council on National Issues. The Canadian economy, it was argued, would benefit from breaking free of all restraints on international trade, especially so-called nontariff barriers. The economic common market with the United States was established in January 1989 and extended to include Mexico in the North American Free Trade Agreement (NAFTA) in 1992. These agreements did not sweep away all protectionist barriers to world trade; however, as predicted by skeptical commentators, the common market did encourage Canadian capitalists to accelerate their demands for the slashing of social-security measures and of protective legislation for workers to enable companies to compete with U.S. and Mexican businesses, which faced fewer constraints on their profit-making. As we saw, most governments have been moving steadily along this path of public policy.

By the mid-1990s, the Canadian labour movement had been battered and buffeted by an aggressive counterattack from capital and the state for some twenty years. State policies had deliberately weakened workers' collective power to deflate their aspirations. Employers had made great strides towards restructuring power relations in the workplace to give themselves more flexibility for coping with the new international capitalist system.

The Condition of the Working Class in Canada in the 1990s

Every time the economy undergoes restructuring, the general shape of working-class life is broken down and put together again in a new form. Since the 1970s working-class Canada has been shaken to its roots. Wage-earners now live with much less job security. Men who grew up in an economy committed to relatively full employment for male breadwinners and who expected to hold a steady job until retirement (most of them are now over age thirty-five) can no longer be so confident. Nor can the many women who fought their way into better jobs. National unemployment rates in Canada have not dropped much below 8 per cent since the 1970s. In the mid-1990s, as business productivity and profits bounced back and business commentators promised an end to the recession, almost one in ten workers was looking for a job. More than a one-quarter of the unemployed had been out of work for more than six months. Workers under age twenty-five, especially those without a university or college degree, were hardest hit (13 per cent of people between the ages of twenty and twenty-four were offically unemployed in mid-1995, but huge numbers had stopped looking for jobs altogether). Overall, if those who had given up the search for work ("discouraged" workers) and those who were involuntarily stuck with part-time jobs were added in, actual unemployment levels could be double the official figures.

The explanations are not hard to find. In the slump of the early 1990s, many factories closed permanently, either dragged down by the weak economy and high interest rates or relocated to new low-wage areas within the new free-trade zone. Others shed thousands of employees and either replaced them with machines or simply inten-sified work for those who remained. Articles proliferate in the busi-ness press about the continuation of unemployment to the turn of the century in the midst of a "jobless recovery." The government offers nothing more than tokenistic, ineffective policies to tackle unem-ployment; indeed, a relatively large pool of jobless workers is now assumed to be normal and effective in allowing Canadian employers more flexibility to reposition themselves in the global economy.

Far more workers are stuck in part-time or short-term jobs, the "nonstandard workforce," which has grown much faster since the mid-1980s than the full-time workforce. Part-timers comprised more than one-fifth of the paid workforce by the early 1990s. Some like the flexibility of short-term contracts, perhaps working at home. Many others, such as parents who need more time with their children or students who have to balance time in the classroom, find it convenient to work fewer hours a week. But at least one-quarter of part-time workers regularly report that they would prefer to work full time, and nearly half would like to work longer hours. The majority of part-timers are women. Wages for these jobs tend to hover just above the mini-mum wage, at seven or eight dollars an hour, and come with few fringe benefits. Employers like the flexibility and low cost of these workers and try to shift as much work into their hands as possible.

As a result, the well-paid, full-time jobs at the heart of the postwar economy — in manufacturing, resource extraction, transportation, communications, and public service — are shrinking as a proportion of total employment. Seven out of ten jobs are now in the service sector. Public service now represents a much larger proportion of the labour market. In older, lunch-bucket cities such as Hamilton and Sudbury, the public-sector workers now outnumber those of the leading industrial employers; nevertheless, because of government cuts, it too is declining, albeit more slowly. Most new jobs now appear in the private-service sector, in smaller units of employment — the economy's rapidly growing numbers of "McJobs." The media have been fascinated with a concurrent trend towards working in the home — sewing garments, taking orders for pizza deliveries, word-processing, editing books, and much more — though they rarely focus on the long hours, lower and more precarious wages, isolation, frequent strains in combining domestic and wage-earning tasks, and overhead costs (such as equipment, furniture, heat, and electricity).

For full-time workers, the changes in the workplace have also been remarkable. Computerized technology is everywhere, most often for gathering and disseminating information, and for monitoring and controlling employees, as part of the long arm of management. Despite the new managerial vocabulary of "participation" and "teamwork," the cold reality is that efforts are under way to improve productivity by intensifying work. Ironically, in a context of widespread unemployment, those with jobs are working as much overtime as ever: the full-time work week has averaged more than forty-two hours since 1975, according to a 1994 federal study.

For some, these changes have brought job enrichment and new skills; others face low-wage tedium. In many cases, the range of jobs between these extremes is disappearing. Increasingly the labour market seems to offer only "good" jobs and "bad" jobs. Women and immigrants are most likely to be found in the latter category. Young workers also have trouble obtaining the better jobs. Since the 1970s, employers have steadily raised the level of schooling required for access to these positions, and in the 1990s many more children of working-class families have tried to stay out of full-time employment long enough to get what they hope will be the necessary college or university credentials. (To afford this increasingly expensive option, most of these young people find part-time work, usually in the private-service sector, which, in turn, now depends on the availability of this labour.) The huge costs of this education and reduced earning power while still in school no longer have a big pay-off: in 1993 university graduates between the ages of twenty-five and twenty-nine earned only $1,500 a year more than high-school graduates of the same age in 1979. Steadily rising tuition fees and the threat of a huge burden of debt after graduation may well deter members of hard-pressed working-class families from this prolonged schooling. In any case, downsizing in so many industries leaves far fewer openings for young graduates, who often end up back in uncertain, poorly paid service jobs. A new generation of workers is emerging without their parents' and grandparents' expectations of long-term, full-time employment at one company. Media commentators have taken to scapegoating middle-aged baby boomers (who, as a result of corporate lay-off policies, now hold a large proportion of full-time jobs) for depriving youth of their birthright.

Working-class families have had to adjust rapidly to the dislocations in the world of wage-earning. As male jobs have disappeared much faster than female in recent economic slumps, the myth of the "family wage" carried home each week by a well-paid, full-time male worker is largely dead. In 1991 58 per cent of adult women had paying jobs. For women with children under sixteen, the figure was 71 per cent. In 1992 nearly three-quarters of Canadian households were supported by two incomes, and women were the chief breadwinners, in one out of four, even though they still earn on average only 70 per cent of an average male wage. Most working-class teenagers are expected to begin working at an early age to help cover family costs or, at least, to relieve their parents of some of the responsibility for providing living expenses (an arrangement that may give these young people more freedom in the use of their income than earlier generations were allowed). Seven out of ten teenagers, aged sixteen to seventeen, had jobs in 1993 (earning on average less than $3,700 a year). Partly as a result of these pressures, high-school drop-out rates have been above 30 per cent since the 1980s. Moreover, the limited job prospects for drop-outs mean that they live in their parents' household much longer than earlier postwar generations. The "double day" of paid and domestic labour for working wives and mothers has not disappeared, however. Recent studies reveal that these women still do most of the cooking, cleaning, and laundry.

Despite the fact that family members are collectively putting in more hours of paid labour, working-class family incomes have declined. That is, the money left after deductions does not buy as much as it did in 1980. In the 1970s the pressure on working-class earnings came from inflation; in the 1990s this pressure comes from employers' strategies to combat international low-wage competition. Workers' pay packets have shrunk as a result of wage cuts and freezes across so many sectors. On average, pay increases have been below the rate of inflation since the early 1980s. Between 1989 and 1993 alone median employment income dropped 6.5 per cent. Younger workers have been hit particularly hard, according to Statistics Canada, which reported that incomes for workers ages twenty-five to twenty-nine declined by 27 per cent between 1979 and 1993. Working-class households have suffered most: over the twenty years before 1993, the share of total national income going to the bottom 50 per cent of Canadian families (in terms of income level) shrank from 30 to 27 per cent, while the top 30 per cent increased their share from 49 to 52 per cent. If the business community's demand for abolition of the minimum wage had been implemented, these figures would be lower still. The government has also taken a bigger bite out of workers' incomes, shifting most of the tax burden from businesses onto personal income and consumer sales. The much celebrated postwar standard of living in North America is eroding, and the decline is far from over.

It is hard to generalize about the significance of declining living standards across the working class. These families' strategies for coping are many and varied, reflecting, for example, ethnic traditions, levels of saving, or geographical location (in some parts of the country, for example, farming, fishing, and hunting can supplement wages). Many workers still aspire to the good life promised to them in advertisements for a glittering array of consumer goods, but for younger workers the new home in suburbia, a car, and sundry other signs of postwar working-class prosperity are no longer within easy reach. To help these consumers, many more discount retailers have sprung up. Yet Statistics Canada tells us that consumer spending is slowing dramatically in the 1990s, that savings accounts are dwindling, and that shoppers are relying heavily on credit. Household debt (including mortgages and consumer credit) has reached 92 per cent of after-tax income, and consumer bankruptcies are rising to an unprecedented scale. The Canadian working class is deeply in debt.

Not surprisingly, many of these families will face a major crisis if one wage-earner, especially the worker with the higher income, is knocked out of the labour market. Qualifying for unemployment insurance is now much more difficult: in 1990 three quarters of the unemployed collected insurance, and in 1995 less than half were able to draw on these funds. And even fewer applicants will qualify under the new regulations currently being debated. Payments are also proportionally smaller. And eventually they run out: over the past decade, the ranks of welfare recipients climbed steeply (to nearly three million in 1992), as far more families had no choice but to apply for social assistance. Nearly half of Montreal's population lived below Statistics Canada's poverty line at the end of 1994, and one-quarter of households earned less than $10,000 a year. In the growing number of single-parent families, the majority of which are headed by women, making ends meet can be agonizing. Three out of five of these families live below the poverty line. It is these casualties of the economic and social disruption of the past twenty years who have become the scapegoats of the right-wing political campaigns of the 1990s, especially in Alberta and Ontario. These families are also the main beneficiaries of the now vast national network of food banks; these charities, which did not exist in 1980, now operate in more than four hundred communities, outnumbering McDonald's outlets in Canada. In 1992, 900,000 children in Canada relied on support from food banks. In the greater Toronto area alone, these groups fed 150,000 people (including 60,000 children) every month in 1994. Thousands of people in such desperate straits have joined the ranks of the homeless in Canada's largest cities.

The other vulnerable group is the elderly, who since the 1950s have typically left the paid workforce at age sixty-five. Generally they are much more secure than previous generations thanks to public and private pension plans. Private plans, however, cover less than 40 per cent of the workforce, require long-term employment with one firm (few benefits are portable between jobs), and generally are not indexed to retail price inflation. Elderly women, who usually live longer than elderly men, are disavantaged in both programs, since they have often spent much less time in wage labour and therefore qualify for lower pension benefits. In the future, retirees of both sexes could face a bleaker future since serious discussions about restricting publicly funded pensions are under way in Ottawa and since the number of workers without private pension plans is growing.

Since the 1970s, Canada's wage-earners and their families have had to confront profound changes in their standards of working and living. They are losing the small leverage with their bosses that relatively full employment and a modest welfare state gave the post-war generation of workers. They are being driven to accept more freedom for business and lower expectations for themselves. These are the new realities facing embattled labour movements. Small wonder that the postal workers' former leader, Jean-Claude Parrot, described these times as "a chilly season for labour."

In contrast to the experience of many other countries' labour movements after 1980, membership in Canadian unions continued to rise — from 3.5 million in 1981 to 4 million in 1991 (membership has levelled off in the 1990s). Adding in the non-union workers covered by collective agreements increases these numbers. The overall proportion of unionists in the nonagricultural workforce has changed little, however. Labour Canada reported that the level of unionization in this workforce in 1994 was 37 per cent; this proportion has shown only minor variations since the late 1970s. Behind these figures lie some important shifts in the composition of workers' movements in Canada.

As in the past, Statistics Canada (which produces figures slightly lower than Labour Canada) found these unionists spread unevenly over the industrial landscape. In 1991 the fields with the highest proportions of union members were public administration (78 per cent) and public services such as education (75 per cent) and health (51 per cent). In many cases, these proportions have reached the "saturation" level, and are unlikely to change. Equally constant were unionization rates in finance, retail trade, and private services, where only tiny percentages of workers are union members. The biggest changes occurred in the blue-collar private sector. Declines in membership were steady in forestry (down to 65 per cent of workers in the industry), construction (64 per cent), and transportation, communications, and utilities (55 per cent), but they were precipitous in manufacturing. Unions in manufacturing rapidly lost members; the proportion of union members in the industry fell from 44 per cent in 1982 to 36 per cent in 1991. Moreover, their percentage of the total union membership slid from 39 per cent in 1966 to 17 per cent in 1991. As a result, the old industrial unions of blue-collar workers no longer carry as much weight inside the house of labour, especially compared to public-sector unionists, who now form half the Canadian union membership. Statisticians also report that union members are more likely to be found in the more skilled, full-time manual and professional jobs and to be working for the country's largest employers. Unionists in nonstandard employment and in private-sector clerical work are few and far between.

Unionization rates also varied across the country, as a result of different industrial structures, changing patterns of economic growth (or stagnation) in each region, and divergent labour policies in each province. Rates in the resource-dominated provinces of British Columbia and Newfoundland were above average at 39 and 53 per cent respectively, as was Quebec's rate at 41 per cent. But, as in the past, less than 32 per cent of workers in Ontario, the industrial heartland, were unionized; this figure is the third-lowest proportion in all provinces, surpassing only Nova Scotia and Alberta (which has seen its labour movement collapse since the mid-1980s).

So the unions in Canada have held on and reached out for new members, but they have had increasing difficulty maintaining their strength in the old industrial core of the country. Statistics, however, cannot begin to explain the many ways in which union activists and their leaders have tried to remake the Canadian labour movement since the 1970s.

6

Rebuilding the
House of Labour

The Canadian labour movement has never endured an ordeal by fire
without some serious soul-searching about its organization and direction. The Knights of Labor, the One Big Union, and the Congress
of Industrial Organizations, for example, all embodied new strategies
and visions that tried to take account of changing circumstances in
Canadian workers' lives. Often, as we have seen, these new directions involved confrontations with cautious, entrenched union leaders. Seldom was that leadership more solidly rooted than in the
postwar industrial regime, where union structures and the institutions
of collective bargaining gave great power to a large union bureaucracy. The Canadian labour movement entered the industrial battles
of the last quarter century with remarkably few changes in the structure, ideology, and strategy that had taken shape in the 1940s. By the
1970s, Canada's founding fathers of modern unionism, who could
remember the bitter battles to win union recognition and who had
led their organizations for three decades, began to retire. They were
replaced with a new generation of elected officials who had gradually
risen through the union hierarchy since the 1950s and 1960s, and
who had never known any other style of unionism. The new leaders
altered the union culture primarily by recruiting more highly educated experts onto the staff (some of whom were products of the New
Left political milieu of the late 1960s and early 1970s). It was this
leadership that responded to the rebellious surge of militancy of the
1960s and 1970s and to the counterattack of capital and the state after
1975. Their initial approach was to talk tough from public platforms
and to try to find bureaucratic channels — whether tripartism or a
revitalized NDP — for deflecting both the attacks from without and
the militancy from below. These leaders soon found they had to meet
vigorous challenges from below for a different kind of unionism —
from union activists who were not on the union payroll, who were

far from union headquarters, and who demanded more democracy or more action on key issues. In a few cases, individual unions became rallying points for a new kind of labour movement. As a result, a lot of rebuilding has been going on throughout the house of labour since the 1970s.

Nationalism

One of the new activists' first questions challenged the relationship between Canadian and U.S. unionists. In Canada, international unions have a long history, which reaches back into the nineteenth century. Craft unionists were the first to link their unions with U.S. organizations, but most industrial unionists were just as eager to establish an international connection. Despite the added bargaining strength that international affiliation was believed to bring, relations between Canadian and U.S. unionists within this structure were not always smooth. Tension occasionally developed within international unions and between the national federations in each country.

Craft unions tended to keep a tight rein on their membership in all parts of North America, principally because the labour market for each craft was most often continental. Industrial unions had none of the craftworkers' fears of craft degradation, but nonetheless administered their Canadian locals with a firm hand. In both cases, highly centralized bureaucracies were sensitive to political or personal challenges from the rank and file or from "dual unions" that threatened their unique jurisdiction. Before the 1970s, few international unions had established special organizational structures for their Canadian affiliates, since all locals in North America were supposed to be treated equally. Some of the larger unions had a Canadian vice-president or director (appointed or elected at international conventions), and in rare cases, such as the steelworkers' and autoworkers' unions, a separate Canadian district or regional office that had limited independence existed.

At the national level, the American Federation of Labor consistently treated Canada's Trades and Labor Congress as little more than a state federation and from time to time cracked the whip to make the congress fall in line with AFL policy. The Congress of Industrial Organizations had a looser relationship with its Canadian counterpart, the Canadian Congress of Labor, though attempts to make the Canadians conform again occurred regularly. The 1956 merger of the two wings of the labour movement into the Canadian Labour Congress included a declaration of independence that U.S. labour leaders agreed to respect. However, it took a few more years before these leaders let the congress settle interunion disputes and tolerated the chartering or recognition of independent unions not connected with the internationals. Policy differences over issues including the CLC's support for the social democratic NDP and U.S. labour's support for imperialist ventures such as the Vietnam War continued to divide the national organizations in the two countries.

Critics of this international connection reappeared in the late 1960s. Some were nationalists with a political agenda of complete economic, social, and cultural independence for Canada or for Quebec. Some in western Canada were part of the regional ferment that had fed resentments of central Canadian institutions for decades. Many left-wing activists saw the drive for independence as part of the struggle for socialism. Others combined nationalism with disgruntlement over poor service or undemocratic procedures within international unions; this same dissatisfaction was fuelling new rank-and-file resistance movements in the United States. To add insult to injury, in the emerging economic crisis, U.S. union leaders announced their willingness to support protectionist measures to save the jobs of their members at the expense of the jobs of others, including Canadians who belonged to the same union. In response to these conflicts, two strategies had emerged in Canada by the early 1970s: some locals withdrew from the mainstream labour movement into a new nationalist union centre; others fought for greater independence within the dominant union structures.

The first strategy resulted in the formation of the Council of Canadian Unions (CCU) (renamed a Confederation in 1973). To many younger, nationalistic, left-leaning unionists and intellectuals, the CCU appeared to be a tough little union centre that would lead determined fights in economic sectors where the bigger, older international unions held back. It also claimed to encourage rank-and-file democracy within its affiliates (a necessity, in fact, in such a small organization with few full-time staff). The council was strengthened by several breakaways of union locals in Winnipeg and British Columbia. But after the initial burst of enthusiasm, this nationalist union centre stopped growing. New organizing continued in the mid-1970s, especially in the southern Ontario textile industry, but there were no dramatic breakthroughs into mass membership. Early in 1985, a narrow majority of Cape Breton coal miners defeated the CCU's last concerted effort to reach outside its limited base in Ontario and British Columbia.

This separatist movement failed to gather momentum largely because the Canadian Labour Congress gradually awoke to the nationalist challenge. Much of the pressure for change came from Quebec and from the powerful new public-sector unions, none of which were international. The CLC's approach was to encourage "autonomy" (in this case, partial independence) for Canadians within the internationals without breaking the links. In 1970 and 1974 the congress passed its first autonomy guidelines, called "minimum standards of self-government," according to which affiliated unions had to allow Canadians to elect their own officers, handle national issues on their own, and speak for their union within Canada. In 1973, in the wake of a few highly publicized strikes by CCU affiliates, sixty-five international unions sent representatives to Ottawa to work out a counter-strategy. That same year the CLC executive agreed to readmit the old communist-led unions that had been expelled in the 1940s and early 1950s, in the hopes of keeping them out of the CCU. The 1974 CLC convention mandated the executive to ensure that new, stricter standards for autonomy were being applied and to suspend any unions that did not comply. By 1980 the congress reported that most internationals had taken concrete steps to grant special status to their Canadian members. Some organizations had altered their constitutional structures to allow Canadian leaders more independence and to provide for separate Canadian elections, policy conferences, administrative districts, and research offices to deal with specifically Canadian issues. In only a few cases (such as the Railway, Airline, and Steamship Clerks and the Broadcast Employees and Technicians) did Canadian locals become completely self-governing within the larger international structure. Many of these changes were possible because the membership of international unions was not declining in Canada as it was in the United States and therefore the Canadian unions were proportionally slightly more powerful within the larger organizations.

The loudest complaints about these blandly nationalist measures came from the bastions of highly centralized international unionism, the craft unions (most of them in construction), which rankled at any outside interference. Although craft unions were chafing within the CLC for a variety of reasons, they especially resented the refusal by the CLC to change its procedures to a block-voting system such as that used in the United States (which gives the leadership much more

power) and its political support for the NDP. These issues had provoked craft-industrial tensions for decades. Most disturbing to the
craft unions, however, was the congress's willingness to tolerate
some independence from its Quebec arm, the Quebec Federation of
Labour. That body allowed breakaways from the internationals to
remain affiliated, despite complaints against dual unionism by the
AFL-CIO Building and Construction Trades Department. The Canadian Building Trades Executive Board protested that Quebec's actions violated the CLC's constitution, but congress leaders hesitated
to act. Consequently, in 1980 twelve construction unions, representing 350,000 workers, withheld their congress dues; a year later
they were suspended. In 1982 nine of these unions founded a new
Canadian Federation of Labour based on their commitment to internationalism, bureaucratic centralism, and political nonpartisanship.
After twenty-five years, craft unionism in Canada once again had
a separate home. However, the labourers', carpenters', and iron-
workers' unions remained aloof, and a few of their locals reaffiliated
with the congress.

The departure of the craft unions weakened resistance to the "Canadianization" of the Canadian labour movement. In 1994, less than
30 per cent of organized workers in Canada belonged to international
unions, and the rest were members of Canadian unions — a complete
reversal of the situation in 1966. For the most part that shift reflects
the growth of public-sector unions and the devastating loss of members that the industrial and construction unions suffered in recent
recessions. But there has also been a noticeable trend for some
private-sector unions to cut loose from their international moorings.
The first and more important splits involved the communications
workers in 1972, the brewery, flour, cereal, soft-drink, and distillery
workers in 1974, the paper workers the same year, and energy and
chemical workers in 1980. Many locals also broke away on their
own. By far the most dramatic move was the 1985 decision of the
Canadian district of the United Automobile Workers to withdraw
from the international and create the Canadian Auto Workers Union
(CAW). A year later the large Canadian section of the International
Woodworkers of America took the same step. The issue had also
been raised within the huge United Food and Commercial Workers'
Union, but, in 1987, before a consensus had been reached, one of the
union's Canadian branches, the twenty-three-thousand-member
Newfoundland Fishermen, Food, and Allied Workers, jumped the
gun by announcing its decision to affiliate with the CAW. The two

larger unions plunged immediately into acrimonious contests for the allegiance of individual bargaining units of fishers and fish-plant workers, most of which joined the autoworkers. But this "raid" of one CLC affiliate by another created a new storm within the congress over the issue of Canadian independence in the labour movement. International-union leaders on the congress executive vilified the autoworkers' leader, Bob White, who responded with attacks on the lack of democracy in some of these unions. At the 1988 CLC convention all parties papered over the tension by supporting a resolution that decried union raiding but left the congress with little power to mediate these disputes. The issue is far from dead in the Canadian labour movement. In mid-1995 international unionism moved a step toward greater unity when two of the largest unions, those of the steelworkers and the machinists, announced a gradual merger that would include the U.S. autoworkers' union.

The Canadianization of the labour movement has been a complex phenomenon. It began as a peculiarly Canadian amalgam of anti-imperialism and resentment against bureaucratic centralism and conservatism. Much of the energy that erupted into rank-and-file revolts in the U.S. labour movement (in which some Canadian locals participated) seems to have flowed into the struggle for independence (or "autonomy"). Within the autoworkers' union, for example, the militant left caucus in the Canadian District Council used a nationalist critique of the international leadership to express their dissatisfaction with the leaders' bureaucratic caution. A group of left-wing militants in the steelworkers' Local 1005 in Hamilton, Ontario, also fought most of their battles with the international headquarters over the issue of nationalism. And dissidents who led their locals out of the steelworkers' union in British Columbia similarly cast a nationalist gloss over their frustrations with business unionism as practised by the international.

Behind the movement toward more national independence for Canadian unionists lies a widening ideological gulf between the Canadian and U.S. labour movements. The widespread "social unionism" in Canada has contrasted sharply with the sectional business unionism that is more typical in the United States. Canadian unionists who actively supported the NDP found their social democratic politics unpopular at most American union conventions. Recently, moreover, Canadian unions have generally taken a more militant stance in the face of demands for concessions and have been less accommodating to the new managerial strategies of the 1980s.

This difference was at the core of the Canadian autoworkers' and woodworkers' break from international connections. The ideological gulf was perhaps most stark when the CLC stepped into a leading role in the fight against the free-trade agreement with the United States in the mid-1980s; that struggle culminated in the 1988 federal election. The CLC waged that campaign in cooperation with many other social movements and stressed broad social concerns about continental integration for all workers and other social groups, not merely the narrow interests of particular union members. The vigorous nationalism of these Canadian labour leaders contrasts sharply with the Canadian labour movement's standard defence of cross-border interests only twenty years earlier.

Affiliation with U.S. workers' movements no longer guarantees the strength of numbers that it once brought in the days of the AFL or the CIO. Union membership in the United States has been experiencing a long-term decline that accelerated rapidly in the 1980s and that plummeted to a mere 15 per cent of the nonagricultural workforce in the early 1990s; this pattern runs through all sectors of employment. The U.S. labour movement seems to have lost the vitality it enjoyed in the 1940s and 1950s. A lot of ink has been spilled in attempting to explain these divergent experiences in Canada and the United States. The most compelling explanations focus on the Canadian labour movement's ability to use its important status within the New Democratic Party to ensure tougher labour legislation at the provincial level, where, in contrast to the United States, most labour laws are enacted. As a result of this labour influence in Canada's decentralized legal regime, in Canada, labour-relations boards tend to be more vigilant in monitoring antilabour practices, and public-sector workers have won collective-bargaining rights that are much more substantial than those of their U.S. counterparts. The legal and institutional framework of labour relations in Canada has thus constrained Canadian employers from engaging in the devastating union-bashing that has come to characterize the U.S. experience. Many Canadian unionists have undoubtedly concluded that to maintain the international connection is to cling to a sinking ship.

Of course, cutting or weakening the links with U.S. labour has raised the spectre of many small, isolated, weak fragments north of the forty-ninth parallel. A closely related trend in the Canadian labour movement has therefore been the consolidation of union members into a smaller number of larger units. By the 1990s, more than half of all union members in Canada belonged to organizations with fifty thousand members or more. Once again, the massive public-sector unions are partly responsible for this pattern. But so too are union mergers, which, by the early 1990s, had become one of the central organizational dynamics of Canadian workers' movements, especially among private-sector unions. In fact, in 1992 a CLC task force recommended more mergers to strengthen the labour movement. Traditional union jurisdictions have collapsed, and the largest industrial unions have become "one big unions" with a wide range of white- and blue-collar workers. The autoworkers' union now takes in fishery workers, railway and airline employees, textile workers and electrical-parts makers; the steelworkers' union includes miners, furniture workers, department-store employees, and rubber workers; the formerly autonomous communications, energy, and paper unions have amalgamated (and created the fourth-largest private-sector union in Canada); and the National Union of Provincial Government Employees incorporated brewery workers (and subsequently changed its name to reflect its more general membership). In 1992–93 the CAW even absorbed a number of affiliates of the old beacon of labour nationalism, the Confederation of Canadian Unions. These consolidations make sense if the goal is to simplify and rationalize the union bureaucracies and to create more bargaining clout. But to an astonishing extent this "merger mania" has been the result of fierce union rivalry that has reinforced the pattern of deeply divided, often mutually suspicious organizations in the Canadian labour movement. The scramble to find a new organizing base in the still largely unorganized private-service sector has heightened this competitiveness.

Canadianization has thus been much more than a set of relatively simple institutional changes. Although international unions remain strong among workers in mining, manufacturing, construction, and trade, probably at no point in the past century has such a large segment of the Canadian labour movement been so determined to set an independent course as in the 1990s. The election of Bob White to the presidency of the Canadian Labour Congress in 1992 symbolized the widespread support for this new direction that his union had set. The result has, arguably, been a more determined, uncompromising spirit in the workers' movement, but the cost has been greater fragmentation and bitterness between enthusiasts for the U.S. connection and their opponents and between unions trying to pull together the severed and shrinking pieces.

Quebec

Quebec unionists have also passed through agonizing debates about their future direction. At the centre of their dilemma has been the political project to create a sovereign Quebec. Branches of the labour movement inside Quebec have thus struggled to position themselves in relation to both the rest of the Canadian labour movement and the Quebec independence movement.

Creating some distance between the labour movements in Quebec and in the rest of Canada has been relatively uncontroversial within the province. The strongly nationalist Confederation of National Trade Unions and its break-away, the Confederation of Democratic Trade Unions (CDTU), as well as the powerful teachers' federation, the CEQ, have remained independent and developed their own, often more radical, programs. But the national and international unions affiliated with the Quebec Federation of Labour have insisted on both similar autonomy within the Canadian and North American structures to oversee their own educational, political and organizational programs, and the funds to sustain this work. In the face of considerable hostility, the QFL convinced the Canadian Labour Congress to grant it special status in 1974. The autoworkers' union gave similar powers to a Quebec council within the Canadian region ten years later. Eventually this arrangement proved inadequate, and in 1994 the QFL won a new status of "sovereignty-association," in which the federation handles all Quebec jurisdictional disputes, controls its own education programs, appoints its own representatives to join CLC delegations to international conferences, and has a place reserved for its president on the congress council and executive. Politically, Quebec unions have generally been uninterested in the NDP, which remains a marginal force in the province (despite the QFL's brief, unrewarding flirtation with the party during the 1988 federal election). By 1993 there was far more support for the sovereigntist Bloc Québécois, several of whose candidates and elected MPs were active unionists.

Inside the province, the state of the labour movement is much more complicated. Unions in Quebec do not gather in a single federation, as in the other provinces, and the historic divisions that date back to the days of Catholic and international unions have persisted. All but one of the union centrals in Quebec support independence (and directly or indirectly backed the campaign for sovereignty in the 1980 and 1995 referendums), but the process of reaching that goal has provoked intense debate and division. Sovereigntists are keen to mobilize the provincial state for their cause; yet, for large numbers of Quebec unionists, the state is an employer with a strong antilabour track record. During the 1970s and much of the 1980s, the union centrals with the largest numbers of public-sector workers, the CNTU and the CEQ, led the most vigorous confrontations with the provincial government in their bargaining through the Common Front and were the most vocal about the dangers of submerging working-class concerns in a cross-class nationalist alliance. This militancy cost the CNTU large numbers of private-sector and professional members, who pulled out to form the Confederation of Democratic Trade Unions or who remained independent (one-quarter of Quebec unionists belong to unions that are not affiliated with a union central). The CNTU continued to harbour a deep distrust of the state and of electoral struggles in its attempts to increase workers' power. Private-sector unions, especially those connected to the QFL, have generally been less apprehensive about the provincial state.

The debate inevitably polarized around support for the province's sovereigntist party, the Parti Québécois. Despite open discussion in Quebec labour circles about the formation of an independent workers' party, the QFL was enthusiastic about the social democratic flavour of the PQ's platform, even though, as in the case of the NDP, there was no structural link between unions and the party. In 1976 the federation invested considerable resources in the party's campaign, and many of its activists worked for the election of the Péquistes. Their reward in the PQ's first term in office (1976–81) was the major overhaul in 1977 of the province's labour legislation, which included a ban on strikebreakers. The PQ government's antilabour turn in the early 1980s threw these unions back into opposition, but by the party's return to power in 1994 the QFL was once again solidly in the nationalist alliance. A key symbol of that commitment was the highly successful Solidarity Fund, which the QFL launched in 1983 to invest in Quebec industry and thus promote employment. Ironically, after years of denouncing the PQ and openly opposing it in the 1985 provincial election, leaders of the other two major union centrals (CNTU and CEQ) had also been coaxed into showing more open support for sovereigntist politics, both in the province through the PQ and in Ottawa through the Bloc Québécois. This shift fits a new collaborationist spirit in these unions that we will explore below.

It is difficult to foresee what implications the narrow defeat in the 1995 referendum on sovereignty will have for Quebec unions. The long-term benefits and costs of participating in the nationalist alliance cannot yet be calculated, though the PQ has shown little interest in a more pro-worker political agenda. In any case, there is little likelihood that the most fragmented provincial labour movement in Canada will overcome its divisions.

Women

The "national question" has not been the only hotly debated issue within the house of labour. Across the country, unions and their central federations have had to respond to the upheaval of a rapidly changing membership with different priorities. These concerns are far from new, but the growth of large, independent social movements focused on, for instance, gender relations, racism, and the environment had encouraged groups that have long experienced subordination within the working class and the labour movement to turn their concerns into serious union issues. These groups' battles within the labour movement have not been easy and are far from over, but it is undoubtedly a sign of the vitality of workers' movements in Canada that union leaders have responded to these new pressures from their members as positively as they have, while deflecting consistent attacks from capital and the state. Much of the current labour leadership has learned that its priorities can longer be limited to the bread-and-butter issues of white male breadwinners. These leaders have been willing to devote union resources to new, more broadly political issues raised by their members and to work with other groups that share these new concerns.

Established union policies and leadership faced their greatest challenge from the fastest-growing group of Canadian workers and unionists — women. As we have seen, women have been entering the labour force on a full-time basis in increasing numbers since the 1960s. By the mid-1970s the Canadian labour movement was feeling the first effects of the new feminist politics, which helped to revitalize unions and expand their agenda for action in new directions.

Many sectors of predominantly female employment have been hard to unionize. Thousands of women work on a part-time basis or at unskilled jobs; in such conditions workers — both women and men — feel isolated and vulnerable to managerial control. The burden of domestic responsibilities also limits many women's ability to make commitments outside the home. Only 30 per cent of female workers were unionized by the 1980s (compared to 43 per cent of male workers). Yet female workers have been joining unions rapidly over the past quarter century — in larger numbers than male workers, in fact. Between the 1960s and the 1990s, the proportion of women in the Canadian union membership jumped from one in six to two in five; this growth rate far exceeds that of unionization among male wage-earners. Most of these women are concentrated in job ghettoes. The largest numbers are in unions covering the public and parapublic sectors and work as government secretaries, nurses, teachers, social workers, librarians, and the like.

Since 1975 Canadians have seen the determined faces of tough-minded female strikers on their television screens and in their newspapers. One of the most dramatic examples occurred in a small, southwestern Ontario town in 1978; a few hundred women in the Fleck auto-parts plant, recently organized by the autoworkers, were forced out on strike for a first contract. Strikebreakers arrived, the provincial police treated the strikers roughly, and scores of other unionists and feminists joined the picket lines. The struggle dragged on for months, and the Fleck strikers became symbols of the new female militancy. Two years later, clerical workers in the federal civil service similarly astonished the country with the determination behind their strike. Since then, there have been numerous disputes involving women. The six-month strike at six southern Ontario Eaton's stores won considerable attention in 1984. Nurses' strikes in Nova Scotia in 1975 and 1981, in Alberta in 1982 and 1988, and in Saskatchewan in 1988 revealed how widespread this new spirit had become among working women in Canada. In the majority of these strikes, feminist groups provided crucial morale-building and practical support (from carrying picket signs to organizing child care) and often helped to highlight the issues at stake of particular concern to women.

After a long, uphill battle, women have also begun to play a more active role within their unions. Traditionally, male unionists have never expected women to stay in the workforce and therefore made no effort to integrate them into union activities, beyond the "ladies' auxiliaries" that made the sandwiches and poured the coffee at union social events. Many men were openly hostile to women working outside the home and resisted their involvement in unions. Local meetings were often smoky gatherings held next to a tavern, and national conventions typically involved scenes of boisterous male carousing. No concessions were ever made to women's domestic responsibilities. Meetings were often held after work with no provision of child care; these conditions severely limited women's participation. In many cases the first women to stand at microphones on a union convention floor faced heckling and snickers. They nonetheless worked their way into elected union office, mostly at the local level. More female staff were hired, more women attended union conventions, and more served on local union executives, but almost never in proportion to their numbers in the membership. By the end of the 1980s, although Shirley Carr had become the CLC's first female president, women held only 25 per cent of national executive board positions. Those who made the greatest strides up the elected union hierarchy tended to be single, childless, or old enough not to be burdened with child care.

Increasing female participation in union activities took aggressive organizing. One strategy, developed in British Columbia in 1972, was to organize a separate union, the Service, Office, and Retail Workers Union of Canada, which incorporated many feminist concerns and which began organizing in hitherto ignored sectors with many female workers such as the banks. But this union's success was limited. Another route was to create independent organizations of women within male-dominated unions. The Working Women's Association, started in British Columbia in 1971, and Organized Working Women, formed in Ontario in 1976, enabled two to three hundred female trade unionists to meet outside their union structures. Female activism also emerged inside the main unions that had large female memberships, especially the public-sector unions. In the mid-1970s, women began to form their own caucuses within unions and federations, which quickly evolved into permanent women's committees. These groups often developed close links with the larger women's movement in their communities. Some of their first goals were to help prepare women for union activity by offering training in public speaking and parliamentary procedure, and by familiarizing them with union structures and functions. Furthermore, these groups often held workshops and conferences for members. Caucuses and committees also mobilized support for female candidates in union elections and convinced their unions to implement affirmative-action programs to encourage women's participation. Women have gradually become much more visible in the internal life of Canadian unions. In the 1980s the CLC, most (but not all) provincial federations, and a few of the larger unions began to guarantee a minimum number of seats on executive boards for women.

These new union activists soon pressured their leaders to address issues that were vitally important to women. The agenda of so-called women's issues in the labour movement was developed through active involvement in the broader feminist community, and female trade unionists have often carried on struggles for legislative action on some of these issues within such coalitions as the National Action Committee on the Status of Women.

While unionized women, like unionized men, enjoyed wages, benefits, and working conditions that were better than those of the nonunionized, they were not satisfied that unions were sensitive to the discrimination and oppression they faced on the job and in the labour market. They wanted union leaders to confront problems that were specific to their jobs, such as the effects of microtechnology and the growth of part-time work. Unionized women also wanted affordable day care and paid parental leave, which would allow them to maintain their jobs while carrying on their domestic responsibilities. They wanted protection from sexual harassment at work and, in many cases, reproductive rights. And they wanted dramatic measures to help them break out of low-wage job ghettoes, where most women find work. This labour-market discrimination is largely responsible for the average female employee earning only 70 per cent of the average male wage in the mid-1990s. In tackling this concern, activists focused on affirmative-action programs both to open up male-dominated jobs to women and to compare male and female wage rates to establish equal pay for work of equal value. In the 1980s many negotiations over collective agreements centred on these issues, though success was limited in the face of employers' rising demands for concessions and the economic slumps of the early 1980s and early 1990s. As a result of agitation by women's groups and unions, most provinces and the federal government have passed some kind of "pay-equity" legislation intended to break through these structural inequalities. (Only in Ontario, however, did this law extend beyond the public sector before it was scrapped by the new Tory government in 1995).

Feminist trade unionists have convinced many union leaders and fellow members of the need for a completely new labour agenda to ensure the equality of women and men in the workplace and society. Many of these women also recognize that much work remains to be done before these issues become a top priority in labour's struggles.

Many still find their union culture to be exclusively male and feel that they must prove themselves as "one of the boys" to survive. Many still face sexual harassment within union settings. To varying degrees, however, working-class feminism is still vigorously challenging such problems and helping to reshape what it means to be a union member.

Minorities

Women played a crucial role in sensitizing their union leaders to the fact that not all members were white, English-speaking, heterosexual men. From the late 1970s, minority groups began to meet in caucuses in some of the national and provincial federations and in a few unions, especially in the public sector. Visible minorities were the first to demand action, followed by lesbians and gays and the disabled. The official response was slow and uneven, but by the mid-1990s the concern for minority rights had found its way into a more prominent place on union agendas.

Canadian labour leaders have had to recognize that, thanks to the less restricted immigration policies of the past twenty years, the ethnic mix of the working class is much greater than it has ever been, and that workers from native, Asian, and black populations still face systemic discrimination in the work world, as in broader society. Women of colour in particular have to bear the combined oppression of their sex and their race, and often find themselves in poorly paid, physically demanding, part-time or casual jobs. Some minority groups created support organizations and caucuses, such as the Workers of Colour Support Network in Manitoba in 1985 and the Ontario Coalition of Black Trade Unionists in 1986, to pressure the labour movement to recognize their needs. Other groups have earned their spurs in bitter organizing campaigns or strikes involving immigrant workers in small-scale manufacturing or the private-service sector (such as the cleaners at First Canadian Place, an office tower in Toronto). These struggles, like many women's strikes in the 1970s and 1980s, often drew political strength from the wider community. Unionists of colour wanted action from legislatures to curb discrimination more effectively and to promote a wider range of occupational opportunities. And they wanted better treatment for minorities within their own unions.

Several provincial federations and a few unions used human rights committees to deal with issues of racism. These committees have been much less common in the labour movement than women's committees and in some cases have had a more sporadic existence. But some have become the focus of significant initiatives for combating discrimination. Most work has been done in attempting to confront racism against Canada's native peoples and racial minorities. Several unions and federations have adopted strong antidiscrimination policies and sponsored antiracist education within their ranks through conferences, seminars, booklets, videos, and, in Ontario, literacy courses. In 1987 the Ontario Federation of Labour became the first labour organization in the country to reserve a seat on its executive for a visible-minority representative. Five years later the Canadian Labour Congress created two such positions (one man and one woman); the Canadian Union of Public Employees now has a similar provision. In addition, in the provinces with the largest new populations of colour, Ontario and British Columbia, the provincial federations hired more staff during the 1980s to work on these issues, launched antiracist publicity campaigns, and worked with community groups to promote affirmative-action programs for visible minorities (with some success federally and in Ontario). In some of the larger unions, antidiscrimination clauses have been on the bargaining table more often in recent years. However, in far too many union locals, these concerns have not yet made a dent in collective-bargaining priorities, and subtle (and sometimes overt) discrimination has not yet been acknowledged in, let alone eliminated from, internal union practices. Among the more promising initiatives, however, are the organization of predominantly Asian farm labourers in British Columbia, the unionization by CUPE Local 79 of part-time nursing aides (half of which are immigrants) in Metropolitan Toronto's old-age homes, and the rebuilding of the Montreal and Toronto locals of the garment workers as multi-ethnic and multiracial organizations that are much more sensitive to the problems of the many female employees from southern Europe and Asia (new union programs run the gamut from day care to English-language classes).

Much more belatedly and with a great deal less energy, some federations and unions have become more sensitive to the problems of the disabled and of lesbians and gays. Issues regarding the disabled tend to be subsumed under general human rights committee activities, and lesbian and gay concerns most often fall to women's committees. Nevertheless, in some unions, organized groups of these workers have lobbied for union policies that are more sensitive to their needs.

The challenge for the current leadership of the Canadian workers' movements is to make their organizations open, democratic structures that welcome all wage-earners and respond to workers' concerns sincerely and consistently. Achieving these goals requires battle on two fronts: with employers and the state, whose policies shape the larger patterns of discrimination in the workplace and the labour market, and with union members, who have too often confronted minorities with racism, homophobia, and other forms of intolerance. In a time of precarious employment, the labour movement will have to squelch the tendency to scapegoat minorities, especially immigrants of colour (an undercurrent of which percolated through Tory and Reform electoral campaigns in the mid-1990s). A revitalized form of solidarity has been proposed that recognizes differences among workers and that sees diversity as a strength rather than a weakness for the labour movement.

Health and Safety Activists

Another area of conflict within the Canadian labour movement centres around standards for health and safety in the workplace. Occupational health and safety has always been a difficult issue for unions to bargain over, since it challenges the determination of capitalist owners and managers to maintain exclusive control over the labour process. Before the 1970s, few collective agreements mentioned the issue, and regulation of the workplace environment was generally left to state inspectors and workers' compensation boards. The human costs mounted nonetheless. Canada has long had one of the worst records of industrial accidents in the Western World. By the early 1970s, some workers had had enough. In 1972 a group of northern Ontario miners broke through their leaders' complacency on the issue with a wildcat strike over unsafe working conditions. The result was an Ontario royal commission and eventually new legislation to regulate occupational health and safety. Many wildcat construction strikes were undoubtedly also protests against unsafe working conditions.

In 1973 Saskatchewan's NDP government pioneered the legislative model that soon spread to most other provinces and the federal government. The new system shifted responsibility for monitoring health and safety onto labour-management committees inside the workplace, and gave workers the right to refuse to work in unsafe settings. Committees have operated outside the collective-bargaining system and have often been hamstrung by employers' refusals to carry out any clean-up in the workplace that seemed too expensive or that was detrimental to flexibility and productivity. But this new system motivated hundreds of rank-and-file unionists across the country, especially those working in mining and manufacturing, to challenge their employers' managerial practices and to demand support from their unions in the form of training programs and staff resources. Many unions and federations introduced such programs, and the Ontario labour movement currently runs a Workers' Health and Safety Centre in Hamilton.

This grass-roots activism began to escape the control of union leaders in the 1980s when workers used the new legislation to stage wildcat strikes against unsafe conditions. In 1985 nearly four hundred pulp and paper workers in Prince Albert, Saskatchewan, walked out in support of a fellow worker who refused to work in an asbestos-contaminated area. In Ontario, the next year Toronto sewer workers and Oakville autoworkers held short strikes to protest hazards in their jobs. In 1987 more than three thousand workers at the McDonnell Douglas aircraft plant in Brampton, Ontario, left their jobs for several days rather than work with toxic chemicals that, tests had shown, were hazardous to their health. And in the small northern Ontario mining town of Elliot Lake, the local labour council even threatened a general strike on the grounds that the lack of an anesthetist in town was too great an occupational risk. In the larger picture, these high-profile challenges were not typical cases, but they drew attention to serious workplace problems and probably helped to establish national right-to-know regulations on chemical hazards in the workplace (known as the Workplace Hazardous Material Information System).

These defiant workers also flew headlong against corporate intentions to reduce this sort of demand on their operations and profits. Revisions to the health-and-safety legislation in the late 1980s and early 1990s attempted to curtail workers' independence by limiting the right to refuse to work and to stop production to specially trained union and management personnel in each workplace. The bleak economic context has also drained much of the momentum around these workplace issues. The driving concerns raised by these rank-and-file activists nonetheless represented revitalization of unions at the base. In recognition of the struggle, workers' movements in Canada now acknowledge April 28 as an annual day of remembrance of those killed on the job.

Culture

The 1980s also saw serious rethinking of what it meant to belong to a union. For many years, most workers expected their relationship with the union to be based on services: good wages and benefits obtained through collective bargaining in return for union dues. But in the heat of new struggles and challenges, some unionists and staff began to look for ways to enrich union culture with new approaches to labour education and cultural life, so that union membership could have a wider meaning.

Unions in Canada had been running educational programs for their members for decades. So, too, had provincial federations and local labour councils. The CLC sponsored a six-week Labour College in Ottawa each summer for local union executives and shop stewards. Unions generally ran what have come to be known as "tool" courses, intended to teach collective-bargaining skills. These courses remain crucial to contemporary labour education, but in the 1980s the range of courses began to expand to include economics, sociology, labour history, and labour law, as well as such contemporary concerns as technological change, occupational health, women's rights, and racism. These programs were designed to teach unionists how to confront the broad issues facing workers in Canada. In 1977 the autoworkers became the first union in Canada to win contract clauses providing paid educational leave for members to attend an extensive program at Port Elgin, Ontario. In 1987 several labour organizations launched an even more ambitious campaign to teach literacy skills in the workplace, to help empower disadvantaged workers. Some of these efforts garnered considerable financial support from governments on the assumption that they would turn out better informed, more responsible unionists and thereby promote greater stability in labour relations. The real thrust of this new direction in labour education, however, was to move away from the notion that union members were simply consumers of services to one in which they became socially aware activists within their organizations and in society.

In the late 1980s, other union officials and staff members attempted to develop a specific union culture that could feed a broader working-class culture. They developed links with musicians, film-makers, and other cultural workers to promote artistic work that reflected the experience and aspirations of working people. In Toronto these efforts blossomed into the Mayworks Festival, held each spring since 1986. Similar events were later staged in Vancouver, London, Cobourg, Windsor, and Ottawa. The Artists and the Workplace Program, promoted by labour and funded by the Ontario Arts Council, facilitated this cooperation between artists and unions and has resulted in writing and photography workshops and the production of sculptures, murals, and union banners, among other things. Many unions now have arts committees and sponsor programs to highlight their members' cultural activities. Similarly a project launched in 1988 to create the Workers' Arts and Heritage Centre in Ontario reached fruition in 1995 with the acquisition of start-up funds and a historic building in Hamilton. The organizers of these programs wanted to encourage the development of an alternative culture that values labour, justice, equality, and struggle and that is collective in nature. The gulf separating workers in the arts from other workers has certainly not been closed completely, but these first brave steps suggest that in many more union offices there is a clearer understanding that the labour movement must move beyond its status as simply a service organization and fill a larger role in the lives of workers — as it once did in most mining towns and many other working-class communities before their dispersion to suburbs and the expansion of commercialized mass culture.

Workplace Struggles

Since the mid-1970s, both individual unions and the national and provincial federations have been reacting to internal challenges over how to change the direction of the labour movement. As we saw in the last chapter, however, these debates took place while the house of labour was buffeted and battered by aggressive attacks by the state and capital. For the past twenty years, Canadian unionists have been challenged to abandon the ramparts of industrial conflict, to bury their "selfish" demands, to take less — all in the name of the collective good of killing inflation, wiping out the deficit, and strengthening the profit-making potential of capitalists. When the state undermined unions' bargaining power or when employers threatened to close up shop and move elsewhere, many unionists paused to think twice about pushing for higher wages or affirmative action, and about using strikes to win concessions. In the 1990s, unions have undoubtedly adopted a defensive stance. Yet the spirit of the Canadian workers' movements has not died. In the face of overwhelming odds, Canadian unionists have protected their interests as aggressively as conditions allowed.

The leaders of Canada's strongest unions were perplexed and uneasy as the assault on their organizations took shape after 1975. Their thirty years of closed-door negotiations to win concessions for workers left them poorly prepared for the task of resisting such major changes in the industrial regime. Confrontations erupted at CLC conventions as postal workers and other members of new left-wing caucuses challenged the leaders' emphasis on quiet discussions of tripartism and on trying to elect an NDP government, neither of which showed any sign of success. Many unionists favoured the tougher alternative of organizing workers to resist the attack on living standards, workplace rights, and civil liberties. The national general strike of October 14, 1976, could be a model for further action rather than a one-shot event, they argued. By the early 1980s, the labour leadership, especially the CLC executive and its colourful president, Dennis McDermott, could no longer refuse to at least make a gesture toward this more militant response.

The 1980s began with one of the most impressive displays of anger and solidarity in Canadian labour history: in 1981 one-hundred thousand people responded to the call by the CLC to demonstrate on Parliament Hill against the Canadian government's monetarist policies. Unfortunately for these workers, the dramatic protest did not stop the economy's slide into deep recession. At the 1982 congress convention, delegates announced their collective resistance to concessions and wage controls, though with no clear plan of action; in contrast, the U.S. labour movement responded to these impositions with a conciliatory tone. Canadian unionists had difficulty carrying out their pledge within the fragmented collective-bargaining system. Their success depended to a great extent on the market situation of individual employers. Autoworkers and woodworkers proudly held their ground against most U.S.-style concessions, but workers in more troubled industries, especially construction, resources, and large parts of manufacturing, had more difficulty. A daring band of autoparts workers in Oshawa occupied the Houdaille plant that was being shut down, and thereby not only wrenched better severance pay and pension arrangements out of the employer, but also, along with several other groups that occupied their plants, helped to convince the Ontario government to improve its severance-pay legislation. Yet few workers followed the autoworkers' example, and, since there was no effective legislation governing shut-downs, most workers watched helplessly as the plant gates were locked behind them. Many of the unemployed could not keep up payments on cars and homes. The number of strikes dropped off drastically, and far fewer new union locals were organized and certified. The level of unionization, which had been rising throughout the 1970s, peaked at 40 per cent in 1983, and then, after 1985, fell back to the level in the late 1970s of 37 per cent. Unionized workers had to scale down their demands drastically. Employers took comfort from the fact that wage settlements were far lower. Unit labour costs stabilized, and productivity increased steadily.

Yet unions had not given up the fight. As the economic gloom began to lift (in central Canada, at least) in the mid-1980s, a new wave of union organizing and striking developed. Retail workers, notably at the mighty Eaton's and Simpson's stores, won bargaining rights in 1984. The Union of Bank Employees made breakthroughs among clerical workers in the head office of the Canadian Imperial Bank of Commerce in 1985. Garment workers broke decades of industrial peace with tumultuous strikes in Montreal in 1983 and in Toronto in 1986. Cleaners employed by contractors launched strikes to win decent wages and job security. The workers at Gainers in Edmonton prevented owner Peter Pocklington from destroying their union and helped to revitalize the Alberta labour movement. In a new spirit of defiance, the province's nurses walked out on an illegal strike in 1988. In fact, nurses were among the most militant workers across the country at the end of the 1980s. Numerous other public-sector workers challenged the tight controls that had been clamped on them. In Newfoundland, several thousand workers defied new restrictions on their right to strike and walked out twice in 1986. British Columbia's workers staged a massive one-day general strike in 1987 to protest their government's Draconian new labour legislation. By 1988 even the hard-pressed construction workers were on strike to regain some of their losses. Early in 1989 Newfoundland's fish-plant workers also held a strike to break out of a five-year wage freeze. Thousands of angry education and health care workers in Quebec also walked out that year. A survey conducted in June 1988 revealed that, of two thousand Canadians polled, half the private-sector workers and nearly as many public-sector workers were prepared to strike to defend their interests, especially to shore up their sagging incomes.

The antilabour offensive had nonetheless taken its toll. Canadian unions were still alive and kicking, but their goals had become more defensive. In many cases, they had not been able to prevent their employers from implementing measures to cut labour costs and increase flexibility in their employment practices. Many settlements were tailored to the specific problems of individual firms, rather than to industry-wide patterns. In some cases, employers were able to play locals off against each other. Unions managed to emerge from agonizing strikes at Eaton's in 1984, Gainers in 1986, and CFTO in 1988 with their locals intact, but with pitifully weak contracts. At the end of the 1980s, industrial-relations experts and business journalists talked confidently about the "new realism" and "pragmatism" of private-sector unions. Public-sector workers failed to change restrictive legislation that stripped so many of them of their rights to strike and to bargain collectively. Workers' primary concern in the resurgent militancy of the 1980s necessarily became holding on to their jobs in the face of lay-offs, technological change, contracting out, privatization, and part-time employment. In many cases, union negotiators and determined picketers succeeded in having some demands for security accepted. For example, as a result of an autoworkers' victory in a 1987 strike against Chrysler, many unions in other sectors began to strengthen the security of retired workers by winning at least partial indexing of pensions.

At the end of the 1980s, Canadian unions were struck with a double blow that once again gave them cause to rethink their militancy. First, the governor of the Bank of Canada intensified his stubborn campaign to reduce inflation by forcing up interest rates once again. The rapid economic slow-down that followed was Canada's version of an international recession, with unemployment soaring above 12 per cent nationally. Second, at almost the same time, the Canadian government agreed to dismantle most of the remaining barriers to continental free trade first with the United States and then with Mexico. The subsequent rationalization of business enterprise hurt the southern Ontario manufacturing sector in particular. Half a million jobs disappeared from the Canadian economy between 1989 and 1993; much of this loss resulted from permanent shut-downs rather than short-term lay-offs (in contrast to the recession a decade earlier). There were a few dramatic flashpoints of industrial conflict — notably the national strike of federal public employees in 1991 and the battle of some railway unions early in 1995, both of which the government ended with back-to-work legislation. But strikes became much less common, as many locals assumed a more prudent position. In a highly symbolic contrast with past negotiations, in 1995, postal workers took the unprecedented step of signing an agreement before the old one had expired.

In this context, corporate employers increased the pressure on unions to accept some form of workplace reorganization. Initially Canadian unions rejected the new managerial schemes, but many of their locals were forced to accept them to save their jobs. As companies began to whipsaw locals against each other, national union leaders began to see the need for more coherent, comprehensive policies on workplace reorganization that went beyond defensive militancy. Several unions participated in the Technology Adjustment Research Program funded by the Ontario government in the early 1990s, to thoroughly research the implications of workplace changes. In 1989 the autoworkers prepared the first policy statement, which was soon followed by statements from unions of steelworkers and of communications, energy, and paper workers. The details varied, and there were important political differences in the level of accommodation in each case. But essentially these unions wanted to ensure that the design and implementation of workplace changes were negotiated through (not around) collective-bargaining structures and that workers had access to adequate resources and information to participate in these discussions. Union leaders wanted to use this reorganization process to promote health and safety, retraining and the upgrading of skills, equal rights for disadvantaged groups, and increased overall democracy in the workplace. In the same spirit, the Confederation of National Trade Unions in Quebec undertook to negotiate social contracts with employers to guarantee worker input and protection. The autoworkers led a successful strike against the joint GM–Suzuki venture known as CAMI to bring the new managerial practices within the bounds of collective bargaining. Although few corporations have shown the willingness to steer their reorganization plans in the direction of genuine industrial democracy, unions and employers in a variety of industries have reached a consensus about workplace reorganization, especially around retraining. In short, some unions have recognized the need to take a proactive position in the face of workplace restructuring. These initiatives have paralleled the broader-based discussions over restructuring in which unions have participated in specific industries since the late 1980s (with varying degrees of cooperative spirit and suspicion). In contrast to the U.S. unions' approach, however, Canadian unions have insisted on establishing that workers' interests and needs cannot be subsumed in the corporate drive for higher productivity and lower labour costs.

The immediate results of two decades of determined resistance to the powerful assault on workers' bargaining power are not easy to gauge. But it is clear that, compared to workers' experience in the United States, the concessions made in Canada have been much less substantial and have involved much less compliance with the new managerial agenda of workplace innovation. Wages and benefits have generally been reduced, cost-of-living clauses have disappeared from many collective agreements, and contracting out has increased. But Canadian unions have been more successful than their U.S. counterparts in resisting the widespread introduction of two-tiered wage structures, lump-sum payments, profit-sharing, and other productivity-based payment systems. Moreover, contract clauses affecting women, such as pay equity, sexual harassment, and family leave, as well as those concerning training, have spread in the late 1980s and early 1990s. In this same period, unions have intensified efforts to organize new locals and obtain certification; as a consequence, despite the job losses, the level of unionization by the mid-1990s had not dropped. In the immediate future a critical factor in maintaining this organizing momentum may be how drastically provincial governments weaken collective-bargaining legislation. Ontario's Conservative government has set the pace by drastically weakening the province's labour laws.

In the mid-1990s the crisis is far from over, and the long-term prospects for workplace struggles in Canada are still uncertain. What is clear is that, except where employers shut down or relocate in a low-wage environment, most union locals are surviving, trying to promote and defend their members' interests in the best way they can. Some of the largest unions are trying to develop creative policy that recognizes economic instability. Are the mid-1990s simply a period of waiting and watching that will end with fuller employment and renewed militancy? Or have increasing legal constraints, the dismantling of the social safety net (especially unemployment insurance), and twenty years of unemployment above 7 per cent had a permanent, sobering effect on collective bargaining? The history of workers' movements in Canada suggests that any firm prediction is ill advised.

Politics

Many labour leaders have realized over the past twenty years that a workers' movement cannot win its battles alone. In fact, the social unionism that many leaders promoted recognized that collective bargaining was only one front in a broader campaign to reform capitalist society. The most important alliance that Canadian unions have entered into is their affiliation with the NDP, and, through the bleakest years, the labour leadership regularly urged members to channel their anger and frustration into votes for the NDP on election day. Across the country, rank-and-file unionists have thrown themselves into electoral battles for the party. In Quebec, members of unions in the QFL invested the same energy into the PQ. During the 1980s the pay-off was limited, since the PQ lost power in 1985 and the country's only NDP government suffered defeat in 1988. That year the NDP also ran a distant third in the federal election. More disturbingly, the party leadership maintained a careful distance from the agonizing labour battles of the 1970s and 1980s. From the opposition benches the social democrats did little to defend unions against the many attacks they have faced in recent years. In addition, NDP spokespersons seemed uneasy with the intensity of confrontation, and avoided highlighting the labour movement's plight for fear of alienating non-union or middle-class voters. Some labour leaders were particularly upset at the NDP's weak attack on free trade in the 1988 federal election; the party's poor showing allowed the Liberals to rise to the head of the anti-free-trade forces. Open letters from the leaders of the autoworkers' and the steelworkers' unions, the NDP's two main sources of labour support, condemned this lacklustre performance and prompted the creation of an internal task force to assess the relationship between the party and the unions.

The issue became more immediate when the NDP came to power in Ontario in 1990, in Saskatchewan and British Columbia in 1991, and in the Yukon in 1992 (thus bringing a majority of the Canadian population under social democratic governments), and when the PQ returned to office in 1994. In all cases unions managed to persuade these governments to introduce prolabour legislation — notably a measure against strikebreaking in Ontario. But, in the grip of a deep recession and international financial pressure, the state opted to control public-sector wages. Ontario's NDP government went the furthest with the Social Contract, a wage-constraint program that involved reopening collective agreements and freezing wages by creating unpaid days off. The Ontario labour movement angrily denounced this move. Some unions, especially in the public sector, severed their affiliations with the party or refused to support the provincial wing. The NDP met defeat in Ontario in 1995 for many reasons, not the least of which was the deep disillusionment of many unionists.

Alongside this frustrating political relationship, another approach developed. In the mid-1980s, in the context of NDP electoral weakness and inadequate defence of union concerns, labour leaders began to look elsewhere for allies in short-term battles. Those allies were not difficult to find, since monetarism, privatization, deregulation, and the slashing of social welfare expenditures angered many other groups and social movements, among them, women, environmentalists, churches, consumers' organizations, seniors, artists, native peoples, farmers, and ethnic and racial minorities. During the 1980s labour leaders more regularly committed their organizations' resources to campaigns based on a single issue, such as abortion rights or nuclear disarmament. The first substantial coalescence of these movements with labour occurred in the Solidarity Coalition in British Columbia in 1983. Similar organizations eventually appeared in other provinces, such as the Coalition for Equality in Newfoundland. The most significant national coalition of this kind was the broad-based movement against free trade with the United States.

In building these links, the labour movement uncovered promising possibilities for overcoming its isolation and victimization, and for broadening its struggle against the agenda of the New Right. But there were problems. Because of its extensive financial and organizational resources, labour was usually the senior partner in these coalitions, and was occasionally uncooperative. Union leaders brought an approach to organizational practices that differed from those of most other coalition partners. In contrast to many of the social movements, which emphasized mobilizing their membership in mass protest or direct action, labour leaders preferred to flex their organizational power in private negotiations or to channel dissent into electoral support for the NDP. In popular coalitions they were unwilling to marshal the industrial power of the strike in support of political objectives shared by their coalition allies (admittedly, Canada's restrictive labour legislation makes it almost impossible to hold political strikes and stay within the law). The coalition strategy also remained an alliance at the leadership level, without much activity within the individual locals. The most dramatic example of these problems occurred in British Columbia, where confrontation with the Social Credit government was developing into a general strike in 1983. Jack Munro, leader of the province's woodworkers, reached a settlement of the labour issues in a private meeting with the premier, and left the other participants in the Solidarity movement convinced that he had abandoned the broader social concerns (human rights, women's issues, and so on). Both sides were still wary a decade later.

Yet, by the late 1980s and early 1990s, many labour leaders were becoming more sensitive and more committed to working in coalitions for broad social goals. The anti-free-trade forces created both a permanent national organization, the Action Canada Network, and provincial and municipal counterparts to fight the right-wing agenda that was spreading through Canadian politics. In 1991 the CLC hosted a huge conference to draft the People's Agenda; six hundred representatives of labour and social movements met to chart a common course. The following year the CLC's revamped constitution made clear its incorporation of coalition-building into its long-range strategy for social change. Perhaps even more important has been the growing tendency for many rank-and-file union activists to involve themselves in other social movements, thereby participating in a broad-based campaign for social justice. These unionists are also likely to be active supporters of the NDP, but this combination of allegiances has proven to be frustrating since, once in power, the NDP has distanced itself from extraparliamentary social movements.

In the mid-1990s the politics of Canadian workers' movements follows two paths: social democratic electoralism and coalition-building. For many unionists, these paths are compatible and mutually supportive. But, in the bitter debates over the NDP's record on labour issues in recent years, these two approaches have often been pitted against each other. In the wake of devastating defeats for the NDP — on a federal level in 1993 (when it was reduced to nine seats) and in Ontario in 1995 (when it fell to third place with only seventeen seats) — voices arguing for a stronger emphasis on coalitions are claiming much attention. At the same time, the widespread working-class support for parties of the centre and right may produce a backlash and a demand for a less overtly political labour movement, such as that espoused by the conservative Canadian Federation of Labour. The leadership of the Oshawa CAW local has already moved in this direction. So far there is no indication that this swing to the right has momentum or significant support among labour activists at any level. The spread of the politics of the New Right is more likely to bolster resistance than to intimidate unionists to back down. Indeed, in Ontario in the winter of 1995–96, anger against the so-called Common Sense Revolution of Mike Harris's Conservative government prompted all parts of the labour movement to close ranks in massive protests. Unions led other social movements in a one-day general strike in London in December 1995 and a two-day demonstration in February 1996 that drew 100,000 people into the streets of Hamilton.

7

A New Agenda for Labour

Unions in Canada set sail into the new troubled waters of labour relations in the 1970s as highly bureaucratized organizations, strait-jacketed by the legal regime governing collective bargaining but adept at using it to promote and defend their interests. Twenty years later, they have moved some distance from that narrow, complacent perspective. The attacks on workers' postwar gains and on the broader economic and social consensus that sustained them have thrown Canada's labour leaders and their active rank-and-file members into a crucible of learning and rethinking. Simultaneously a new activism that demands a broader agenda has percolated through the ranks of workers' movements. Has the Canadian labour movement evolved into a different kind of animal from what it was in the 1960s? Only partially. It has distanced itself increasingly from its weak, accommodationist U.S. counterpart and created larger, less frag-mented blocs of union power in Canada. It has broadened its horizons to respond to pressure from new workers and rank-and-file activists, and to address concerns that were not on the collective-bargaining agenda twenty or thirty years ago. It has loudly denounced the anti-labour campaigns of the 1980s and spearheaded the defence of en-dangered social programs. At Canadian Labour Congress and provincial federation conventions the rhetoric is angrier and more strident, and resolutions are now routinely passed in support of a broad range of reforms and expressions of solidarity.

Yet this tougher rhetoric masks some basic similarities with labour movements of the past. Fundamentally the Canadian labour move-ment's structure and style of operation have not changed. Unions still jealously guard their individual power and influence. In fact the antilabour offensive of the 1980s and 1990s may have made them even more competitive and insular. Certainly the current merger campaigns and the scramble to organize the private-service sector have sharpened these lines. Most unions cooperate only in symbolic events such as CLC conventions or Labour Day parades; they more rarely join forces in pressing for common demands (beyond the initial angry responses to new provincial labour legislation). The congress, the provincial federations, and the labour councils are still relatively weak organizations with little effective power to coordinate labour's battles. (In contrast, the Quebec centrals have more power to direct the whole labour movement.) The congress now represents only three out of five unionized wage-earners. At the local level, most workers still view their unions as distant, though vital, service organizations.

Many union leaders have not been able to see a way out of the crisis they find themselves in. They have only reacted, reasserting their general faith in the legalism and gradualism of the postwar collective-bargaining system and social democratic politics. Yet increasing numbers of union leaders and staff have begun to recognize that the future of workers' movements in the country requires more fundamental rethinking. The pressures from inside and outside the house of labour have created momentum that has already begun to transform the long-term agenda for labour. A few unions, including those of the autoworkers, the postal workers, and the garment workers, have been particularly innovative. Some items on the new agenda are clear and well articulated; other parts are still half formed. In particular, unionists are only gradually coming to terms with the new economy, the new workplace, the reorganized labour market, and the new worker. In implementing this new agenda, labour leaders will no doubt have to use some form of structured collective-bargaining system as the main bulwark in defence of standards of living and working, though this system need not be as restrictive as the present regime. But they will also need to build on the widespread, deeply felt sense that a well-articulated vision of a popular, practical alternative can challenge the corporate agenda. The outlines of this new unionism are appearing, but the edges are still blurry.

The New Economy

At the commanding heights of the Canadian economy, the key assumptions of the postwar period have largely been scrapped in recent years. Labour now has to accommodate two profound changes: integration into the global economy and the decline of state intervention and regulation. The initial response of the labour movement to monetarism was to defend the Keynesian approach of stimulating the economy; its antidote to free trade seemed to be little more than vague protectionism for Canadians. In the mid-1990s it is no longer adequate to fall back on economic policies that always had inherent problems for workers and that cannot address how profoundly the Canadian economy has already changed. Labour and its allies will have to announce a new economic strategy that credibly charts an alternative path forward. This plan must guarantee jobs and income security by focusing on community economic development (rather than corporate rationalization), find a central role for workers in shaping economic decisions, and incorporate a role for the state in ensuring social responsibility in economic decision making. This strategic direction is certainly not the same as simply buying into the corporate agenda to increase competitiveness, since the logic of that route veers away from maintaining a decent standard of living and the dignity of toil that labour has promoted.

At the same time, labour will have to do more than rush to the defence of the existing ragged patchwork of the social safety net. There is nothing sacred about the programs pieced together by successive governments between the 1940s and the 1970s. Labour and its allies need not be drowned out by the rising chorus of voices calling for the "reform" of this system from provincial capitals across the country. Labour leaders can respond first with an equally loud defence of the principle of social security for all and follow with their own clear reforms that respond more effectively and more humanely to the needs of economically disadvantaged workers and their families. The result could be the progressive overhaul of an inadequate welfare state.

The New World of Work

Earlier generations of unionists recognized that they would have to negotiate hard to find a proper place for themselves within rapidly changing industrial structures. Their experience is still relevant. Today, more unions will have to follow the lead of those that have been trying to develop flexible, creative responses to the new wave of managerial innovations, both technological and organizational, since the mid-1980s. Union leaders and their staff will now have to be much more knowledgeable about these issues, and union resources will have to be directed into educational programs to help members deal with the waves of change washing over them. Unions can no longer bargain just to save existing jobs; they will have to find ways to fight the trend toward cheapening and intensifying labour. With an aggressive strategy of proactive bargaining, unions can draw the issues of workplace restructuring back into collective bargaining (which employers ensured did not cover reorganization). In this way, they can make sure that "lean production" also means a safer, healthier workplace with more scope for regular skill upgrading, fairness in job distribution, and worker input into decision making. This framework will require restructuring within the union to revitalize the position of stewards as representatives of work groups and teams. It will also require industry-wide approaches, so that individual locals or groups within locals are not pitted against each other. Ideally, it should also involve coordinated strategies among distinct unions, probably through national and provincial federations. Many employers will stubbornly resist this renegotiation of "management rights." Many, however, are now committed to a new human-resource policy that recognizes the importance of the "smart worker" for high-quality products. This is the crack in the door that unions can widen with a serious push.

The New Worker

In the nineteenth century the typical unionist was a skilled, white male, practising his craft in a labour-intensive workshop or mine. For much of the twentieth century the dominant figure in workers' movements was the semiskilled, blue-collar, white, male worker, usually of British origins, with a job in a highly mechanized, large-scale workplace in transportation, a resource industry, or a mass-production factory. Both of these unionists saw themselves as breadwinners with wives and children who were dependent on them for their economic survival. Craft and industrial unions reflected the central concerns of these two particular groups of workingmen and tended to neglect wage-earners in other settings. In the 1960s thousands of workers in the new public-sector unions began to challenge the dominance of male, blue-collar workers. Many of these newcomers to the house of labour worked in offices, not factories or mines, and many were women. Nevertheless, the ideology of the male breadwinner and his family wage persisted, until feminists inside and outside the labour movement began to confront these patriarchal assumptions in the 1970s and 1980s.

By the 1990s economic, social, and cultural changes had eroded the old basis of a labour movement run mainly by men from crafts, large-scale industries, and government offices. Technological change, plant closures, and general downsizing have cut the size of the blue-collar workforce, and state employment continues to shrink. The primary growth area for at least twenty years has been the private-service sector, which employs large numbers of women, youth, and immigrants, especially people of colour. These employees work for low wages frequently on a part-time or casual basis, and are often scattered through many small-scale workplaces. The labour market is becoming polarized, with a shrinking number of high-income, more secure jobs at one end and low-paid, more uncertain positions in service and other sectors at the other. Moreover, the myth that a man can support his family on his wages alone is completely dead, as the majority of families now rely on incomes from two wage-earners, and from teenagers who move into regular part-time work at an early age.

The challenge for the labour movement is to acknowledge this recomposition of working-class life in Canada and to develop effective strategies for organizing and representing the new workers and linking them to workers with better union protection. Some unions have already recognized that this new strategic direction will require an effort to organize part-time workers and to overcome the fragmented plant-by-plant bargaining structure by means of composite union locals and broader-based bargaining; as a result, for example, a handful of workers in one retail outlet will not be completely isolated and victimized by an employer with many separate outlets. In addition, given the high turnover in service-sector jobs, the time has arrived to consider reviving the universal union-membership card that craft unionists and the Industrial Workers of the World used to enrol transient workers. With this card, a worker could move between jobs and in and out of the labour market and remain a full member of the union. Above all, the labour movement has to accept that the Third Industrial Revolution that is rolling through the economy at the close of the twentieth century is bringing new kinds of workers who must be represented inside the house of labour if it is to survive.

Beyond the Workplace

For most of the nineteenth and twentieth centuries, unions in Canada committed themselves first and foremost to issues surrounding wage-earning and relations with employers. Most of their demands for state legislation were also efforts to strengthen the legal framework for collective bargaining and for social security measures to buttress the breadwinner's ability to support a family (or to fill in for the missing breadwinner). One of the healthiest developments within workers' movements in Canada over the past decade has been the increasing attention paid to workers' lives beyond the paid workplace. Women have been the most important force in pressuring their fellow unionists to recognize the issues of home and family, such as child care, and family violence. Minority groups, especially ethnic and racial minorities, have also demonstrated that their concerns are not limited to the work environment. Some unions, locals, and labour councils now recognize this wider world of workers' lives and provide such services as nonprofit housing or employment counselling. Others, especially outside the big cities, continue active social programs through union halls. The autoworkers' union provides an interesting example of reaching beyond the wage-earner, by integrating entire families into their educational programs at Port Elgin. Some unionists have also been building links with musicians, playwrights, filmmakers, and other artists to cultivate the creative expression of workers' experience off the job. Since 1992 the autoworkers have amassed a large number of volunteer, community-based organizers who not only help friends and neighbours build new locals but also develop better links between the union and the community. In short, to meet current challenges, more unions will have to follow the example of these innovative labour organizations and become social, cultural, and community institutions promoting the interests of both the waged and the unwaged. In particular, they will have to develop ways to work more effectively with the unemployed and the underemployed, who justifiably resent the still-privileged enclaves of unionized work.

In fact, for generations, many Canadian unionists have recognized that they must carry this larger perspective beyond the confines of their own unions. This idea is the essence of social unionism. The slogan What We Want For Ourselves We Want For All has carried workers' movements into campaigns for full civil rights for women and minorities (though belatedly in both cases) and for many measures of social security, including free education, old-age pensions, unemployment insurance, and health insurance. Furthermore, many public-sector unions now regularly reach out to other workers with demands for better services for the tax-paying public, from the post office to hospitals and schools, and for a more democratic government. More generally, the mainstream of the workers' movements in Quebec and in English Canada still sees itself as part of a broad movement for social justice. Unions will have to invest greater efforts in solidifying the alliances and coalitions that sustain that broader movement and especially in making it a grass-roots project in individual working-class communities.

Solidarity

Labour's anthem begins, "When the union's inspiration through the workers' blood shall run / There can be no power greater anywhere beneath the sun." Working-class solidarity has been the goal of workers' movements in Canada since the mid-nineteenth century. Transforming that goal from a pious wish into a dynamic reality has never been easy, as plenty of cross-currents promote tensions and animosities among workers. Many divisions have emerged out of frictions in the workplace and the labour market: skilled versus unskilled, full-time versus part-time, male versus female, adult versus youth, anglophone versus non-English-speaking, white versus visible-minority, Canadian-born versus immigrant, unionized versus non-unionized. Many of these tensions have been combined to create deep divisions between groups of workers. Recently, some sections of the workers' movements have made great efforts to overcome these difficulties by creating inclusive organizations that restrict neither membership nor the level of participation and that see diversity within the ranks as a part of the foundation for a healthy, responsive labour movement. These efforts must be consolidated and expanded throughout individual unions and federations. But consolidation is no easy task. The previous basis for unity was a craft, an occupation, or an industrial product; these distinctions no longer exist among the diverse memberships of most unions. Building consensus and solidarity will depend on appealing to a stronger sense of working-class identity. Somehow that appeal must also reach across the great occupational gulf to the marginally employed, poorly paid workers in the nonstandard workforce. Otherwise unions will become organizations serving only the better-off workers in the economy's remaining "good" jobs. In a bold departure from union traditions, the International Ladies' Garment Workers Union has reached out to organize home workers, most of them recent immigrants, even though these individuals cannot legally be certified as unionists. On a larger scale, a broad-based political campaign for "wage solidarity" could involve higher minimum wages and other efforts to narrow the income gaps through fairer taxation. Concerted efforts to shorten hours of work could also help to create jobs for the unemployed and the underemployed.

Even within the house of labour, where solidarity is expected to overcome divisions, tensions over strategy and tactics continue to drive groups of workers apart. And the splits seem to be deepening in the 1990s. Supporters of international and national unions eye each other warily at best. The social democratic leadership of the main workers' organizations faces cold indifference among the business unionists of many construction unions. Public-sector unionists who have battled with the state over numerous issues explode in anger at their erstwhile social democratic partners in NDP governments, while most private-sector unions welcome the more liberal collective-bargaining legislation that those governments have put on the statute books. As union jurisdictional boundaries collapse, a new rivalry is emerging among the consolidated unions, which are now eager to take in almost any group of workers. The highest councils of the workers' movements in Canada will have to directly address this fragmentation to bring together warring factions. A divided labour movement will be ill prepared for ongoing assaults from the state and from employers.

Unions will also have to find effective ways to coordinate their efforts with labour organizations in other countries that face common concerns about globalization. A protectionist perspective that focuses only on Canadian unionists is doomed in a world where transnational corporations move freely between continents. National labour organizations will suffer if they are pitted against each other in a fruitless game of international capitalist competition.

A Vision

Workers participate in modern capitalist society in many different ways, as citizens, consumers, parents, producers, members of ethnic

groups, and so on. In each of these separate realms, efforts are made
to organize workers into a particular kind of social consensus. Sometimes that consensus is achieved through appeals to ethnic identity,
through lifestyle promises, through anticrime campaigns or through
appeals to "honest toilers" that accompany cuts in welfare spending.
The central reality in the midst of these multiple identities, however,
is workers' dependence on wage-earning for their survival. Even
with high levels of unemployment, most adult workers derive a large
part of their self-worth in earning a wage or salary. It is on this terrain
that the New Right has managed to fashion its powerful appeal.
Corporations now reach out to their employees with regular appeals
to link their wage-earning experience to a common struggle for the
survival of industry. National and provincial politicians similarly
urge workers to help make "our" economy internationally competitive. At the same time, a business community that wants to eliminate
government regulation and dismantle the welfare state works to build
a consensus around lower taxes, which have become a heavy drain
on shrinking working-class incomes and which, as a target, are more
visible than corporate profits. Politicians play into this refrain with
their relentless, oversimplified attacks on deficits in government
spending. This vision of a society with a weaker government, a
stronger private sector, family-based social welfare, and untram-
melled individualism is repeated like a mantra in the mass media and
has been turned into the new "common sense" that workers use to
understand the world.

Recent opinion polls have often revealed that popular support for
some of the main priorities in the corporate agenda, especially deficit-
bashing, is actually quite limited. Since the free-trade election of
1988, many voices within the labour movement have been struggling
to provide a credible alternative vision. This effort has a long history
in and around workers' movements in Canada. Early in the twentieth
century, labourists stressed the social value of labour, but proposed
little more than legislative reforms to democratize electoral politics
and to protect those unable to organize for their own protection
(women, children, the aged). The role of these political activists
faded along with the craftworkers who articulated these ideas. Marx-
ists in early socialist and later communist parties called for a much
more thorough transformation of society to replace capitalist power
with working-class control and management. Their influence waned
during the Cold War and, despite the blossoming of new marxist
currents in the 1960s and 1970s, suffered serious damage with the

international collapse of communism after 1989. Social democrats once shared with communists a moral rejection of capitalism and projected a stirring vision of an alternative society based on considerable state ownership, centralized planning, and extensive social-security programs. By the birth of the NDP in 1961, however, they had jettisoned nationalization and state planning in favour of Keynesian regulation of the economy and concentrated on a package of reforms for making capitalism more humane. The workers' movements in Canada in the 1990s rest on the residue of these older left-wing traditions, but the word *socialism* no longer describes an alternative world view for most unionists (indeed, it has come to represent "big government"). Yet the convergence of labour with new social movements offers a rich opportunity for creating a new kind of socialist politics that retains the traditional labour concerns with economic security, the dignity of labour, fairness, and democracy and that weaves in the values and lessons of feminists, antiracists, environmental activists, gays and lesbians, radical Catholics, and many more. A new politics of democracy, social responsibility, and social justice is possible, and many within the current labour movement are struggling to put it together in an articulate form.

This vision must be more than a convention document or manifesto (though a widely distributed, readable statement would certainly be useful). It must be built into the immediate, short-term campaigns and ongoing programs that unions and their federations undertake. It must encourage workers to identify primarily with other workers and their allies, rather than with the élitist forces of the New Right.

In the middle of 1995 a group of casino workers in Montreal were locked in a prolonged strike over a four-day work week. Their struggle stood squarely in the tradition of movements towards shorter hours in Canada that runs back more than a century. As the founders of May Day argued in 1890 and many unionists learned in their struggles to get more time away from waged work, this is an extremely pregnant issue that can open up beyond an immediate demand to the larger vision of a more humane society. The demand for shorter hours touches all workers regardless of occupation and speaks to their common condition as wage-earners. It connects with both the pressures of intensified paid work and the demands of home and community. It can be used to pose alternative uses of human labour, to share paid and unpaid work and leisure more equitably. It can open up vistas of different, creative uses of time not driven by the relentless logic of private profit-making. It can encourage workers to imagine a brighter future. If unions are to survive as more than meek, marginal partners in a corporately controlled world, it will be this kind of visionary organizing that will carry them into the twenty-first century.

Glossary of Labour Centrals

ACCL All-Canadian Congress of Labour (1927–1940)

Organized in 1927, the ACCL drew together several small independent Canadian unions that had been organized outside, or had separated from, the international unions affiliated with the AFL and the TLC. Initially these unions included those led by communist labour leaders, but in 1929 these militants organized the WUL. The ACCL merged with the Canadian affiliates of the CIO in 1940 to form the CCL.

AFL   American Federation of Labor (1886–1955)

A national federation of craft unions in the United States, the AFL gave its affiliates jurisdiction over Canadian workers. In 1902 the TLC expelled all unions in competition with AFL affiliates. In 1935 the CIO first emerged within the AFL and two years later was expelled. The AFL and CIO merged again in 1955. The new organization was known simply as the AFL-CIO.

CCCL Canadian and Catholic Confederation of Labour /
Confédération des travailleurs catholiques du Canada
(1921–1960)

The CCCL was founded in 1921 as a result of vigorous efforts by the Catholic Church in Quebec to create a labour organization under its ideological direction. Clerical control had waned by the 1940s and in 1960 all references to Catholicism were finally removed. The organization was renamed the CNTU.

CCU Council/Confederation of Canadian Unions (1969–present)

The CCU was founded in 1969 when a small number of independent Canadian unions decided to create a new centre of nationalist unionism. The name was changed to the Confederation of Canadian Unions in 1973. A few more breakaway unions joined in the early 1970s, but the organization was never able to attract a wide enough following to challenge the CLC.

CFL　Canadian Federation of Labour (1902–1927)

Initially known as the National Trades and Labour Congress of Canada, the CFL was organized from those unions expelled by the TLC in 1902. Other unions outside the international union movement eventually joined, but the federation remained small and merged into the ACCL in 1927.

CFL　Canadian Federation of Labour (1981–present)

This version of the CFL was organized in 1981 by Canadian affiliates of international building-trades unions, which had withdrawn from the CLC.

CCL　Canadian Congress of Labour (1940–1956)

The CCL was created in 1940 when the Canadian affiliates of the CIO merged with the ACCL to create a new national central dedicated to industrial unionism. It merged with the TLC in 1956 to create the CLC.

CIO　Congress of Industrial Organizations (1935–1955)

The CIO began in 1935 as the Committee for Industrial Organization within the AFL, dedicated to organizing industrial unions. After being expelled from the AFL in 1937, the CIO became an independent national central in the United States with a new name — the Congress of Industrial Organizations. Its Canadian counterpart after 1940 was the CCL. In 1955 the CIO merged with the AFL to form the AFL-CIO.

CLC　Canadian Labour Congress (1956–present)

The CLC resulted from a merger of the TLC and the CCL in 1956. Until 1981, when the CFL was organized, the CLC was the single national voice of labour in Canada. It remains the largest and most influential.

CNTU　Confederation of National Trade Unions / Confédération des syndicats nationaux (1960–present)

The CNTU emerged when the CCCL shed its Catholicism in 1960. Its basis of unity was a commitment to organizing Quebec workers and promoting their particular concerns. It remains a union with few members outside Quebec.

IWW   Industrial Workers of the World (1905–present)

The IWW was organized in 1905 by U.S. radicals as a centre of militant revolutionary unionism. It soon extended into the Canadian West, but suffered dramatic defeats in the years immediately before and after World War I. For the rest of the twentieth century, it remained more an inspiration for new generations of radicals than an effective labour central.

OBU   One Big Union (1919–1956)

The OBU was organized in 1919 when affiliates of the TLC and AFL in western Canada withdrew to create a more radical organization with a greater commitment to industrial union-ism and socialism. Initially quite popular, it was attacked by employers, craft unions, and the state and in the 1920s quicky shrank to tiny proportions. It merged first with the ACCL in 1927, but, after expulsion in 1936, survived as a marginal organization in the Canadian labour movement, until it merged into the CLC in 1956.

TLC   Trades and Labor Congress of Canada (1886–1956)

The TLC was organized in 1886 by craft unions and assem-blies of the Knights of Labor. It united both independent unions in Canada and international unions affiliated with the Knights and the AFL. In 1902 it accepted the AFL brand of craft unionism and expelled all unions in competition with AFL affiliates. Formally, the TLC was the national voice of the Canadian labour movement in approaching the govern-ment, but in practice the AFL most often treated it as little more than another state federation of labour. In 1939 the AFL convinced the TLC to expel the Canadian locals of the CIO. In 1956 the TLC merged with the CCL to create a single national labour central, the CLC.

WUL   Workers' Unity League (1929–1935)

The WUL was the national central of the communist labour movement in Canada in the early 1930s. It dissolved in 1935 and its members and affiliates rejoined the TLC and the new CIO unions.

Further Reading

General

Abella, Irving, ed. *On Strike: Six Key Labour Struggles in Canada, 1919–1949* (Toronto: James Lorimer 1974).

Abella, Irving, and David Millar, eds. *The Canadian Worker in the Twentieth Century* (Toronto: Oxford University Press 1978).

Avakumovic, Ivan. *The Communist Party in Canada: A History* (Toronto: McClelland and Stewart 1975).

———. *Socialism in Canada: A Study of the CCF-NDP in Federal and Provincial Politics* (Toronto: McClelland and Stewart 1978).

Bercuson, David J., ed. *Canadian Labour History: Selected Readings* (Toronto: Copp Clark Pitman 1987).

Bernard, Elaine. *The Long Distance Feeling: A History of the Telecommunications Union* (Vancouver: New Star Books 1982).

Brennan, William J., ed. *"Building the Co-operative Commonwealth": Essays on the Democratic Socialist Tradition in Canada* (Regina: Canadian Plains Research Centre 1984).

Briskin, Linda, and Lynda Yantz, eds. *Union Sisters: Women in the Labour Movement* (Toronto: Women's Press 1983).

Brody, Janine, and Jane Jensen. *Crisis, Challenge, and Change: Party and Class in Canada Revisited* (Ottawa: Carleton University Press 1988).

Buck, Tim. *Yours in the Struggle: Reminiscences of Tim Buck*, ed. William Beeching and Phyllis Clarke (Toronto: NC Press 1977).

Caragata, Warren. *Alberta Labour: A Heritage Untold* (Toronto: James Lorimer 1979).

Chafe, W.J. *I've Been Working on the Railroad: Memoirs of a Railwayman, 1911–1962* (St. John's: Canadian Committee on Labour History 1987).

Charland, Jean-Pierre. *Les pâtes et papiers au Québec, 1880–1980: technologies, travail et travailleurs* (Québec: Institut québécois de recherche sur la culture 1990).

Charpentier, Alfred. *Cinquante ans d'action ouvrier: les memoires d'Alfred Charpentier* (Quebec: Les Presses de l'Université Laval 1971).

Cherwinski, W.J.C., and G.S. Kealey, eds. *Lectures in Canadian Labour and Working-Class History* (St. John's: Committee on Canadian Labour History 1985).

Communist Party of Canada. *Canada's Party of Socialism: History of the Communist Party of Canada, 1921–1976* (Toronto: Progress Books 1982).

Confédération des syndicats nationaux and Centrale de l'enseignement du Québec. *The History of the Labour Movement in Quebec* (Montreal: Black Rose Books 1987).

Cruikshank, Douglas, and Gregory S. Kealey. "Canadian Strike Statistics, 1891–1950," *Labour/Le Travail*, 20 (Fall 1987), 85-145.

Davis, N. Brian, ed. *The Poetry of the Canadian People: 1720–1920: Two Hundred Years of Hard Work* (Toronto: NC Press 1976).

———. *The Poetry of the Canadian People, 1900–1950* (Toronto: NC Press, 1978).

Earle, Michael. *Workers and the State in Twentieth Century Nova Scotia* (Fredericton: Acadiensis Press 1989).

Fifty Years of Labour in Algoma: Essays on Aspects of Algoma's Working-Class History (Sault Ste. Marie: Algoma University College 1978).

Frager, Ruth. *Sweatshop Strife: Class, Ethnicity, and Gender in the Jewish Labour Movement of Toronto, 1900–1939* (Toronto: University of Toronto Press 1992).

Gillespie, Bill. *A Class Act: An Illustrated History of the Labour Movement in Newfoundland and Labrador* (St. John's: Newfoundland and Labrador Federation of Labour 1986).

Greening, William E. *Paper Makers in Canada: A History of the Paper Makers Union in Canada* (Cornwall: International Brotherhood of Paper Makers 1952).

Greening, William E., with M.M. McLean. *It Was Never Easy, 1908–1958: A History of the Canadian Brotherhood of Railway, Transport and General Workers* (Quebec: Mutual Press 1961).

Harvey, Fernand, ed. *Aspects historiques du mouvement ouvrier au Québec* (Montreal: Boreal Express 1973).

———. *Le mouvement ouvrier au Québec* (Montreal: Boreal Express 1980).

Heron, Craig, and Robert Storey, eds. *On the Job: Confronting the Labour Process in Canada* (Kingston and Montreal: McGill-Queen's University Press 1986).

Heron, Craig, et al. *All That Our Hands Have Done: A Pictorial History of the Hamilton Workers* (Oakville, Ontario: Mosaic Press 1981).

Hopkin, Deian, and Gregory S. Kealey, eds. *Class, Community, and the Labour Movement: Wales and Canada, 1850–1930* (Aberystwyth: Llafur and Committee on Canadian Labour History 1989).

ILWU Local 500 Pensioners. *"Man along the Shore": The Story of the Vancouver Waterfront as Told by Longshoremen Themselves, 1860s–1975* (Vancouver: ILWU Local 500 Pensioners 1975).

Jamieson, Stuart Marshall. "Some Reflections on Violence and the Law in Industrial Relations," in D.J. Bercuson and L.A. Knafla, eds., *Law and Society in Historical Perspective* (Calgary: University of Calgary 1979), 141-56.

———. *Times of Trouble: Labour Unrest and Industrial Conflict in Canada, 1900–66* (Ottawa: Queen's Printer 1968).

Kealey, Gregory S., ed. *Class, Gender, and Region: Essays in Canadian Historical Sociology* (St. John's: Canadian Committee on Labour History 1988).

Kealey, Gregory S., and Peter Warrian, eds. *Essays in Canadian Working-Class History* (Toronto: McClelland and Stewart 1976).

Knight, Rolf. *A Man of Our Times: The Life-History of a Japanese-Canadian Fisherman* (Vancouver: New Star Books 1976).

MacDowell, Laurel Sefton, and Ian Radforth, eds. *Canadian Working Class History: Selected Readings* (Toronto: Canadian Scholar's Press 1992).

MacEwan, Paul. *Miners and Steelworkers: Labour in Cape Breton* (Toronto: Hakkert 1976).

MacPherson, Ian. *Each for All: A History of the Co-operative Movement in English Canada, 1900–1945* (Toronto: Macmillan 1979).

McKay, Ian. *The Craft Transformed: An Essay on the Carpenters of Halifax, 1885–1985* (Halifax: Holdfast Press 1985).

McNaught, Kenneth. *A Prophet in Politics: A Biography of J.S. Woodsworth* (Toronto: University of Toronto Press 1959).

Mills, Allen. *Fool for Christ: The Political Thought of J.S. Woodsworth* (Toronto: University of Toronto Press 1991).

Montero, Gloria, ed. *We Stood Together: First-Hand Accounts of Dramatic Events in Canada's Labour Past* (Toronto: James Lorimer 1979).

Morley, J.T. *Secular Socialists: The CCF/NDP in Ontario, A Biography* (Kingston and Montreal: McGill-Queen's University Press, 1984).

Morton, Desmond. *NDP: The Dream of Power* (Toronto: Hakkert 1974).

————. "Aid to the Civil Power: The Canadian Militia in Support of Social Order, 1867-1914," in Michiel Horn and Ronald Sabourin, eds., *Studies in Canadian Social History* (Toronto: McClelland and Stewart 1974), 417-34.

————. *The New Democrats, 1961–1986: The Politics of Change* (Toronto: Copp Clark Pitman 1987).

Morton, Desmond, with Terry Copp. *Working People: An Illustrated History of the Canadian Labour Movement* (Ottawa: Deneau 1984).

Moscovitch, Allan, and Jim Albert, eds. *The "Benevolent" State: The Growth of Welfare in Canada* (Toronto: Garamond Press 1987).

Palmer, Bryan D., ed. *The Character of Class Struggle: Essays in Canadian Working-Class History* (Toronto: McClelland and Stewart 1986).

————. *Working-Class Experience: Rethinking the History of Canadian Labour, 1800–1991* (Toronto: McClelland and Stewart 1992).

Parr, Joy. *The Gender of Breadwinners: Women, Men, and Change in Two Industrial Towns, 1880–1950* (Toronto: University of Toronto Press 1990).

Penner, Norman. *The Canadian Left: A Critical Analysis* (Scarborough: Prentice Hall 1977).

Phillips, Paul. *No Power Greater: A Century of Labour in British Columbia* (Vancouver: British Columbia Federation of Labour 1967).

Pringle, Jim. *United We Stand: A History of Winnipeg's Civic Workers* (Winnipeg: Manitoba Labour Education Centre 1991).

Radforth, Ian. *Bushworkers and Bosses: Logging in Northern Ontario, 1900–1980* (Toronto: University of Toronto Press 1987).

Roberts, Wayne, and John Bullen. "A Heritage of Hope and Struggle: Workers, Unions, and Politics in Canada, 1930–1982," in Michael S. Cross and Gregory S. Kealey, eds., *Readings in Canadian Social History, Vol.5: Modern Canada, 1930-1980s* (Toronto: McClelland and Stewart 1984), 105-40.

Rouillard, Jacques. *Histoire du syndicalisme québécois: des origines à nos jours* (Montréal: Boréal 1989).

Russell, Bob. *Back to Work? Labour, State, and Industrial Relations* (Toronto: Nelson 1990).

Ryan, Judith Hoegg. *Coal in Our Blood: 200 Years of Coal Mining in Nova Scotia's Pictou County* (Halifax: Formac Publishing 1992).

Salutin, Rick. *Kent Rowley, the Organizer: A Canadian Union Life* (Toronto: James Lorimer 1980).

Scott, Jack. *A Communist Life: Jack Scott and the Canadian Workers' Movement, 1927–1985,* ed. Bryan D. Palmer (St. John's: Committee on Canadian Labour History 1988).

Smith, Doug. *Let Us Rise: An Illustrated History of the Manitoba Labour Movement* (Vancouver: New Star Books 1985).

Sobel, David, and Susan Meurer. *Working at Inglis: The Life and Death of a Canadian Factory* (Toronto: James Lorimer 1994).

Stanton, John. *Never Say Die!: The Life and Times of a Pioneer Labour Lawyer* (Ottawa: Steel Rail Publishing 1987).

Steeves, Dorothy G. *The Compassionate Rebel: Ernest Winch and the Growth of Socialism in Western Canada* (Vancouver: J.J. Douglas 1977).

Strong, Cyril W. *My Life as a Newfoundland Organizer: The Memoirs of Cyril W. Strong, 1912–1987* (St. John's: Committee on Canadian Labour History 1987).

Struthers, James. *The Limits of Affluence: Welfare in Ontario, 1920–1970* (Toronto: University of Toronto Press 1994).

Vanasse, Gilbert. *Histoire de la Fédération des travailleurs du papier et de la forêt, Tome 1 (1907–1958)* (Montreal: Les Editions Saint Martin 1986).

Warburton, Rennie, and David Coburn, eds. *Workers, Capital, and the State in British Columbia: Selected Papers* (Vancouver: University of British Columbia Press 1988).

Wiseman, Nelson. *Social Democracy in Manitoba: A History of the CCF/NDP* (Winnipeg: University of Manitoba Press 1983).

Women at Work: Ontario, 1850–1930 (Toronto: Women's Press 1974).

Working Lives Collective. *Working Lives: Vancouver, 1886–1986* (Vancouver: New Star Books 1985).

Zerker, Sally F. *The Rise and Fall of Toronto Typographical Union, 1832–1972: A Case Study of Foreign Domination* (Toronto: University of Toronto Press 1982).

Nineteenth Century

Battye, John. "The Nine-Hour Pioneers: The Genesis of the Canadian Labour Movement," *Labour/Le Travail*, 4 (1979),

Belanger, Noel, et al. *Les travailleurs québécois, 1851–1896* (Montréal: Les Presses de l'Université du Québec 1973).

Bitterman, Rusty. "Farm Households and Wage Labour in the Northeastern Maritimes in the Early 19th Century," *Labour/Le Travail*, 31 (Spring 1993), 13-45.

Bradbury, Bettina. *Working Families: Age, Gender, and Daily Survival in Industrializing Montreal* (Toronto: McClelland and Stewart 1993).

Cohen, Marjorie Griffith. *Women's Work, Markets and Economic Development in Nineteenth Century Ontario* (Toronto: University of Toronto Press 1988).

Crave, Paul. "The Law of Master and Servant in Mid-Nineteenth-Century Ontario," in David Flaherty, ed., *Essays in the History of Canadian Law* (Toronto: University of Toronto Press 1981), 175-211.

———. "Workers' Conspiracies in Toronto, 1854–72," *Labour/Le Travail*, 14 (Fall 1984), 49-70.

Craven, Paul, ed. *Labouring Lives: Work and Workers in Nineteenth-Century Ontario* (Toronto: University of Toronto Press 1995).

Cross, Michael S., ed. *The Workingman in the Nineteenth Century* (Toronto: Oxford University Press 1974).

De Bonville, Jean. *Jean-Baptiste Gagnepetit: Les travailleurs montréalais à la fin du XIXe siècle* (Montréal: Les Editions de l'Aurore 1975).

Fingard, Judith. *Jack in Port: Sailortowns of Eastern Canada* (Toronto: University of Toronto Press 1982).

Forsey, Eugene. *Trade Unions in Canada, 1812–1902* (Toronto: University of Toronto Press 1981).

Harvey, Fernand. *Révolution industrielle et travailleurs: une enquête sur les rapports entre le capital et le travail au Québec à la fin du 19e siècle* (Montréal: Boréal Express 1978).

Kealey, Gregory S., ed. *Canada Investigates Industrialism: The Royal Commission on the Relations of Labor and Capital, 1889 (Abridged)* (Toronto: University of Toronto Press 1973).

———. *Toronto Workers Respond to Industrial Capitalism, 1867–1892* (Toronto: University of Toronto Press 1980).

Kealey, Gregory S., and Bryan D. Palmer. *Dreaming of What Might Be: The Knights of Labour in Ontario, 1880–1900* (New York: Cambridge University Press 1982).

Knight, Rolf. *Indians at Work: An Informal History of Native Indian Labour in British Columbia, 1858—1930* (Vancouver: New Star Books 1978).

Langdon, Stephen. "The Emergence of the Canadian Working-Class Movement, 1845-75," Parts 1 and 2. *Journal of Canadian Studies*, (May 1973), 3-13; (August 1973), 8-25.

Lutz, John. "After the Fur Trade: The Aboriginal Labouring Class of British Columbia, 1849–1890," Canadian Historical Association, *Journal*, New Series, Vol. 3 (1992), 69-94.

McKay, Ian. "'By Wisdom, Wile or War': The Provincial Workmen's Association and the Struggle for Working-Class Independence in Nova Scotia, 1879–97," *Labour/Le Travail*, 18 (Fall 1986), 13-62.

Newsome, Eric. *The Coal Coast: The History of Coal Mining in B.C. — 1835–1900* (Victoria: Orca Books 1989).

Pentland, H. Clare. *Labour and Capital in Canada, 1650–1860* (Toronto: James Lorimer 1981).

Palmer, Bryan D. *A Culture in Conflict: Skilled Workers and Industrial Capitalism in Hamilton, Ontario, 1860–1914* (Kingston and Montreal: McGill-Queen's University Press 1979).

———. "Labour Protest and Organization in Nineteenth-Century Canada," *Labour/Le Travail*, 20 (Fall 1987), 61-83.

Sager, Eric W. *Seafaring Labour: The Merchant Marine of Atlantic Canada, 1820–1914* (Kingston and Montreal: McGill-Queen's University Press 1989).

Tremblay, Robert. "Un aspect de la consolidation du pouvoir d'Etat de la bourgeoisie coloniale: la législation anti-ouvrière dans le Bas-Canada, 1800–50," *Labour/Le Travail*, 8/9 (Autumn/Spring 1981–82), 243-52.

Tucker, Eric. *Administering Danger in the Workplace: The Law and Politics of Occupational Health and Safety Regulation in Ontario, 1850–1914* (Toronto: University of Toronto Press 1990).

———. "'That Indefinite Area of Toleration': Criminal Conspiracy and Trade Unions in Ontario, 1837–77," *Labour/Le Travail*, 27 (Spring 1991), 15-54

Verzuh, Ron. *Radical Rag: The Pioneer Labour Press in Canada* (Ottawa: Steel Rail Press 1988).

1900–25

Avery, Donald. *"Dangerous Foreigners": European Immigrant Workers and Labour Radicalism in Canada, 1896–1932* (Toronto: McClelland and Stewart 1972).

Babcock, Robert. *Gompers in Canada: A Study in American Continentalism Before the First World War* (Toronto: University of Toronto Press 1974).

Bercuson, David Jay. *Confrontation at Winnipeg: Labour, Industrial Relations, and the General Strike* (Kingston and Montreal: McGill-Queen's University Press 1973).

———. *Fools and Wise Men: The Rise and Fall of the One Big Union* (Toronto: McGraw-Hill Ryerson 1978).

Bowen, Lynne. *Boss Whistle: The Coal Miners of Vancouver Island Remember* (Lantzville, B.C.: Oolichan Press 1982).

Bumsted, J.M. *The Winnipeg General Strike of 1919: An Illustrated History* (Winnipeg: Watson Dwyer 1994).

Copp, Terry. *The Anatomy of Poverty: The Condition of the Working Class in Montreal, 1897–1929* (Toronto: McClelland and Stewart 1974).

Craven, Paul. *An Impartial Umpire: Industrial Relations and the Canadian State, 1900–1911* (Toronto: University of Toronto Press 1980).

Doherty, Bill. *Slaves of the Lamp: A History of the Federal Civil Service Organizations, 1865–1924* (Victoria: Orca Books 1991).

Fillmore, Nicholas. *Maritime Radical: The Life and Times of Roscoe Fillmore* (Toronto: Between the Lines 1992).

Frank, David, and Nolan Reilly. "The Emergence of the Socialist Movement in the Maritimes, 1899–1916," in Robert J. Brym and R.J. Sacouman, eds., *Underdevelopment and Social Movements in Atlantic Canada* (Toronto: New Hogtown Press 1979), 81-105.

Fraser, Dawn. *Echoes from Labour's Wars: Industrial Cape Breton in the 1920s* (Toronto: New Hogtown Press 1976).

Heron, Craig. "Labourism and the Canadian Working Class," *Labour/Le Travail*, 13 (Spring 1984), 45-75.

———. *Working in Steel: The Early Years in Canada, 1883–1935* (Toronto: McClelland and Stewart 1988).

Heron, Craig, ed. *The Workers' Revolt in Canada, 1917–25* (forthcoming).

Kealey, Linda. "Canadian Socialism and the Woman Question, 1900–1914," *Labour/Le Travail*, 13 (Spring 1984), 77-100.

Krawchuk, Peter. *The Ukrainian Socialist Movement in Canada (1907–1918)* (Toronto: Progress Books 1979).

Larivière, Claude. *Albert Saint-Martin, militant d'avant-garde, 1865–1947* (Laval: Editions coopératives Albert Saint-Martin 1979).

Leier, Mark. *Where the Fraser River Flows: The Industrial Workers of the World in British Columbia* (Vancouver: New Star Books 1990).

Mardiros, Anthony. *William Irvine: The Life of a Prairie Radical* (Toronto: James Lorimer 1979).

Mayse, Susan. *Ginger: The Life and Death of Albert Goodwin* (Madeira Park, B.C.: Harbour Publishing 1990).

McCormack, A. Ross. *Reformers, Rebels, and Revolutionaries: The Western Canadian Radical Movement, 1899–1919* (Toronto: University of Toronto Press 1977).

McDonald, Ian D.H. *"To Each His Own": William Coaker and the Fishermen's Protective Union in Newfoundland Politics, 1908–1925* (St. John's: Institute of Social and Economic Research, Memorial University of Newfoundland 1987).

Mouat, Jeremy. *Roaring Days: Rossland's Mines and the History of British Columbia* (Vancouver: University of British Columbia Press 1995).

Naylor, James. *The New Democracy: Challenging the Social Order in Industrial Ontario, 1914–25* (Toronto: University of Toronto Press 1991).

Newton, Janice. *The Feminist Challenge to the Canadian Left, 1900–1918* (Kingston and Montreal: McGill-Queen's University Press 1995).

Penner, Norman, ed. *Winnipeg 1919: The Strikers' Own History of the Winnipeg General Strike* (Toronto: James Lorimer 1973).

Piva, Michael J. *The Condition of the Working Class in Toronto — 1900–1921* (Ottawa: University of Ottawa Press 1979).

Roberts, Wayne. *Honest Womanhood: Feminism, Femininity, and Class Consciousness among Toronto Working Women, 1893–1914* (Toronto: New Hogtown Press 1976).

Robin, Martin. *Radical Politics and Canadian Labour, 1880–1930* (Kingston: Industrial Relations Centre, Queen's University 1968).

Rouillard, Jacques. *Les travailleurs du coton au Québec, 1900–1915* (Montréal: Les Presses de l'Université du Québec 1974).

———. *Les Syndicats nationaux au Québec de 1900 à 1930* (Québec: Les Presses de l'Université Laval 1979).

Schwantes, Carlos. *Radical Heritage: Labor, Socialism, and Reform in Washington and British Columbia* (Vancouver: Douglas and McIntyre 1979).

Seager, Allen. "Socialists and Workers: The Western Canadian Coal Miners, 1900–21," *Labour/Le Travail*, 16 (Fall 1985), 23-59.

1925–50

Abella, Irving. *Nationalism, Communism, and Canadian Labour: The CIO, the Communist Party, and the Canadian Congress of Labour, 1935–1956* (Toronto: University of Toronto Press 1973).

Angus, Ian. *Canadian Bolsheviks: The Early Years of the Communist Party of Canada* (Montreal: Vanguard Publications 1981).

Bergren, Myrtle Woodward. *Tough Timber: The Loggers of B.C. — Their Story* (Toronto: Progress Books 1967).

Betcherman, Leta-Rose. *The Little Band: The Clashes Between the Communists and the Political and Legal Establishment in Canada, 1928–1932* (Ottawa: Deneau 1980).

Bosnich, Milan. *One Man's War: Reflections of a Rough Diamond* (Toronto: Lugus Productions 1988).

Brown, Lorne. *When Freedom Was Lost: The Unemployed, the Agitator, and the State* (Montreal: Black Rose Books 1987).

Caplan, Gerald C. *The Dilemma of Canadian Socialism: The CCF in Ontario* (Toronto: McClelland and Stewart 1973).

Colling, Herb. *Ninety-Nine Days: The Ford Strike in Windsor, 1945* (Toronto: NC Press 1995).

Comeau, Robert, and Bernard Dionne. *Communists in Quebec, 1936–1956: The Communist Party of Canada/Labour Progressive Party* (Montréal: Presses de l'Unité 1982).

Copp, Terry, ed. *Industrial Unionism in Kitchener, 1937–47* (Elora: Cumnock Press 1976).

———. *The I.U.E. in Canada* (Elora: Cumnock Press 1980).

Cox, Mark. "The Limits of Reform: Industrial Regulation and Management Rights in Ontario," *Canadian Historical Review*, 68 (1987), 552-75.

Crowley, Terry. *Agnes Macphail and the Politics of Equality* (Toronto: James Lorimer 1990).

Dumas, Evelyn. *The Bitter Thirties in Quebec* (Montreal: Black Rose Books 1975).

Finkel, Alvin. "The Cold War, Alberta Labour, and the Social Credit Regime," *Labour/Le Travail*, 21 (Spring 1988), pp.123-52.

Green, Jim. *Against the Tide: The Story of the Canadian Seamen's Union* (Toronto: Progress Books 1986).

Guest, Dennis. *The Emergence of Social Security in Canada* (Vancouver: University of British Columbia Press 1979).

Fortin, Gerard, and Boyce Richardson. *Life of the Party* (Montreal: Vehicule Press 1984).

Heaps, Leo. *The Rebel in the House: The Life and Times of A.A. Heaps, MP* (London: Niccolo Publishing 1970).

Horowitz, Gad. *Canadian Labour and Politics* (Toronto: University of Toronto Press 1968).

Howard, Victor. *"We Were the Salt of the Earth!": The On-to-Ottawa Trek and the Regina Riot* (Regina: Canadian Plains Research Centre 1985).

Hunter, Peter. *Which Side Are You On Boys: Canadian Life on the Left* (Toronto: Lugus Productions 1988).

Kaplan, William. *Everything That Floats: Pat Sullican, Hal Banks, and the Seamen's Unions of Canada* (Toronto: University of Toronto Press 1987).

Kolasky, John. *The Shattered Illusion: The History of Ukrainian Pro-Communist Organizations in Canada* (Toronto: PMA Books 1979).

Lembke, Jerry, and William M. Tattam. *One Union in Wood: A Political History of the International Woodworkers of America* (New York: International Publishers 1984).

Lévesque, Andrée. *Virage à gauche interdit: Les communists, les socialistes, et leurs ennemis au Québec, 1929–1939* (Montréal: Boréal Express 1984).

Lewis, David, *The Good Fight: Political Memoirs, 1909–1958* (Toronto: Macmillan 1981).

Logan, Harold. *State Intervention and Assistance in Collective Bargaining: The Canadian Experience, 1943–54* (Toronto: University of Toronto Press 1956).

MacDowell, Laurel Sefton. *"Remember Kirkland Lake": The Golf Miners' Strike of 1941–42* (Toronto: University of Toronto Press 1983).

————. "Relief Camp Workers in Ontario During the Great Depression of the 1930s," *Canadian Historical Review*, 76, no.2 (June 1995), 205–28.

MacEachern, George. *George MacEachern: An Autobiography; The Story of a Cape Breton Radical*, ed., David Frank and Donald MacGillivray (Sydney: College of Cape Breton Press 1987).

Manley, John. "Canadian Communists, Revolutionary Unionism, and the 'Third Period': The Workers' Unity League, 1929–1935," Canadian Historical Association, *Journal*, 1994, 167–91.

McEwen, Tom. *The Forge Glows Red: From Blacksmith to Revolutionary* (Toronto: Progress Books 1974).

Miner, Bob. *Miner's Life: Bob Miner and Union Organizing in Timmins, Kirkland Lake, and Sudbury*, ed. Wayne Roberts (Hamilton: Labour Studies Program, McMaster University 1979).

Penner, Norman. *Canadian Communism: The Stalin Years and Beyond* (Toronto: Methuen 1988).

Ready, Alf. *Organizing Westinghouse: Alf Ready's Story* (Hamilton: Labour Studies Program, McMaster University 1979).

Roberts, Wayne. *Baptism of a Union: Stelco Strike of 1946* (Hamilton: Labour Studies Program, McMaster University 1981).

Rodney, William. *Soldiers of the International: A History of the Communist Party of Canada, 1919–1929* (Toronto: University of Toronto Press 1968).

Sangster, Joan. *Dreams of Equality: Women on the Canadian Left, 1920–1950* (Toronto: McClelland and Stewart 1989).

———. *Earning Respect: The Lives of Working Women in Small-Town Ontario, 1920–1960* (Toronto: University of Toronto Press 1995).

Schultz, Patricia V. *The East York Workers' Association: A Response to the Great Depression* (Toronto: New Hogtown Press 1975).

Sheils, Jean Evans, and Ben Swankey. *"Work and Wages!": Semi-Documentary Account of the Life and Times of Arthur H. (Slim) Evans* (Vancouver: Trade Union Research Bureau 1977).

Solski, Mike, and John Smaller, *Mine Mill: The History of the International Union of Mine, Mill, and Smelter Workers in Canada since 1895* (Ottawa: Steel Rail Press 1984).

Struthers, James. *No Fault of Their Own: Unemployment and the Canadian Welfare State, 1914–1941* (Toronto: University of Toronto Press 1983).

Sufrin, Eileen. *The Eaton Drive: The Campaign to Organize Canada's Largest Department Store, 1948 to 1952* (Toronto: Fitzhenry and Whiteside 1982).

Sugiman, Pamela. *Labour's Dilemma: The Gender Politics of Auto Workers in Canada, 1937–1979* (Toronto: University of Toronto Press 1994).

Taylor, Don, and Bradley Dow. *The Rise of Industrial Unionism in Canada — A History of the CIO* (Kingston: Industrial Relations Centre, Queen's University 1988).

Trudeau, Pierre Elliott. *The Asbestos Strike* (Toronto: James Lorimer 1974).

Vance, Catharine. *Not by Gods but by People: The Story of Bella Hall Gauld* (Toronto: Progress Books 1968).

Walsh, Mark, and Mary E. Baruth-Walsh. *Strike! Ninety-Nine Days on the Line: The Workers' Own Story of the 1945 Windsor Ford Strike* (Penumbra Press 1995).

Watson, Louise. *She Was Never Afraid: The Biography of Annie Buller* (Toronto: Progress Books 1976).

Weisbord, Merrily. *The Strangest Dream: Canadian Communists, the Spy Trials, and the Cold War* (Toronto: Lester and Orpen Dennys 1983).

White, Howard. *A Hard Man to Beat: The Story of Bill White, Labour Leader, Historian, Shipyard Worker, Raconteur* (Vancouver: Pulp Press 1983).

Young, Walter D. *The Anatomy of a Party: The National CCF, 1932–61* (Toronto: University of Toronto Press 1969).

1950–75

Black Rose Books Editorial Collective, ed. *Quebec Labour: The Confederation of National Trade Unions Yesterday and Today* (Montreal: Black Rose Books 1972).

Calhoun, Sue. *A Word to Say: The Story of the Maritime Fishermen's Union* (Halifax: Nimbus Publishing 1991).

Cameron, Silver Donald. *The Education of Everett Richardson: The Nova Scotia Fishermen's Strike, 1970–71* (Toronto: McClelland and Stewart 1977).

Canada, Task Force on Labour Relations. *Labour Relations in Canada* (Ottawa: Queen's Printer 1968).

Crispo, John, and Harry Arthurs. "Industrial Unrest in Canada: A Diagnosis of Recent Experience," *Relations industrielles/Industrial Relations*, 23, no. 2 (1968), 237-64

Davidson, Joe, and John Deverell. *Joe Davidson* (Toronto: James Lorimer 1978).

Drache, Daniel, ed. *Only the Beginning: The Manifestoes of the Common Front* (Toronto: New Press 1972).

Edwards, Peter. *Waterfront Warlord: The Life and Violent Times of Hal C. Banks* (Toronto: Key Porter Books 1987).

Freeman, Bill. *1005: Political Life in a Union Local* (Toronto: James Lorimer 1982).

Gerin-Lajoie, Jean. *Les métallos, 1936–1981* (Montréal: Boréal Express 1982).

Goldenberg, Carl, and John Crispo. *Construction Labour Relations* (Toronto 1968).

Iacovetta, Franca. *Such Hardworking People: Italian Immigrants in Postwar Toronto* (Kingston and Montreal: McGill-Queen's University Press 1992).

Inglis, Gordon. *More Than Just a Union: The Story of the NFFAWU* (St. John's: Jesperson Press 1985).

Jamieson, Stuart. *Industrial Conflict in Canada, 1966–75* (Ottawa: Economic Council of Canada 1979).

Johnson, Walter, ed. *Working in Canada* (Montreal: Black Rose Press 1975).

———. *The Trade Unions and the State* (Montreal: Black Rose Press 1978).

Kwavnick, David. *Organized Labour and Pressure Politics: The Canadian Labour Congress, 1956–1968* (Montreal: McGill-Queen's University Press 1972).

Laxer, Robert. *Canada's Unions* (Toronto: James Lorimer 1976).

Macdonald, David A. *Power Begins at the Cod End: The Newfoundland Trawlermen's Strike, 1974–75* (St. John's: Institute of Social and Economic Research, Memorial University of Newfoundland 1980).

MacDowell, G.F. *The Brandon Packers' Strike: A Tragedy of Errors* (Toronto: McClelland and Stewart 1971).

Magnuson, Bruce. *The Untold Story of Ontario's Bushworkers: A Political Memoir* (Toronto 1990).

Roberts, Wayne. *Cracking the Canadian Formula: The Making of the Energy and Chemical Workers Union* (Toronto: Between the Lines 1990).

Swerdlow, Max. *Brother Max: Labour Organizer and Educator* (St. John's: Committee on Canadian Labour History 1990).

Yates, Charlotte. *From Plant to Politics: The Autoworkers Union in Postwar Canada* (Philadelphia: Temple University Press 1993).

1975–95

Albo, Gregory. "The 'New Realism' and Canadian Workers," in Alain-G. Gagnon and James P. Bickerton, eds., *Canadian Politics: An Introduction to the Discipline* (Peterborough: Broadview Press 1990), 471-504.

Advisory Group on Working Time and the Distribution of Work. *Report* (Ottawa 1994).

Archer, Keith. *Political Choices and Electoral Consequences: A Study of Organized Labour and the New Democratic Party* (Montreal and Kingston: McGill-Queen's University Press 1990).

Argue, Robert, Charlene Gannage, and D.W. Livingston, eds. *Working People and Hard Times: Canadian Perspectives* (Toronto: Garamond Press 1987).

Armstrong, Pat, and Hugh Armstrong. *The Double Ghetto: Canadian Women and Their Segmented Work* (Toronto: McClelland and Stewart 1984).

Arthurs, Harry, et al. *Labour Law and Industrial Relations in Canada* (Toronto: Butterworth's 1988). ·

Black, Errol, and Jim Silver, eds. *Hard Bargains: The Manitoba Labour Movement Confronts the 1990s* (Winnipeg: Committee on Manitoba's Labour History n.d.).

Bleyer, Peter. "Coalitions of Social Movements as Agencies for Social Change: The Action Canada Network," in W.K. Carroll, ed., *Organizing Dissent* (Toronto 1992).

Briskin, Linda, and Patricia McDermott, eds. *Women Challenging Unions: Feminism, Democracy, and Miltancy* (Toronto: University of Toronto Press 1993).

Carroll, William K., and R.S. Ratner. "Old Unions and New Social Movements," *Labour/Le Travail*, 35 (Spring 1995), 195–221.

Chaykowski, Richard P., and Anil Verna, eds. *Industrial Relations in Canadian Industry* (Toronto: Holt, Rinehart and Winston 1992).

Clement, Wallace. *Hardrock Mining: Industrial Relations and Technological Change at INCO* (Toronto: McClelland and Stewart 1981).

———. *The Struggle to Organize: Resistance in Canada's Fishery* (Toronto: McClelland and Stewart 1986).

Comish, Shaun. *The Westray Tragedy: A Miner's Story* (Halifax: Fernwood Publishing 1993).

Corman, June, et al. *Recasting Steel Labour: The Stelco Story* (Halifax: Fernwood Publishing 1993).

Drache, Daniel. *Getting on Track: Social Democratic Strategies for Ontario* (Kingston and Montreal: McGill-Queen's University Press 1992).

Drache, Daniel, and Meric Gertler, eds. *The New Era of Global Competition: State Policy and Market Power* (Kingston and Montreal: McGill-Queen's University Press 1991).

Drache, Daniel, and Harry Glasbeek. *The Changing Workplace: Reshaping Canada's Industrial Relations System* (Toronto: James Lorimer 1993).

Duffy, Ann, and Norene Pupo. *Part-Time Paradox: Connecting Gender, Work, and Family* (Toronto: McClelland and Stewart 1992).

Economic Council of Canada. *Good Jobs, Bad Jobs: Employment in the Service Economy* (Ottawa: Ministry of Supply and Services 1990).

Forrest, Anne. "The Rise and Fall of National Bargaining in the Canadian Meat-Packing Industry," *Relations industrielles/Industrial Relations*, 44 (1989), 393-406.

Fudge, Judy, and Patricia McDermott, eds. *Just Wages: A Feminist Assessment of Pay Equity* (Toronto: University of Toronto Press 1991).

Gannage, Charlene. *Double Day, Double Bind: Women Garment Workers* (Toronto: Women's Press 1986).

Giles, Anthony. "The Canadian Labour Congress and Tripartism," *Industrial Relations* 37 (1982), 93-125.

Gilson, C.H.J. *Strikes: Industrial Relations in Nova Scotia, 1957–1987* (Hantsport: Lancelot Press 1987).

Gindin, Sam. *The Canadian Auto Workers* (Toronto: James Lorimer 1995).

Globe and Mail (Toronto), 11 October 1993, A9; 27 Novemebr 1993, A1; 3 March 1994, A1; 4 March 1994, A7; 25 May 1994, A2; 22 December 1994, A1, B5; 3 February 1995, A2; 6 February 1995, A17; 13 February 1995, B1; 10 April 1995, B1, B4; 12 April 1995, A26; 31 May 1995, A1; 7 June 1995, A7, A13; 15 June 1995, A4; 26 June 1995, A9; 8 July 1995, B5; 24 July 1995, A9; 2 August 1995, B19; 5 August 1995, B3; 6 September 1995, A4; 14 September 1995, B3; 2 October 1995, C6; 9 October 1995, B1; 25 October 1995, A1.

Gunderson, Morley, and Allen Ponak, eds. *Union-Management Relations in Canada* 3rd ed., (Don Mills: Addison-Wesley 1995).

Haiven, Larry, Stephen McBride, and John Shields, eds. *Regulating Labour: The State, Neo-Conservatism, and Industrial Relations* (Toronto: Garamond Press 1991).

Ismael, Jacqueline S., ed. *The Canadian Welfare State: Evolution and Transition* (Edmonton: University of Alberta Press 1987).

Jenson, Jane, and Rianne Mahon, eds. *The Challenge of Restructuring: North American Labor Movements Respond* (Philadelphia: Temple University Press 1993).

Kettler, David, et al. "Unionization and Labour Regimes in Canada and the United States: Considerations for Comparative Research," *Labour/Le Travail*, 25 (Spring 1990), 161–87.

Kumar, Pradeep, and Dennis Ryan, eds. *Canadian Union Movement in the 1980s: Perspectives from Union Leaders* (Kingston: Industrial Relations Centre, Queen's University 1988).

Kumar, Pradeep. *From Uniformity to Divergence: Industrial Relations in Canada and the United States* (Kingston: IRC Press 1993).

Leah, Ronnie. "Linking the Struggles: Racism, Sexism and the Union Movement," in Jessie Vorst, ed., *Race, Class, and Gender: Bonds and Barriers* (Toronto and Winnipeg: Garamond Press and Society for Socialist Studies 1991), 169–200.

Lowe, Graham S. *Bank Unionization in Canada: A Preliminary Analysis* (Toronto: Centre for Industrial Relations 1980).

Lowe, Graham S., and Harvey J. Krahn, eds. *Working Canadians: Readings in the Sociology of Work and Industry* (Scarborough: Nelson Canada 1991).

Magnusson, Warren, et al., eds. *The New Reality: The Politics of Restraint in British Columbia* (Vancouver: New Star 1984).

Maslove, Allan M., and Gene Swimmer. *Wage Controls in Canada, 1975–78: A Study in Public Decision-Making* (Montreal: Institute for Research on Public Policy 1980).

McBride, Stephen. *Not Working: State, Unemployment, and Neo-Conservatism in Canada* (Toronto: University of Toronto Press 1992).

Menzies, Heather. *Fast Forward out of Control* (Toronto: Macmillan 1989).

Munro, Jack, and Jane O'Hara. *Union Jack: Labour Leader Jack Munro* (Vancouver: Douglas and McIntyre 1988).

Murray, Gregor. "Union Culture and Organizational Change in Ontario and Quebec," in Colin Leys and Marguerite Mendell, eds., *Culture and Social Change: Social Movements in Quebec and Ontario* (Montreal: Black Rose Books 1992), 39–61.

Noel, Alain, and Keith Gardner. "The Gainers Strike: Capitalist Offensive, Militancy, and the Politics of Industrial Relations in Canada," *Studies in Political Economy*, 31 (Spring 1990), 31–72.

Palmer, Bryan D. *Solidarity: The Rise and Fall of an Opposition in British Columbia* (Vancouver: New Star Books 1987).

————. *Capitalism Comes to the Backcountry: The Goodyear Invasion of Napanee* (Toronto: Between the Lines 1994).

Panitch, Leo, and Donald Swartz. *The Assault on Trade Union Freedoms: From Wage Controls to Social Contract* (Toronto: Garamond Press 1993).

Phillips, Paul, and Erin Phillips. *Women and Work: Inequality in the Canadian Labour Market* (Toronto: James Lorimer 1993).

Reasons, Charles E., et al. *Assault on the Worker: Occupational Health and Safety in Canada* (Toronto: Butterworths 1981).

Reiter, Ester. *Making Fast Food: From the Frying Pan into the Fryer* (Kingston and Montreal: McGill-Queen's University Press 1991).

Robertson, David, and Jeff Wareham. *Technological Change in he Auto Industry* (Toronto: Canadian Auto Workers 1987).

Schenk, Christopher, and John Anderson, eds. *Re-shaping Work: Union Responses to Technological Change* (Toronto: Ontario Federation of Labour 1995).

Smith, Miriam. "The Canadian Labour Congress: From Continentalism to Economic Nationalism," *Studies in Political Economy*, 38 (Summer 1992), 35–60.

Steedman, Mercedes, Peter Suschnigg, and Dieter K. Buse, eds. *Hard Lessons: The Mine Mill Union in the Canadian Labour Movement* (Toronto: Dundurn Press 1995).

Swift, Jamie. *Wheel of Fortune: Work and Life in the Age of Falling Expectations* (Toronto: Between the Lines 1995).

Thompson, Mark, and Gene Swimmer, eds. *Conflict or Compromise: The Future of Public Sector Industrial Relations* (Montreal: Institute for Research on Public Policy 1984).

Warskett, Rosemary. "Bank Worker Unionization and the Law," *Studies in Political Economy*, 25 (Spring 1988), 41–73.

————. "Defining Who We Are: Solidarity through Diversity in the Ontario Labour Movement," in Colin Leys and Marguerite Mendell, eds., *Culture and Social Change: Social Movements in Que-bec and Ontario* (Montreal: Black Rose Books 1992), 109–27.

Wells, Donald M. *Empty Promises: Quality of Working Life Programs and the Labor Movement* (New York: Monthly Review Press 1987).

White, Bob. *Hard Bargains: My Life on the Line* (Toronto: McClelland and Stewart 1987).

White, Jerry. *Hospital Strike: Women, Unions, and Public Sector Conflict* (Toronto: Thompson Educational Publishing 1990).

White, Julie. *Male and Female: Women and the Canadian Union of Postal Workers* (Toronto: Thompson Educational Publishing 1990).

———. *Sisters and Solidarity: Women and Unions in Canada* (Toronto: Thompson Educational Publishing 1993).

White, R.D. *Law, Capitalism, and the Right to Work* (Toronto: Garamond 1986).

Yalnizyan, Armine, T.Ran Ide, and Arthur J. Cordell. *Shifting Time: Social Policy and the Future of Work* (Toronto: Between the Lines 1994).

Yates, Charlotte. "The Internal Dynamics of Union Power: Explaining Canadian Autoworkers' Militancy in the 1980s," *Studies in Political Economy*, 31 (Spring 1990), 73–105.

Index